Radicals, Reformers and Socialists

Radicals, Reformers and Socialists

FROM THE FABIAN BIOGRAPHICAL SERIES

Edited by Michael Katanka
Introduction by Dame Margaret Cole

CHARLES KNIGHT & CO LTD
London 1973

Charles Knight & Co. Ltd.
11/12 Bury Street, London EC3A 5AP
Copyright © 1973
Charles Knight & Co. Ltd.
ISBN 0 85314 185 1

Printed in Great Britain by
Brown, Knight & Truscott Ltd., London and Tonbridge

CONTENTS

FOREWORD

The Fabian Biographical Series, consisting of short biographies of pioneer radicals, socialists and social reformers, has been in constant demand since the first tract was published in October, 1912. Some of the early tracts were reprinted again and again, but for many years the whole of the series has been out of print. Nor has it been possible, except rarely, to obtain them from secondhand bookshops where occasional copies, listed in catalogues, have fetched high prices as collectors' items. Very few libraries have sets as this is the first time they are available in book form.

There were 15 pamphlets in the original series. In this first selection there are studies of Tom Paine, Francis Place, Robert Owen, William Lovett, Keir Hardie, John Burns and Beatrice and Sidney Webb. Others will be published in a subsequent volume.

Eminent writers and historians, including G. D. H. and M. I. Cole, St. John G. Ervine, Mrs. Barbara Hammond and Kingsley Martin, were commissioned to write the series and the quality of their work was such that subsequent full-length works were able to add only little which had not already been touched upon in these essays. Indeed, on Place, Lovett and the Webbs, there have been no full-length studies published since these pamphlets were first written.

For greater legibility the originals have been re-set in new type, but apart from the correction of a few misprints, nothing has been changed. We have retained, for example, the form of spelling favoured by Mr. George Standring, the printer of many Fabian publications. Standring, a member of the executive committee of the Fabian Society, was naturally supported in this by his fellow-Fabian, Bernard Shaw. We have added new bibliographies and notes on contributors to replace those which have become out of date.

In preparing this volume we have been fortunate in having the advice and co-operation of Dame Margaret Cole, President of the Fabian Society. Her lively introduction places these essays firmly in their Fabian background. Tom Ponsonby, General Secretary of the Fabian Society, has been enthusiastic and helpful from the beginning. Edmund Frow has supplied elusive texts from his vast collection. H. W. Bailey-King and the staff at Charles Knight made light of any difficulties and thus overcame them.

M.K.

I Margaret Cole
INTRODUCTION

It was late in 1912 that the Fabian Society, then 28 years old, brought out the first of its new series of *Tracts*—Biographical Tracts—of which 15 appeared between then and 1955 : all but one are reproduced in these volumes. The time needed for the writing and printing of these Tracts meant, obviously, that the decision to launch out in this line must have been taken some time previously; and in fact it was not unconnected with the period of sudden growth and inner turbulence in the Society, of which the first part was described by Edward Pease, its official historian, as "The Episode of Mr. Wells", and which, in my *Story of Fabian Socialism,* I called "The Second Blooming"— the first "blooming" having taken place nearly 20 years before, after the publication of *Fabian Essays.*

The radical revival which was so startlingly manifested in the general election of 1906 brought something like 2,000 or 3,000 new recruits to the Fabian Society—"the *little boom"*, as Beatrice Webb correctly if patronisingly described it—but they tended to be recruits of a rather different stamp from those who had been admitted, after careful scrutiny by the Executive, in earlier years. Many of them were young. They were restive and critical, anxious to transform the Society in one way or another, to widen its scope, to force it to take up attitudes and enter upon activities not hitherto contemplated. In the first clash, as all social historians know well, the rebels lined up under the banner of H. G. Wells, whose lively memorandum, *The Faults of the Fabian,* loudly demanded that Fabians should cease to be a grubby collection of coral-insects endeavouring to build a new world unseen, but should learn to think big and talk big, move into large bright offices and produce large bright publications on all the burning issues—in short, modernise and make a splash in

1

the world. Wells lost his battle, defeated, as he himself admitted in later years, largely through his own incapacity to handle a public meeting when self-pitted against such formidably-equipped adversaries as Bernard Shaw and Sidney Webb. After a brief period of recrimination he stormed out of the Society and showered abuse on its Old Gang in the pages of that rather over-lengthy political novel, *The New Machiavelli*. But, as Shaw pointed out to Beatrice Webb in a letter—in which he was later reinforced by the very near victory of those superior and more persistent tacticians the Guild Socialists, only a few years afterwards—the victory of the Old Gang was really only a paper victory, for the membership largely sympathised with what Wells was trying to do, even though it could not honestly support his detailed and wildly impracticable proposals. Realising this, in the years immediately following, the Society, as well as putting into effect one or two minor changes in organisation (and for the first time declaring itself in favour of votes for women), began to widen its scope somewhat; a Fabian Arts Group made its appearance, and several local Fabian dramatic societies—and the Biographical Tracts attesting new interest in the human side of radical history. To mark the occasion as a new departure —and also to draw the sting of a motion that "the appearance of Fabian publications be made less repellent"—the new series was equipped with covers containing portraits of its subjects, and a penny added to the selling price.

The series started well, with five studies appearing in the first 14 months. But then came the war, and most of the potential Fabian writers both Left and Right were engulfed in it, if not in the armed forces themselves, then as administrators or in course of time as opponents. The two Tracts which appeared while the war was on show a clear falling-off; one, indeed (No. 7) is so slight and has so little relevance to the main purpose of the series that it has been excluded from this reprint. Only when the war and the post-war turmoil were safely over was the series resumed with three more important Tracts. One, however, was not specially written, but was the printed text of a lecture given by G. D. H. Cole which, though its subject, William Cobbett, had little that was Fabian about him, signified the author's reconciliation, after the collapse of the Building Guilds and the eclipse for a very long while of the doctrines of Guild Socialism

2

and workers' control, with his former antagonists of the Old Guard. The two other Tracts of the twenties, on William Lovett and Tom Paine, were excellent value, but there was only a faint revival of the Fabian Society to support them.

With the rise, and subsequent crash, of the Labour Party and the conversion of the Webb Partnership to whole-hearted interest in and devotion to the principles and practice of Soviet Communism, the Society entered the long period of inertia from which it was only rescued, on the verge of a new world war, by amalgamation with the vigorous group of younger men and women which called itself the New Fabian Research Bureau, and from whom sprang so many of the parliamentarians and civil servants of the wartime coalition and of the Labour Government of 1945. The unquestioned leader in the regenerated Society was G. D. H. Cole, for so many years its chairman; so one is not surprised to find that the resumption of the series between 1941 and 1943 consisted of just three Tracts from that prolific pen. Finally, after the war was over, the Webb Partnership safely in Westminster Abbey and the Labour Government already fallen, Margaret Cole contributed *Beatrice and Sidney Webb,* the 15th and last of the Tracts.

There were no more, which is sad, for they sold well, and as a whole were very helpful to the reader, well-written by persons who had troubled to get up their subjects properly if they did not know them well already; they have dated little and contain a good deal which is still apposite, even after the passage of 60 years of violent change in society. This is not, of course, equally true of all of them; a small struggling society with scanty financial resources, as the Fabian Society has always been, cannot carry out a completely ordered plan of publication, but must depend, both for subject and for author, on the willingness and availability of writers to carry out the original design.

In this particular series, the intention was to choose subjects whose life and work would have a particular appeal to Fabian Socialists and those whom they hoped to enrol or to influence; and the first, in which St. John Ervine, the Edwardian dramatist who later published the best, so far, biography of Bernard Shaw, studied that masterly Radical wire-puller, Francis Place "The Tailor of Charing Cross", fulfilled that intention admirably. Place, though he came from a much lower stratum and had

3

known real degrading poverty, might almost have sat as a model for Sidney Webb, so far as his political energies were concerned; and Ervine is at pains to drive this home. "An Early Victorian Fabian", he calls him, one of the men who came after the first pioneers and built upon their faith without ever despising them for their errors; and he describes him as "full of rare courage and rare faith"—sentiments which in his later disillusioned years Ervine might well have felt like revising. His Tract does not, of course, go deeply into the vast mass of personal material in the British Museum which is known as the Place MSS; but the vividly-told story of the organisational effort which led to the 1824 repeal of the Combination Acts and prevented their reimposition in the following year might well carry lessons for trade union leaders of the present day. Technology may have helped striking miners to produce a much more rapid effect on the economy, but it does not appear to have had any comparable effect on the abilities of trade union organisers to plan campaigns.

The subject of the second of the Tracts, Beatrice Hutchins's *Robert Owen,* is a less obvious candidate, whose inclusion some would actually find surprising. The last 35 years of Owen's long life, from the settlement of New Harmony in Indiana through the co-operative and trade union boom and crash at the beginning of the 1830s to the millennial aberrations of its closing years, suggest anything rather than Fabianism. But those latter years were not covered by the Fabian Tract at all, which confined itself, as the sub-title states clearly, to *Robert Owen, Social Reformer.* (A footnote promised a supplement on Owen's later life, which did appear as *Robert Owen, Idealist;* but this was so sketchy and so largely concerned with experiments other than Owen's, that it has not been included in this collection.) As Social Reformer, however, Owen's claim is clear. In his brain, and in part in his practice, he pioneered almost all the ideas of social reformers for generations to come; in such diverse spheres as school education, its purpose, content, and method, state training of teachers, the proper attitude towards children and criminals, town planning and garden cities and communal services, high wages, short hours, factory conditions, the use of leisure, the reform of the Poor Law and the prevention of unemployment, his suggestions were so far in advance of his own day that some are still awaiting implementation even in our own. Beatrice Hutchins, co-author of the then standard history of factory legislation, was eminently fitted to describe them; and though her account of Owen's personal history needs supplementation from recent research into the finance of his various businesses, including New Lanark, the main picture stands today.

The inclusion of *John Stuart Mill,* by Julius West, first secretary of the Fabian Research Committee and later one of the historians of Chartism, as No. 4 in the series, needs no justification. Mill was undoubtedly a Fabian born prematurely, unfortunate to have died 10 years too early to have been one of the founding fathers. Some of his observations, such as that the Combination Laws were "enacted and maintained for the declared purpose of keeping wages low", and that "what is called morality in these times is a regulated sensuality" have a remarkably modern ring. He was ahead of his Utilitarian friends—and anticipatory of Bernard Shaw—in finding the problem of poverty fundamental to his social thought; and the very apposite fact that the father of Sidney Webb helped in his election campaign in Westminster only points the moral.

The third Tract, however, on William Morris, shows quite clearly that in this Second Blooming there were two classes of Fabian "heroes". Mrs. Emily Townshend was not a young Rebel, but a lady of past middle age, whose daughter was married to a young manager of one of the Liberal government's newly-created Labour Exchanges; but she was heart and soul with G. D. H. Cole and William Mellor in their revolt. The Tract on Morris, with its eulogistic appraisal of him as "the greatest Englishman who has passed out of our ranks", with his *Pilgrims of Hope* as a magnificent poem which "will kindle warm interest in our great-grandchildren", could only have been written by a fervent Guild Socialist; and it goes so far as to describe Morris's joining the Fabian Society as "a kind of death-bed repentance", adding that if he had lived into the new century he would assuredly have been a Syndicalist—a remark calculated to give the maximum annoyance to the Fabian elders. (The younger ones enjoyed it: it ran through five editions.) C. E. Vulliamy's *Charles Kingsley and Christian Socialism,* which was the last of the first batch, also derives from the Guild Socialist arguments. Kingsley was not anything approaching a Fabian, and the Christian Socialist movement of the mid-nineteenth century was neither long-lived nor of great importance in its history. But the Anglican social reformers of the next reign, members of the Church Socialist League, men like J. N. Figgis, the author of *Church and State,* or Conrad Noel, the Red Vicar of Thaxted in Essex, found that the philosophy of Guild Socialism, with its emphasis on functional autonomy for guilds of producers, chimed in very well with their own views for the future of the churches. So Kingsley enters the pantheon. The sixth Tract, in which Professor Edith Morley wrote on *John Ruskin and Social Ethics,* is also a trifle eclectic. The Fabians had never got "on terms" with Ruskin. They had to admit, because it was a fact, that his ideas, and the torrent of eloquence in which he expressed them, had played a great part in the "climate of thought" of radicals—working-class as well as middle-class radicals, many of whom went out of their way to acknowledge a deep debt to Ruskin without being quite certain what it was; but they did not really see why this should be so, and were cross about it—and for Ruskin for not being, as he clearly ought to have been, a socialist, but at best a sociologist, before sociology became a proud profession. Yet, surely, Ruskin's conviction that one cannot separate economic man from emotional man, and his insistence that proper consumption was a field of legitimate study, and that consumption must be clearly distinguished from fatal and disgusting "covetousness", was well worth the attention of bright young Fabians—as indeed it still is today. But the Fabians, as a whole, did not take to it—not because they knew much about the storms of Ruskin's own personal life, which had not in 1916 been disclosed in detail, but because they resented his general attitude; and this may account for a slight defensiveness in Professor Morley's treatment of her subject, a slight over-enthusiasm. She calls him, for example, "the pioneer of technical education"—an encomium more suited to Prince Albert; and ascribes to his influence "almost every modern measure of social improvement", a staggering assertion which in time of peace would certainly have been resisted by critics within the Society. It is a measure of its catholicity, perhaps, that the Tract was published.

In the twenties, however, orderly progress was resumed. Tract 9, on Cobbett, has already been mentioned, and however explosively Cobbett's ghost would have reacted if it had found itself in the company of Fabians, whom he would certainly have classed with the "feelthy philosophers" of the *Edinburgh Review,* there can be no doubt about his status as a radical pioneer. *William Lovett* (No. 8) and *Tom Paine* (No. 10), are both very competent pieces of work, the one written by Barbara Hammond, whose historical reputation as co-author of *The Village Labourer* and *The Town Labourer* was unimpeachable, and the other by the young Kingsley Martin, six years away from becoming the unexpected editor of the *New Statesman,* but already an eager and vivid writer on radical socialism. Modern research has added little to the picture of Lovett, Fabian alike in his tactics and his enthusiasm for education; as to Paine, the man whose journalism upheld one group of successful revolutionaries in the dark days of Valley Forge, who was elected to the directing Committee of another in Paris, and who first demanded that the State should regulate the rights and relationships of property—Paine was so much the epitome of radical social-democracy, its programmes and its hoped-for practice, that it is only surprising that he was not included earlier. Victor Cohen's *Jeremy Bentham* is a slightly more off-beat choice. It may have been partly influenced by the rude remarks which the author of the Mill pamphlet had made about Bentham : but though he would not have been pleased to be called a Socialist, Bentham's mode of thought, his mathematical calculations, his continuous inventiveness of social devices and of neologisms like "international" which are now deeply embedded in the speech of all countries, clearly foreshadows the coining by the Webbs a century later of the phrase *"Measurement and Publicity"* as a suitable motto for the Labour movement.

The productions of the last phase mirror clearly G. D. H. Cole's leadership in the revived Society : the choice of subjects is his, and the evident erudition his. Here then is Keir Hardie, at the time the unquestioned onlie begetter of the Labour Party itself and of Labour in Parliament, waging a continuous battle with moderate unimaginative trade union leaders on the one hand and "no-compromise" socialists of *Tribune* type on the other, and establishing a compromise which according to his biographer here may not have been "correct" but was assuredly the only course possible at the time. Hardie's language, with its strong reminiscence of his Biblical upbringing dates today—though the descriptions of poverty quoted in Tract 12 still have power to make the blood boil—and more is known today about his tactical (and practical) discussions with prominent Liberals; but the picture of the man the very mention of whose name, many years after his death, had the emotional power to make a Labour meeting rise to its feet in homage or protest against attempts at innovation in the Labour Party, remains effectively unimpaired.

There follows Richard Carlile—the bookseller and publisher who claimed with some but not complete truth that with his printing of Tom Paine's work he had single-handed won the battle for the free press, and whom we might well celebrate today for his dictum that the common law in reality is "judge-made abuse"—and John Burns. John Burns, the "lost leader", the first man who had worked with his hands (at Price's Candle Factory in Battersea) to become a cabinet minister, the man who earned working-class hatred by "dishing the Webbs" over poor law reform, the only character of the 15 to have a really hostile biography written by a member of his own side (Joseph Burgess of the *Workman's Times*); John Burns the red-faced white-hatted traitor who for so many years after he had abandoned national politics out of principle in August, 1914, maintained that he might soon come back to lead a working-class party "without any of Hyndman's nonsense". Yet John Burns was a real leader, in politics as well as in industry, not just a waxwork in Madame Tussaud's, but the first trade union leader since the days of Owen who had performed the indispensable task of catching the public eye, with the "silver gleam of the docker's tanner"; and his life, inexcusably neglected by later historians, could be an important subject of study.

The Webbs were the last to be chronicled. The fifteenth of the Tracts is rather different from the rest in that it was written and appeared only a few years after Bernard Shaw's insistent propaganda and the existence of the first Labour government with a clear majority had laid the Partnership to rest under the flags of Westminster Abbey—where Ernest Bevin was so soon to be laid beside them. Beatrice had died President of the revived Fabian Society : there was therefore no need to remind the membership of the Webbs' existence or even to argue their importance. They were still living forces, whereas Burns, though he died in the same year as Beatrice, had been for nearly thirty years, as G. D. H. Cole had written "an historical monument rather than a man;" the job of their author then was rather to sort out and present in handy and significant form the main items of their multifarious works and days. This, since their scope was so wide and their energy so shattering, inevitably involved compression and omission; but Beatrice's Diaries, opened after her death, provided so great a mass of contemporary information that the only really fresh story which has come to light since the Tract was published is the magnificently machiavellian—and Fabian to the nth degree—Saga of the Hutchinson Trust, of the way in which Sidney clandestinely converted Hutchinson's legacy to the setting up of a School of Economics and Political Science—an idea of which the testator could hardly have dreamed—and of the host of pump-priming and camouflaging devices whereby he fed and nourished the struggling infant until it became the formidable institution which is called the L.S.E.

With this Tract the series once more comes to an end—a misfortune, to my mind. For taking account the intention of the series, there are a good number of other characters whose names cry out for inclusion : Robert Blatchford of the *Clarion,* Feargus O'Connor, H. G. Wells, George Lansbury, a founding Co-operator less idiosyncratic than Owen, Arthur Henderson, Ernest Bevin, Tom Mann, to take only a few examples. Even granting that Shaw has been over-written and that Ramsay MacDonald may still be too dangerous a proposition, short studies of these men and any of half-a-dozen others who could be mentioned would be welcomed by embryo Socialists. But they will have to wait a long while and pay a good deal more for their construction. For the reason for the stop was not, as some have conjectured, that the Society could not go beyond its founders : rather it was that the proliferation, just beginning in the fifties, of university departments of social history with their courses, degrees and diplomas, and even more, as time went on, of research theses financially grant-aided and painstakingly compiled with the object of obtaining doctorates and therewith advancement in the profession, has radically changed the pattern of publication. To-day, the brief narrative and characterising biography has all too often given place to the learned monograph, weighed down with detailed library and museum references and swelled out with huge footnotes and lengthy quotations from tape-recordings or contemporary newspapers or other documents recently unearthed

—the whole gritty mass costing three or four pounds to buy. It seems a pity.

It was the end, however; and all that remains for one re-reading the whole at the present time, is to add one or two general comments. What must strike everyone at first reading is—how little these apostles of brotherly love loved one another. Were there a Valhalla for Radicals, they would hardly have fraternised happily in its halls—nor would many of the others who might have been included. Burns and Hardie, when both were M.Ps., despised and disliked each other; Robert Owen thought the Benthamites, including Place, poor misguided fellows who based the whole of their philosophic system upon a misapprehension; Place found Owen an amiable impossibilist, Lovett found him overbearing, and Cobbett called him "a beastly writer". Few of his contemporaries could put up with Cobbett for long, and he poured abuse on Tom Paine until, having abruptly changed his own political views, in rather flamboyant repentance he brought Paine's bones back to his native land—where they were lost. Carlile had an obscure but fierce quarrel with William Hetherington; H. G. Wells thought the Webbs wicked intriguing old spoilsports, and they found him an irresponsible ill-mannered libertine. And so it goes on. Those who to-day deplore the seeming desire of Socialist propagandists to prove to the world at large that the vast majority of Labour and trade union politicians are fools or liars or traitors or all three, should look back on the records; it has happened before.

Yet it was not quite the same—at least, reading the story again, I do not feel that it was. Through all the recriminations of the past one seems to catch a sense of common purpose commonly felt, a consciousness that we are all really driving to one end, and that the aberrationists, by whatever names it was necessary (and desirable!) to call them, were in the last resort mistaken rather than damned, and might easily be—as often they were—reconciled with their antagonists when the scene changed. This is what camp-followers and rank-and-file workers meant when they spoke of "the Movement". The word is not popular with recent historians, some of whom have been busy pecking at it, Namier-wise, until they have proved that, as it lacks definition, it must have lacked existence also—that it was a sentimental fantasy as much as *News from Nowhere*. But it was not; there was no

10

fantasy in the way in which Arthur Henderson, a tough Trade Union politician if ever there was one, used to refer to "our great movement", which he served with faith and conviction until his death. Much of what has been written recently on the history of the Labour Party and other working-class organisations seems to suggest that the writers (unlike John Ruskin) have no grasp of the emotional content of the word—it may be that one of the results of technological development is to destroy it altogether, which would also be a pity. Meantime, these short lives remain readably attestant to it.

MARGARET COLE.

2 Kingsley Martin
THOMAS PAINE

Few great writers have lived so adventurously as Tom Paine. His great books, "Common Sense," "The Rights of Man," and "The Age of Reason," were only incidental to his career as an active revolutionist. The first made him a leader of the American Revolution, the second, the chief spokesman of the French Revolution, and, by the third, he brought to the working classes the new scientific outlook which had up till then been the preserve of the upper classes in England and France. He is one of the greatest English pamphleteers. Few men have so possessed the faculty for summarising in an unforgetable phrase the thought for which other men were groping, or been able so convincingly to reveal to their contemporaries the relation between the immediate issue and the general march of events. With him a general philosophy was always coupled with a practical activity, and to share his revolutionary enthusiasm was to be led to battle in the glorious certainty that the cause of the revolution was "the cause of all mankind." This is the reason why Paine was a greater man than his younger contemporary, Cobbett. For Cobbett fought always for a past which could not, in any case, be retained. Paine, with a truer, though too optimistic vision, was also conscious of the evils which resulted from the industrial and democratic upheaval of his age, but looked for help not to the dying forces of the past, but to the creative elements in the chaotic present. Thus, while Cobbett declaimed against the corruption of ministers and the immorality and obstructionism of George IV., Paine argued that these were the necessary results of aristocracy and hereditary monarchy. While Cobbett deplored bad landlordism and the degradation of the labourer through machinery, Paine declared himself for land taxes, motherhood endowment, and old age pensions, and looked forward to a time when machinery would bring wealth and not misery to the workers. While Cobbett hated the parsons who neglected and fleeced their flocks, Paine taught the workers to ridicule the superstitious doctrines of the Church, and to demand popular education, and a civilisation based on the knowledge which science could bring. Cobbett, as Mr. Cole has said, was a survival, even though a great one. Paine was a prophet. Both Cobbett and Paine were persecuted during their lives, but while most of Cobbett's writing died with him and the England he fought to preserve, Paine's works lived on. If we may judge by their enormous sale in cheap editions and the persecution which the upper classes thought it worth while to enforce against those who circulated them, Paine's influence over the working classes grew steadily after his death, and was perhaps, on the whole, greater than that of any other single revolutionary writer in nineteenth century England.

OBSCURITY AND FAILURE, 1737-1774

No one could have prophesied a great future for Paine when he arrived in America in 1774. He was already 37 years old, and his career had been singular but not promising. He had ventured upon many professions. He had been a sailor, a maker of ladies' stays, an exciseman, a schoolmaster; he had tried his hand at the evangelical novelty of lay preaching, and appears to have been prevented from taking holy orders only by his ignorance of Latin. He had been a shopkeeper and had gone bankrupt, and had lost one wife and unsuccessfully married another. His parents were small Quaker folk, who lived in the little town of Thetford in Norfolk. Paine does not seem to have enjoyed his mother's society or his father's trade of staymaking, and at seventeen escaped to sea on a privateer to fight against the French. Of his adventures as a sailor we know nothing. He seems soon to have returned, got married, and found employment as a staymaker in London. His spare time was devoted to science. He purchased a "pair of globes, and attended the philosophic lectures of Martin and Ferguson," made the acquaintance of Dr. Bevis, the astronomer, and followed the proceedings of the Royal Society. In 1760, however, his wife died, and Paine abandoned staymaking and procured a position as exciseman. He was soon dismissed for a species of negligence which was probably commonly practised by

13

excise officials, but after an interval in which he starved as a teacher in Kensington, he obtained reappointment as excise officer, this time at Lewes. In 1771 he married a second time, and joined with his wife and her widowed mother in keeping a small shop and "tobacco-mill." He spent much of his time in the White Hart Tavern with a group of friends, with whom he composed humorous verses and patriotic songs. For the first time his ability seems to have been discovered, and he was chosen by his fellow excisemen to act as their spokesman in an agitation for higher wages and an improved status. In 1772 he wrote and presented to the Government an elaborate memorandum setting forth their grievances.

Whilst ineffectively pressing his suit in London, his shop and work were both neglected, and on his return he was finally dismissed from the Excise. The year 1774 saw the climax of his misfortunes; not only was he once more without employment, but he was separated from his wife, with whom he had never been more than formally married, and he found it necessary to sell all his goods to avoid arrest from debt. Thus, already nearly middle aged, Paine found himself penniless and alone. He had, however, one asset—the acquaintance of Benjamin Franklin, who was then in London and at the height of his fame. Franklin had watched with interest Paine's efforts on behalf of the excisemen, and agreed with him in detesting the personal rule of George III. and the corruption of aristocratic politics. He suggested to Paine that he should seek his fortune in America, and supplied him with an introduction to his son-in-law in Philadelphia, to whom he described Paine as an "ingenious, worthy young man," who would do well "as a clerk or assistant tutor in a school or assistant surveyor."

THE AMERICAN REVOLUTION, 1774-1787

"It was the cause of America," Paine once wrote, "which made me an author." He had already learned to condemn the Government of England, which had so signally failed to utilise his ability. In America he found anger against England already uncontrollable, and he immediately set to work to gather together the forces of the New World to pit them against the Old. Europe was decadent: America offered hope and opportunity. Dr. Franklin's introduction immediately obtained him work as a journalist, and in 1775 he became editor of a new paper called the "Pennsylvania Magazine." "Probably," says Mr. Moncure Conway, "there never was an equal amount of good literary work done on a salary of £50 a year." "America," he wrote in the first number, "yet inherits a large portion of her first imported virtue. Degeneracy is here almost a useless word. Those who are conversant with Europe would be tempted to believe that even the air of the Atlantic disagrees with the constitution of foreign vices; if they survive the voyage they either expire on their arrival, or linger away in an incurable consumption. There is a happy something in the climate of America which disarms them of all their power both of infection and attraction." In one instance, however, he saw that a foreign vice had survived and even thriven on the passage to America, and he opened with a denunciation of the slave trade, and suggested practical means of abolishing slavery where it was already established. Five weeks later the first American Anti-slavery society was formed in Philadelphia. Paine's other articles were equally before their time. His "Occasional Letter on the Female Sex" and his article on "Unhappy Marriages" were among the earliest expressions of the modern feminist movement. Paine here anticipated in many ways the "Rights of Woman" which Mary Wollstencroft, later to be his friend in Paris, published in 1792. He went on to expose the absurdity of duelling, to plead for humane treatment of animals, and to advocate international arbitration as a means of preventing war. Most important, however, was his support of the American cause against England. He believed from the beginning that separation was inevitable, and, while Americans were still strongly royalist, he wrote, "Call it independence or what you will . . . if it is the cause of God and humanity it will go on." After the skirmish of Lexington he had no more doubts : it was the cause of God and humanity.

In January, 1776, he published "Common Sense." It is one of the world's great political pamphlets, and Paine's friends and enemies have agreed in ascribing to it an extraordinary influence. Cheetham, Paine's most hostile biographer, admits that "Common Sense," by "speaking a language which the colonists had felt but not thought," had a "popularity which was unexampled in the history of the Press, and terrible in its consequences to the parent country."

To understand its effects we must remember that even after Lexington few Americans had faced the idea of separation. Jefferson was still writing to ask John Randolph in London if he could help towards a reconciliation with England. Washington declared that if ever he was heard talking of separation he might be put down as "everything wicked." Americans had grown accustomed to the idea of armed resistance against bad government. Paine forced them to realise that this meant separation or ignominy. Reconciliation was an "agreeable dream" which had necessarily passed away. England, said Paine prophetically, offered "protection not from friendship but from self-interest. She would have defended Turkey from the same motive, viz., the sake of trade and dominion." Protection of this kind was no longer of any service to America. All Europe was waiting to trade with her when English interference was removed. Moreover, it was time America realised her maturity, and slipped the leading strings of the Mother Country. "A greater absurdity cannot be conceived of than three millions of people running to their seacoast every time a ship arrives from London to know what portion of liberty they should enjoy... The sun never shone on a cause of greater worth... It is not the affairs of a city, a country, a province or a kingdom but a continent; not the concern of a day, a year or an age : posterity are involved in the contest, and will be more or less affected even to the end of time. Now is the seed time of continental union, faith and honour. The least fracture now will be like a name engraved with the point of a pin on the tender rind of a young oak : the wound will enlarge with the tree, and posterity read it in full-grown characters."

In his plea for independence Paine carried with him the majority of Americans. Many loyalists, it is true remained, but the choice had to be made, and the cause of revolution triumphed. "Common Sense," however, had a second message to convey. The war to Paine was not merely a war against George III., but also one against monarchy : not only against a corrupt oligarchic government, but against all attempts by a privileged few to govern the majority. He made the cause of the American revolution also the cause of democracy and republicanism.

In this second part of his message Paine was not uniting Americans but dividing them. For the moment they could agree

16

on the issue of separation. But there were many who were willing to repudiate the government of England over America and yet continued to believe in the principles on which the constitution of that government rested. In opposition to these Paine may be said to have founded and led the Jeffersonian party. John Adams and those leaders who were afterwards to be known as Federalists, although united with Paine in the struggle with England, were at heart bitterly opposed to his principles. They believed in the English type of government portrayed in the writings of Montesquieu and Blackstone. They were, in fact, fighting to substitute an American President for an English King, not to overthrow aristocracy and establish democracy in its stead.

Paine, on the other hand, knew that English government was not as Blackstone painted it. Moreover, he was an admirer of Rousseau rather than Montesquieu. But he found one grave defect in Rousseau. By repudiating the principle of representation he refused the only mechanism which could have made democracy possible in the eighteenth century. "We find," Paine wrote later, "in the writings of Rousseau and the Abbé Raynal a loveliness of sentiment in favour of liberty that excites respect and elevates the human faculties, but having raised this animation they do not direct its operations, and leave the mind in love with an object without describing the means of possessing it."

For himself he saw no difficulty in achieving liberty. He was uninterested in Rousseau's argument that the general will could only be found in the city state. Majority government was the necessary political practice, and representation must take the place of the direct vote of the market place. In his account of the origin of society he closely follows the picture painted by Rousseau in the "Origin of Inequality," and does not try, as Rousseau tried in the "Social Contract," to found a society in which all men surrender their rights and yet retain their liberty unimpaired. "Society," he wrote, "is produced by our wants, government by our wickedness." The manifold advantages of co-operative life had irresistably led men to form societies. But government, "like dress, is the badge of lost innocence; the palaces of kings are built on the ruins of the bowers of paradise. For were the impulses of conscience clear, uniform and irresistably obeyed man would need no other lawgiver: that not being the case, he finds it necessary to surrender a part of his property to furnish means

17

for the protection of the rest." Government, therefore, is a necessary evil, whose sole justification is the protection of the rights of
individuals. If it fails to fulfil this function they have the right to
institute a different one. Tried by this democratic test, the English
government will not stand analysis. What is wanted in a government, if it is to safeguard the welfare of the people, is wisdom
and responsibility. Hereditary monarchy and aristocratic government have neither of these qualifications. "There is something
exceedingly ridiculous," he tells us, "in the composition of
monarchy." It first excludes a man from the means of information, and then empowers him to act in cases where the highest
judgment is required. "The state of a king shuts him from the
world, yet the business of a king requires him to know it
thoroughly." But if monarchy is bad, hereditary monarchy is the
last of absurdities. "The idea of hereditary legislators," he wrote
later, "is as absurd as an hereditary mathematician, or an hereditary wise man; and as ridiculous as an hereditary poet-
laureate." Any wisdom that exists in the English monarchy or
House of Lords is therefore purely accidental. And if wisdom is
unlikely to exist, the second important attribute of government—
responsibility—is wholly absent from the British Constitution. It
is so complex that no one can say who is accountable for anything. Montesquieu's view that liberty was the result of a "separation of powers," and the praise which Blackstone and De Lolme
bestowed upon a system of "checks and balances" seemed to
Paine therefore wholly absurd. A mechanism in which every part
was invented to check another must surely be a farce. If the
people did not trust their king, why did they have him at all? If
they had representatives, ought these not to have the power to
govern unhampered by a House of Lords, and responsible only
to those who have elected them? Why disguise it any longer?
The only glorious part of the British Constitution was the democratic part, the right which the people had, in some measure at
least, of electing their own House of Commons. Paine, therefore,
advocated a single democratic chamber, with a plural executive
responsible to no one except the representatives of the people.
The American Constitution of 1789, therefore, although embodying some of Paine's principles, displeased him by the autocratic
and lonely position of the President as well as by the existence of

the Senate. The Constitutions of many of the States were, however, exactly founded on Paine's model.

The identity of "Common Sense" was not hidden, and Dr.
William Smith, the President of the University of Philadelphia,
attacked Paine's writings as the "foul pages of interested writers
and strangers intermeddling in our affairs." Paine answered with
a bitter assault upon the Tories, but he did not then mention that
he had given the copyright and all profits from "Common Sense"
to the cause of Independence. Dr. Smith's sneer was certainly
unfortunate, for no one was ever more disinterested than Paine.
Within three months a hundred and twenty thousand copies of
"Common Sense" were sold at two shillings each, and the sale
probably reached about half a million copies in all, so that Paine,
who had never yet had enough to live upon and who remained a
poor man to the end of his life, had made and given away a
fortune for the cause he loved.

Less than a year after the appearance of "Common Sense" its
principles were incorporated in the Declaration of Independence.
It appears to have been the work of Thomas Jefferson, who had
become a friend of Paine's, and one paragraph, devoted to condemnation of the slave-trade, was, perhaps, composed by Paine
himself. But most Americans held that liberty, as James Russell
Lowell remarked, was "a kind of thing that don't agree with
niggers," and the paragraph was cut out. By this time, however,
Paine had given up his paper and joined the ragged and dis-
jointed ranks of the revolutionary army.

Fighting by day did not prevent Paine writing by night. During the critical days when Washington was struggling, in the face
of State jealousies and Congressional incompetency to keep the
cause of America alive, nothing so effectively inspirited the army
as the pamphlets which Paine wrote night after night by the
camp-fire. The exhilaration of valiant struggle against odds never
leaves Paine's pages. "These are the times that try men's souls,"
the "Crisis" begins. "I love the man who can smile at trouble,
that can gather strength from distress and grow brave from
reflection." He knew all the tricks of war propaganda. There is
always the assumption that America must win, coupled with the
reminder that the enemy, though feeble, can only be defeated by
their best efforts. English "atrocities" are described, and Lord
Howe reminded that England is used to winning in battle only

19

because she is usually opposed by mercenary armies, not by a nation in arms. "After all," he adds, "Englishmen always travel for knowledge, and your lordship, I hope, will return, if you return at all, much wiser than you came." But Paine's best abuse is reserved for the Americans who stood aside in the struggle. Perhaps it was because he was himself brought up as a Quaker, and had, until now, believed himself a pacifist that he found it so difficult to be just to the non-resister, and so readily assumed that he was a coward or a traitor. Refusal to join the American cause he declared to be disloyalty, and the Quakers, who claimed the virtue of consistency when they remained pacifists in war-time, were "like antiquated virgins who see not the havoc deformity has made upon them, but pleasantly mistaking wrinkles for dimples, conceive themselves yet lovely, and wonder at the stupid world for not admiring them."

Ability to write like this was rare, and Paine was called from the ranks to help the government more directly. He continued to write the "Crisis" and, in addition, became in effect Secretary of State for Foreign Affairs. He was sent on various missions, including one to France, and was in part responsible for the negotiation of the French loan. At a most critical moment, when money was urgently needed, he opened a private subscription list with a gift of £100 himself and obtained from others a sum sufficient to tide over the emergency. After the establishment of peace Paine's services were not forgotten, though it seemed for some months as if a somewhat indiscreet though zealous watching over American interests which led to his losing favour in Congress, would prevent his obtaining due recognition. In the end, however, he was voted considerable sums of money and presented with a farm at New Rochelle, which remained his small but sufficient source of income for the rest of his life.

THE FRENCH REVOLUTION

In 1787 Paine returned to Europe. During his last months in America he had been much occupied with a new kind of invention—an iron suspension bridge. He seems to have been anxious to get the approval of French and English authorities for his invention, and he came also with a diplomatic mission. His bridge was exhibited at Hammersmith, its principles much praised, and, with improvements, generally adopted. His diplomatic mission brought him into contact with the leaders of the Whig opposition, and amongst other visits he spent a week with Edmund Burke. Of English politicians Burke stood highest in Paine's opinion : his American speeches had seemed to Paine incomparably fine. But though they had been at one about stamp duties, no two men could really have been farther apart. Writing to Jefferson at this time, Paine remarked that democratic changes were coming to pass, and that these might involve some disturbances. Rulers, he added, ought not to fear these for "the creation we enjoy arose out of chaos." The rulers of eighteenth century Europe, however, were satisfied with things as they were, and were not prepared to welcome the element of creation discernible in the French Revolution. Paine himself was so interested that he left the fascinating pursuit of bridge-building to visit Paris. In November, 1790, he returned in time for the publication of Burke's "Reflections on the French Revolution." It was a magnificent piece of rhetoric, exactly calculated to rouse the aristocracies of Europe to the dangers of the democratic principles which had been implicit in his own "Speeches on America." "The forms of a free and the ends of an arbitrary government are things not altogether compatible," he had written. Could the Revolution then stop at establishing the forms of a free government? Burke still thought not, but whereas in the case of America this was an argument for reform, in France, it seemed, repression was the only alternative to chaos. The strength of Burke's appeal did not lie in its argument. It was obviously inconsistent to denounce Dr. Price for declaring that the people of England by once choosing their own governors, "cashiering them for misconduct," and "framing a government for themselves" had forever forfeited their right to do so again. To claim finality for the "Contract" of 1689 was as absurd as Hobbes' effort to bind posterity to a monarch because our forefathers once accepted one. In such cases Paine's question, "Who is to decide, the living or the dead?" is a final answer. But Burke's appeal was an emotional one. He drew a picture of the young Queen of France, whose beauty had so enchanted him on a visit to France some years before, and her kindly and well-intentioned husband now helpless in the hands of revengeful and ignorant sansculottes : he prophesied that extreme would follow extreme till France was destroyed, and, through their example, drag other countries

21

down to their own degradation. Such a picture could only rouse anger and horror in the minds of men who were ignorant of the actual conditions of France and were accustomed to identify a nation with its rulers. In the "Rights of Man" Paine answered on behalf of those who had in mind the common people of France. Burke, indeed, knew little of France, and, as Paine remarked, "When the tongue or the pen is let loose in a frenzy of passion, it is the man and not the subject that becomes exhausted." It was Paine's business to paint a different picture also incomplete, no doubt, but at least founded on some knowledge of the situation. "When Mr. Burke *cast his eyes over the map of Europe and saw a chasm that once was France,* he talked like a dreamer of dreams." The reality was very different. All the essential parts of France were still there—her people and her natural resources were unimpaired, indeed strengthened by the destruction of an arbitrary and corrupt government. To talk of indignity to the Queen of France was surely irrelevant. It was, as Paine said in perhaps the greatest of the phrases which give him immortality, "to pity the plumage and forget the dying bird." Burke's sympathy was concentrated on the plight of one foolish woman. Paine's mind was set on the age-long suffering of a misgoverned and tortured people. Under these circumstances there could be no argument between them, for they could not agree on the essential facts of the situation.

Early in 1791 Paine again crossed to France, leaving the publication of the first part of the "Rights of Man" in the hands of his radical friends, Godwin, Holcroft, and Hollis. He was disappointed to hear that the Parisians has thought it worth while to bring back Louis XVI. when once he had sought safety in flight. In America Paine had been the first to demand the proclamation of a Republic. In the same way Paris was still monarchist in sentiment when Paine arrived there, and begun his career as a French Revolutionist by placarding the streets and even the door of the National Assembly with a manifesto declaring that, while France could not "stoop to degrade herself by a spirit of revenge" she would do well to repudiate "Louis Capet" as soon as possible. Paine never changed his view about this. He was later to engage in controversy with Sieyés, who argued that, though illogical, an hereditary monarchy worked better than an elected one. Paine could see no reason for accepting this choice of evils. Why have any kind of monarch?

This visit to France was also short : he returned to England with Horne Tooke and other English radicals, and proceeded to organise meetings in favour of Republican principles and social reform. In 1792 the second part of the "Rights of Man" appeared. It was an elaboration and expansion of the principles laid down in Part I. Men's rights were of two kinds : some of them, such as the right to free thought and its expression, ought never to be interfered with in any way : others, such as the right to the property whose value a man has enhanced by his labour, can only be secured by government regulation. Government, therefore, is an organisation for the control and security of those rights which men cannot secure for themselves without regulation. All governments except democratic republics are in the interests of a few and the new American Constitution, though not altogether to Paine's liking, supplied Europe with a pattern of a democratic system. Having explained the value of a written Constitution which guarantees the permanent security of rights with which government may not attempt to interfere, Paine proceeded to an amazingly bold series of practical suggestions for a peaceful English revolution. Spence and Ogilvie had already put forward schemes of land nationalisation. Paine was less socialistic but perhaps more practical, and he did not consider the landowner the only source of social evil.

He computed the population of England at about seven millions, and believed that, if the Poor Law was abolished, the four million pounds thus saved would be sufficient for a grant of £4 per head to each child under fourteen, and a pension, beginning at £6 per annum for workers after the age of fifty. The residue of the money saved would be spent in a grant for education, a maternity benefit of £1 at the birth of each child, and the setting up of government work for the unemployed. This, however, was only a beginning. The abolition of sinecure offices and ultimately of kings and their courts would bring further revenue. Most productive of all, however, would be a graded estate-duty, which, beginning with an annual tax of three pence per pound on estates worth £500 a year, would rise on each thousand pounds till it reached twenty shillings in the pound for all annual revenue over £23,000 a year. Thus an estate which brought in this sum annually would be taxed £10,630, and any annual increment beyond this would, in fact, be confiscated by the State. Taxation of this kind would make indirect taxes unnecessary, and ensure the prosperity of the people. Finally, he hoped that reforms of this kind could be accomplished peacefully; that France, England and Holland would see the folly of rival armaments, and when they had formed an alliance and agreed to accept arbitration, be able to abolish their army and navy. What possible arguments, he asks, could his opponents bring against him? Would they dare to say that to "provide against all the misfortunes to which human life is subject" by devoting the national revenue to their prevention "is not a *good thing?*" Europe, in any case, had reached the end of aristocratic government, which alone stood in the way of reform. But "reason and discussion will soon bring things right, however wrong they may begin," and "if the good to be obtained be worthy of a passive, rational and costless Revolution, it would be bad policy to prefer waiting for a calamity that should force a violent one".

The book was an immediate success. Cheap editions were demanded by working class societies all over the country. Paine was burnt in effigy by upper class mobs in Plymouth, Warrington, and other places. The "Rights of Man" was at once translated into French, and so enthusiastically acclaimed that Paine was included in a special vote whereby Washington, Hamilton, Kosciusko, Pestallozzi, Mackintosh, Clarkson, Wilberforce, Bentham and Priestley were made eligible for membership of the National Assembly. He was at once elected as Deputy for four Departments. In England Pitt took alarm and decided to prosecute. Paine appeared and pleaded not guilty at the first summons, but prompted, it is said, by William Blake, who had heard a rumour of his impending arrest, did not wait his trial and fled to France. A letter from Washington amongst his papers induced the Customs Officer to allow him to leave England just before orders for his detention reached Dover. Although defended by Erskine in his absence, Paine was pronounced guilty by a jury which did not even wait to hear the judge sum up against him. Paine was never again able to visit England. This was the first of many trials in which the "Rights of Man" was to appear. It was also the beginning of the Reign of Terror in England which followed the outbreak of war with France.

Outlawed from England, Paine received a triumphal welcome in France. Everywhere he was fêted, and one of his companions wrote home that he seemed "in good spirits though rather fatigued by the kissing". On his arrival in Paris he was asked by Lafayette if he would act as intermediary in the presentation of the key of the Bastille to Washington. It was the proudest moment of Paine's life : he was the acknowledged link between the revolutions in the Old and New Worlds. He became for a time the unofficial ambassador of England in France, and extraordinary stories are told of the almost quixotic generosity he displayed in championing suspects whom he thought unjustly treated, even at the risk of his own life. He was intimately associated with a party of the Gironde, aided Condorcet in drawing up the abortive Constitution of 1793, and found good friends in Madame Roland, Mary Wollstencroft, Captain Imlay, and others of the more moderate revolutionaries. His first act in the National Convention was singularly courageous, and made him suspect in the eyes of Marat, Robespierre, and the party of the Mountain. He was well known as a Republican, but he did all in his power in the Convention as well as outside it to save the life of Louis XVI. Paine was a determined opponent of capital punishment, and his dislike of bloodshed was as sincere and unwavering as his belief in republicanism. His disappointment when Louis was executed changed to a feeling of despair as he watched the growing violence of the Revolution which seemed to be fulfilling Burke's most gloomy prophecies. As the power of the Gironde weakened and the power of Robespierre increased Paine's influence vanished. In any case, he knew no French, and could carry little weight in the Assembly. He devoted himself to writing "The Age of Reason". The revolution at which Paine aimed was always primarily a mental one, and when he saw that the passions and the follies of men could survive a change of their institutions he felt, as Robert Owen felt thirty years later that until men could be released from the bonds of religious superstition they were likely to remain subject to political chicanery.

In the "Age of Reason" Paine attacked Christianity and the accepted interpretation of the Bible in a manner scarcely less trenchant than that of Voltaire. His book did, in fact, for the working classes of nineteenth century England what Voltaire had done for the aristocracy of eighteenth century France. Like Voltaire, too, he believed in God, but his faith was far more fervent and less opportunist than Voltaire's. Neither was his purpose any less serious. He wanted not so much to attack Christianity as to usher in the "Age of Reason", when science and critical habits of thought should overcome political and social prejudices. At the end of 1793 he had just completed the first part of his work when the time came for him to follow his friends to prison.

Paine was not released until November of the next year. As an American citizen he expected the immediate intervention of Washington, who had been his friend in America. The American ambassador, however, was Gouvernor Morris, who disliked Paine and his opinions. He seems to have kept Washington in partial ignorance of the situation, but it is probable that, in any case, Washington, who was at that time seeking to make friends with the English government, was not anxious to offend them by interceding for Paine. For this Paine never forgave him, and his later attacks on Washington's politics were envenomed by a personal contempt for what he regarded as a betrayal of their friendship. It was not until Monroe had taken Morris' place and Robespierre's power was at an end that Paine was released. According to the story Paine was once actually sentenced to the guillotine, and only escaped through the mistake of a warder, who placed the fatal chalk mark on the inner side of his cell door so that in the night when the condemned were taken out to death Paine's door was missed.

One pleasing incident occurred during Paine's imprisonment. His life had so far been romantic in action not in sentiment. But as he lay in prison letters full of hope and friendship reached him in an unknown handwriting. They were signed "The Little Corner of the World". He answered in verse. Later, he discovered that the writer had been Lady Smythe, whose husband he had tried to befriend when he was in danger, and the friendship thus formed continued and grew deeper after his release from prison. Paine was an arrogant man, willing enough to speak of himself and his public services. But he was a lonely man, and except in his letters to Lady Smythe and in one letter to an old friend in America, in which he speaks wistfully of "marriage as the harbour of human life" which he had missed, we have few records of his more intimate desires and regrets.

After his release from prison Paine stayed eighteen months in Monroe's house. Though broken in health he seems to have found a new happiness in friendship, and lost little time in beginning again to write. He composed the second Part of the "Age of Reason", wrote his "Agrarian Justice" and his famous pamphlet on the "Decline and Fall of the English System of Finance". Paine saw at once that the Revolution, made possible by the workers of Paris, was being used only in the interests of the middle-classes. In "Agrarian Justice", published immediately after the failure of Babœuf's insurrection, he declared that God did not, as the Bishop of Llandaff had said, make "rich and poor", but only "male and female, and gave them the earth for their inheritance". Since, however, he deemed it impossible for the land to be shared equally by all, he suggested that a tax should be levied on inheritances. This money was to be expended on money grants of £15 to all citizens when they came of age, and on annuities of £10 for all who reached the age of fifty. In his currency pamphlet he prophecied the suspension of gold payments by the Bank of England, which followed the next year, and declared that inflation was a method of robbing the people in the interests of government bondholders. It was this pamphlet which afterwards changed Cobbett from Paine's enemy to his enthusiastic admirer.

Paine remained in France till 1802. Of his many activities the most curious was his discussion with Napoleon as to the best way of invading England. Paine regarded England as the stumbling-block to the universal establishment of a European Republic, and he was so willing to help to defeat her that he actually went to Belgium to watch the collecting of two hundred and fifty gun-boats destined for the English invasion. Patriotism was never one of Paine's faults. Napoleon, however, without, so far as we know, thinking any apologies due to Paine for his trouble, preferred a descent upon Egypt. Paine returned to Paris to lead an interesting little movement which resembled a pre-Comtist Positivism. The Society of "Theophilanthropists" met together to worship God through his works in the simplest manner possible. It aimed at popular education through lectures upon natural science and "the religion of humanity".[1] In 1801 Theophilanthropy was sup-

---

[1] Mr. Moncure Conway thinks that the Theophilanthropists were the originators of this phrase.

pressed, and in 1802 Paine knew that the Revolution was over.

He decided to return to America. The Revolution in England still tarried, and for France he prophesied that Napoleon would make himself Emperor, and "by his intemperate use of power and thirst of dominion cause the people to wish for their old kings, forgetting what beasts they were." "This is no country for an honest man," he said to a friend, "they do not understand anything at all of the principles of free government. I know of no republic in the world, except America, which is the only country for men such as you and I." "Ah, France! thou hast ruined the character of the Revolution virtuously begun, and destroyed those who produced it. I might almost say like Job's servant, 'I only am escaped!' "

But the cup of Paine's disappointment was not yet full. He found that even in America democracy was but partially established, and that its fruits were not so sweet as he had hoped. He could not approve of the Constitution. It was essentially aristocratic; it was English in structure, and its President was only a "fossilised George III." But democracy disappointed Paine in more momentous ways. He had been among the first advocates of the abolition of negro-slavery, and though his old friend Dr. Franklin was President of the American Anti-Slavery Society, the invention of the cotton gin had made slavery so profitable that he found few supporters. Washington, Madison, even Jefferson evaded the issue, and did nothing to aid the negroes who fled from oppression in Domingo. Finally, Paine found that democracy was not necessarily tolerant. Many who would have welcomed the author of "Common Sense" and "The Rights of Man" were virtuously cold towards the infidel who could write "The Age of Reason."

Paine, however, found friends, one of the best of whom curiously enough was Mr. Willett Hicks, a member of the Society of Friends, amongst whom Paine had been born, and whom he had at one time so manfully abused. But Paine remained a good infidel till his death in 1809 at the age of seventy-two.[2]

---

[2] Biographers have often a mistaken affection for the bodies of their heroes, and like to give us details of their funerals and graves. In Paine's case the future career of his bones was so unusual that it must be recorded. In 1819 Cobbett, then in America, struck with remorse for his early slanders on Paine, obtained permission

SOCIAL PHILOSOPHY AND INFLUENCE

The American and French revolutions brought into prominence three main types of political philosophy. Their best known exponents in England are Burke, Paine and Bentham. Hatred of the French Revolution led Burke to express in language which has become classic the principles of Conservatism. The essence of his doctrine is that at any time the existing régime, though perhaps capable of certain improvements, contains within itself the concentrated wisdom of the past, and must only be touched, if at all, with extreme reverence. Such institutions as private property, marriage, the Church of England and the British Constitution were therefore to him sacred and assured. If it was not always possible

to carry his bones to England. Christian burial had been refused Paine, even the Quakers denying admission to so famous a Deist, and his body had been placed in a corner of his own farm at New Rochelle. Cobbett carried it home to England in triumph, but failed to find anyone to take up his scheme for a mausoleum. Paine's bones remained in the Cobbett family till the bankruptcy of Cobbett's eldest son, when they became, as Mr. Cole remarks, an "unrealisable asset in the hands of the latter's creditors." After this we lose sight of Paine's bones until Mr. Moncure Conway discovered some of them later in the course of his indefatigable researches for traces of Paine. At the time, however, Cobbett's enterprise was a great opportunity for ridicule. Many stories had already grown up of Paine's "death-bed repentance," and the lie that Paine had died in fear of hell fire was the final tribute which outraged Christianity paid to his name. Enemies of Cobbett, who was always a good Churchman, were delighted at the opportunity of bracketing his name with that of Paine not only as a radical, but also as an infidel.

> "O rascal, why my name afresh
> Dost thou lug forth in canting tones?
> The worms content were with my flesh;
> But thou hast robbed me of my bones,"

said the ghost of Paine in one rhyme.

Byron, too, commented on the situation in a verse which he sent to Tom Moore but did not publish, since he did not wish to aid in the clamour against reform.

> "For digging up your bones, Tom Paine   ,
> Will Cobbett has done well;
> You'll visit him on earth again,
> He'll visit you in hell."

(Vide Cole, Life of William Cobbett, pp. 235-236.)

to find justification for them from considerations of immediate utility this was probably the result not of their inadequacy, but of our incapacity to see their true place in the evolution of the social organism. "We have," he wrote, "an inheritable crown, an inheritable peerage : a House of Commons and a people inheriting privileges, franchises and liberties from a long line of ancestors. This policy appears to me to be the result of profound reflection; or rather the happy effect of following nature, which is wisdom without reflection and above it. A spirit of innovation is generally the result of a selfish temper and confined views. People will not look forward to posterity who never look backward to their ancestors." Existing institutions, therefore, have a sanctity which necessarily contains an element of the mysterious, and when the individual finds himself in conflict with them he must learn to bow his reason before the embodied wisdom of the ages.

Against this view Paine opposed the conception of individual rights. The British Constitution did not seem to him either "the result of profound wisdom" or the "happy effect of following nature." He thought it merely a device by which an aristocracy could enjoy leisure at the expense of the people's rights. To Burke the organic flow of social unity was the important affair : to Paine the freedom of the individual in society. Freedom meant the exercise of certain rights which he called natural. According to the bad habit of the eighteenth century, he was apt at times to justify his belief in these rights by reference to a primitive society where they were supposed to have been freely exercised. The introduction of this makeshift support of the golden age and the social contract was unfortunate, because, when the historical fallacy was knocked away, the truth underlying Paine's doctrine was overlooked.

Paine's doctrine springs as Rousseau's did, from a passionate Protestantism. By nature and upbringing he felt it intolerable that any authority should stand between the individual and the use of his own reason. Sixteenth century Protestantism began in the same way but failed in courage, and set up the Bible in place of the Pope. Only Anabaptists and Quakers had accepted the whole faith of Protestantism in matters of religion. Paine, following the Encyclopædists, carried the same spirit into all departments of thought. The methods of science were to him, as to them, the only means of obtaining truth. Authority could order, but it could not prove. "Religion," he said, "is a great affair between man and his maker, and no tribunal or third party has a right to interfere between them." "Who then art thou, vain dust and ashes! by whatever name thou art called, whether a King, a Bishop, a Church or a State, a Parliament or anything else that obtrudest thine insignificance between the soul of men and its maker? Mind thine own concerns. If he believes not as thou believeth, it is a proof that thou believest not as he believeth, and there is no earthly power can determine between you."

With this in mind the doctrine of natural rights becomes intelligible. Its evil lay in an *a priori* mode of expression. But if Paine lacked the historical background of Burke, Burke's method had a corresponding weakness. Burke started no less than Paine from certain *a priori* assumptions, but while Paine left his bare to the most casual glance, Burke covered his with a generous parade of historical generalisations, which were in reality just as much the servants of his philosophy as the simple deductions of Paine. Moreover, it is possible to find just as strong a support in history for Paine's view as for Burke's. Paine might profitably have put the matter thus. Society is made up of individuals who have spiritual as well as economic needs. Now it is of the very nature of a spiritual existence that it develop from within, that no outside force can direct it, and that its development will be individual and unpredictable. Thus, there is a large part of the life of every man which must not be regulated by any government. Any society is self-condemned which does not give an opportunity to this spiritual life to develop, and we have the long record of history to show that men are willing to suffer imprisonment and torture, to give up ease and even life itself in pursuit of this freedom. On Burke's own historical grounds, therefore, it is clear that no government can last which fails to recognise and give scope to these fundamental needs of man. In this sense, therefore, natural rights are, as Paine says, in part at least, anterior to the State, since they arise out of the continuous demands of human nature, and, though the content of these demands change and is in part modified by the State, they remain superior to any other interests of the State and their fulfilment is, in fact, the test by which the State must be judged.

Paine's attack on existing institutions is, therefore, essentially, a moral and not a utilitarian one. So far, his philosophy is identical with that of Rousseau. But both were faced by a dilemma. Pressed to its logical conclusion the doctrine of indefensible natural rights leads to anarchy. Yet both were confronted with the fact of government, and knew that without it rights would not obtain any security. Rousseau solved the dialectical problem of accepting government and yet retaining complete liberty for the individual by a metaphysical juggle which opened the way for Hegelian conservatism. By the fiction of the general will, for whose expression he provided no machinery applicable to the eighteenth century, he claimed that popular sovereignty would restore to each individual the liberty which he had given up when he surrendered his personal rights to the community. Paine was more realistic. He saw that some rights needed governmental regulation if any but the strongest were to exercise them, while others could best be realised if left freely to the discretion of the individual. In this latter class the right to free thought and its expression was paramount. He did not claim that toleration was desirable, because the government was as likely as the individual to be wrong, or because truth was best served by the free interplay of ideas. He would have agreed with these utilitarian arguments but, to him, the heart of the matter was simply that no one, priest or king, could be permitted to stand between that individual and his conscience. "Toleration," he said, "is not the opposite of intolerance, but is the counterfeit of it. Both are despotisms. The one assumes to itself the right of with-holding Liberty of Conscience, and the other of granting it." But there were other rights, such as that of private property, the exercise of which could not be left to the individual's unlimited discretion. Unlike thought, land was limited, and its possession by one individual excluded ownership by another. Its regulation, therefore, Paine wished to entrust to a representative government. But lest this government should forget that some rights were outside its sphere of action, a Constitution must be drawn up and a Bill of Rights declared fundamental. This Constitution, though revisable from time to time by the people, seemed to Paine essential to good government. With Paine there can be no such thing as sovereignty, popular or monarchical, for in the last resort the individual is supreme and no majority, however great, can justly deny to him the ultimate right to follow his own conscience. In teaching this doctrine Paine was once more re-echoing the stoic conception of a Law of Nature as interpreted by English seventeenth century lawyers. There were contemporary Americans who could have expressed his demand for a fundamental law in legal phraseology. In England the result of the seventeenth century battle between Law, Parliament and King had been to establish doctrine of Parliamentary sovereignty. But this doctrine had never reached America, and lawyers there were still quoting Coke's argument that the judiciary had the right to nullify a law which was "against common right and reason," and Chief-Justice Marshall was ready to accept a Constitution which should take the place of the "fundamental law of Magna Carta," against which the passing waves of popular will might beat in vain. The doctrine of judicial revision was quite to Paine's taste, though the subsequent history of its exercise by the Supreme Court would scarcely have pleased him.

No conception of a fundamental bill of rights could find place in England, where Bentham was revising English law on Utilitarian principles. Bentham, in sweeping away the doctrine of natural rights as "nonsense, nonsense on stilts," lost sight of the importance of Paine's attack upon sovereignty. He assumed naturally enough that the democracy for which he worked would safeguard the rights of the individual. But, in truth, as de Tocqueville and John Stuart Mill were to teach later, there is no necessary connection between popular government and individual freedom. John Stuart Mill, indeed, in fear of the tyranny of the majority, was driven to advocate on Utilitarian grounds just that dividing line between the spheres of individual and State action which Paine had championed in the "Rights of Man." Moreover, Mill was led in another direction to revert to Paine's conclusions at the expense of Bentham's philosophy. For before the end of his life, Mill had learned to agree with Paine that the achievement of liberty depends upon a just regulation by the State of rights of private property.

In his analysis of natural rights Paine had seen that there was no sphere in which State interference was so necessary as the economic. Under different circumstances, the doctrine of the greatest happiness of the greatest number might have led Bentham to the same conclusion. But the corrupt incompetence of the eighteenth century State, and the industrial needs of the

33

middle class for whose advantages he was unconsciously theorising, led Bentham to believe that the greatest happiness would best be served by economic individualism. Thus, while agreeing with Paine that the State should not interfere with matters of belief, he differed from him in including the unlimited right to control of private property in the same category. In both these views he was supported by the evangelical thinkers who so much differed from him in theory and yet were so often in practice his allies. So it came about that in nineteenth century England, the thought of which was dominated by evangelicanism and utilitarianism, the doctrine of "laisser-faire" was applied not only to the rights which Paine called "personal," but also to that of private property.

There has, therefore, been a curious complication in English nineteenth century political theory. The battle for the right of free speech put the believers in natural law, the Utilitarians and Evangelicals all into one camp. They were united against the State by a long struggle which had begun in the sixteenth century, when the English Church had first become identified with the English State. Bound up with this was the middle class opposition to State interference in the economic sphere, and it was partly because Paine and Robert Owen after him were both opponents of Christianity while the majority of the working class in England remained evangelical Christians, that English working men have been very slow to accept Paine's conclusions that the State could usefully regulate the rights of property. Socialism and infidelity have been connected in England not only because leading Socialists have often been infidels, but because there has been a traditional belief that State interference with industry also involved interference with those spiritual rights for which nonconformists had fought so boldly in the past. Indeed, until Darwinism had gone far to discredit orthodox religion and the crying evils of industrialism had time after time necessitated the rejection of a "laisser-faire" policy, the workers themselves were commonly united with the middle classes in their dislike of State interference. With the exception of the Tory democrats, there is no English school of thought which looked to the State for help between the early land reformers, the most important of whom was Paine, and the Fabian Society which began its propaganda nearly a century later. It is a significant fact that when at length the connection between non-conformity and laisser-faire should have broken down, the first Labour Prime Minister of England should himself be an Evangelical Christian.

The failure of the Utilitarians to make Paine's distinction between personal rights and rights which the State should regulate had a further interesting result. The absolute right to the control of private property rested in origin upon the double theory of Locke and the Physiocrats that, by mixing his labour with the soil, the worker had a "natural" right to the produce which resulted from his efforts, and that, without this incentive to labour, industry would languish. Thus the right of private property meant, in fact, the right of the peasant to freedom from feudal dues. It was a theory of peasant proprietorship. When the classical economists, stressing the Utilitarian side of this argument, transferred the right of private property to all forms of ownership, they failed to note that the control of industry involves power of a different kind from that of the peasant proprietor. Soon, in fact, with the advance of the new industrialism, Locke's theory was being used in a manner precisely opposite from that for which it was intended, and it was left to Hodgskin and Marx to argue that, if labour created value and was entitled to the produce of industry, this was a condemnation and not a justification of the rights of capitalist ownership. The most remarkable of all Paine's claims to fame is that he, a man of middle class origin himself, saw the distinction between the old and new form of property, and advocated the rights of private property, not as the Utilitarians in practice did, for the advantage of the new industrial capitalist, but also for the wage earner whose only property now was his labour.[1]

[1] The confusion between the right to own what you make and the right to do what you like with what you happen to own still exists. It would be interesting to know, for instance, whether Lord Leverhulme, in claiming for himself the proceeds of negro labour in Nigeria, does so on the grounds that he has a "natural right" to the labour of other people, or whether he takes the Utilitarian view that the constitution of a negro-labourer is so different from a white Capitalist that his industry is stimulated by other persons reaping the fruits of his labour rather than himself.

3 St. John G. Ervine
FRANCIS PLACE

Francis Place was born on November 3rd, 1771, in a "sponging-house," or private debtors' prison, in Vinegar Yard, near Drury Lane, kept by his father, Simon Place, who was at that time a bailiff to the Marshalsea Court. He died on January 1st, 1854, at a house in Foxley Terrace, Earl's Court, at the age of eighty-two. His death attracted almost as little attention as his birth. He might have passed out of the memory of men had not Mr. Graham Wallas dug out the facts of his career from a mass of unattractive manuscripts, and printed them in his admirable "Life of Francis Place." Yet no man of his century was more necessary to the establishment of democracy in England than he. He was essentially the practical man in politics. Other men saw visions and dreamed dreams, but he, when they related their visions and retold their dreams, turned the visions into acts and the dreams into laws. He was an agitator of a totally different type from the agitator of common imagination. He had not the gift of oratory, and was a little distrustful of those who had; he could not stir an audience by emotional appeals, nor did he aspire to do so; he could not force men to deeds by finely written statements, though he tried to do so : he was too prolix, too eager to state all that there was to state, whereas the art of writing consists in knowing what to omit; but he could prepare plans for using to the best advantage the emotion which orators evoked. He made ways for the safe passage of democracy, and devised schemes for its protection while it was still weak. When the visionaries came to him and said, "The people must be free," he replied : "Yes, but how shall we make them free?" And then, so practical was he, instantly set about discovering a means to this end. The idealist and the practical man too frequently work in opposition to each other. It was fortunate for the cause of democracy that Francis Place, entirely practical, should always have desired to work with the idealists who were setting up the structure of a commonwealth in England in the early nineteenth century.

BOYHOOD AND EDUCATION

His father was a rough, careless, and sometimes brutal man, whose habitual method of communicating with his children was to assault them. "If he were coming along a passage or any narrow place such as a doorway, and was met by either me or my brother, he always made a blow at us with his fist for coming in his way. If we attempted to retreat he would make us come forward, and as certainly as we came forward he would knock us down." Mr. Place, after a number of years' service as a keeper of a sponging-house, took a tavern, but he spent so much of his money in the State lotteries that he frequently had to resort to his old trade as a journeyman baker in order to retrieve his losses, his wife in the meantime maintaining their family by needlework. From the age of four until he was nearly fourteen Francis was sent to one of the private adventure schools which abounded in the neighbourhood of Drury Lane and Fleet Street in the eighteenth century. The instruction given to him was of poor quality, but he was quick-witted and eager to know, and he easily became head boy in his school. His thirst for learning, however, did not prevent him from taking part in the street life of his day. He was, writes Mr. Graham Wallas, skilled in street games, a hunter of bullock in the Strand, an obstinate faction fighter, and a daily witness of every form of open crime and debauchery.

When the time came for him to leave school, he being then about fourteen years old, his father decided to apprentice him to a conveyancer, but he refused to become a lawyer; and his father, thus flouted, strode into the bar-parlour and offered him as an apprentice to anyone who would have him. A drunken breeches maker, named France, accepted the offer, and to him the boy was formally bound. During this time he became associated with a "cutter club"—an eight-oared boat's crew—who used to drink and sing together in the evening. The coxswain of this crew was subsequently transported for robbery, and the stroke oar was hanged for murder. A certain quality of pride saved Francis Place from dissoluteness, and in 1790, when he was

37

eighteen, and had given up his indentures, he met his future wife, Elizabeth Chadd.

MARRIAGE

The effect of this meeting was to check any tendency to viciousness he ever had. He then began the career of extraordinary endeavour, which lasted for the remainder of his life. His fortunes at this time were not happy. His trade was a declining industry, and, although he was a highly skilled workman, he could not earn more than fourteen shillings a week. His family was impoverished; his father, in ill-health, had sold his tavern and had lost the proceeds in a lottery, and his mother was obliged to work as a washerwoman. The time did not seem propitious for marriage; but Place, always indomitable and always hopeful, was prepared to take risks which Elizabeth Chadd, unhappy at home, was willing to share, and in March, 1791, when he was nineteen and a-half, and she was not quite seventeen, they married and went to live in one room in a court off the Strand. Their joint earnings were under seventeen shillings a week. "From this we had to pay for lodgings three shillings and sixpence a week, and on an average one shilling and sixpence a week for coals and candles. Thus we had only twelve shillings a week for food and clothes and other necessaries."

When he was twenty-one, and the father of a child, a strike took place in the leather breeches trade. At this time the Combination Laws were still in force. There were, however, a number of societies of a purely benevolent character in existence, and to one of these, the Breeches Makers' Benefit Society, Francis Place belonged. He has left an interesting account of this society and the strike which it caused: "The club, though actually a benefit club, was intended for the purpose of supporting the members in a strike for wages. It had now, in the spring of 1793, about £250 in its chest, which was deemed sufficient. A strike was agreed upon, and the men left their work."

The conditions of labour in this trade were exceedingly bad. A skilled workman, regularly employed, could earn a guinea a week; but regular employment was seldom to be had, and, generally speaking, wages for good workmen, often employed, were never more than eighteen shillings a week, and frequently a good deal less. Unfortunately for the leather breeches makers, the employers made a counter move, which eventually destroyed the strike. They urged their customers to buy stuff breeches instead of leather, and at the same time organized a boycott of all leather breeches makers, whether they were concerned in the strike or not. The Combination Laws theoretically applied to all members of the community, to employers as well as to workmen, but although they were rigorously enforced against workmen, Place, in after life, was unable to discover a single instance of their having been enforced against employers.

FIRST EFFORTS AT ORGANIZATION

Although Place was a member and a regular subscriber to the funds of his society, he seldom attended any of its meetings, and he was unaware of the fact that a strike had been decided upon, or that it had actually taken place, until he received his dismissal from one of his employers. The moment he heard of the strike he went to the club house, where he was informed that every man out of work would receive seven shillings a week from the funds. He made enquiries, and learned that there were as many members of the society as there were pounds in the chest, and saw that the funds would be exhausted in three weeks. His genius for organizing begun to stir. The stewards of the club had no plans laid. It seemed to them that all that was necessary was to declare a strike and pay out seven shillings a week to the members until the funds were depleted. They hoped that by that time the employers would also be exhausted. Place changed all that. He suggested that those members who were prepared to leave London, undertaking not to return for one month, should receive a week's payment in advance. These men would not receive any further sum. A number of the members accepted the offer because of the custom of the trade that a tramping journeyman should receive a day's keep, a night's lodging, and a shilling the next morning, and in some of the larger towns a breakfast and half-a-crown from country leather breeches makers' shops to help him along until he had obtained work.

When this matter was settled, and the fund was thereby relieved, Place proposed another scheme of an ingenious character, whereby each man remaining in London, instead of receiving seven shillings per week, should make up two pairs of breeches of a particular quality, for which he should be allowed four shillings each pair. These breeches were sold in a shop taken for the purpose, Place being employed as manager for twelve shillings a week. The effect of these proposals was that the fund, instead of being exhausted at the end of three weeks, lasted for three months. The strike, however, was unsuccessful. When the money was expended the men had to return to work on the employers' terms, and those of them, like Place, who had been conspicuous in the strike, were refused employment of any sort by any leather breeches maker. The failure of the strike was due to the facts that the industry was a declining one and that the masters, being few in number, were able to combine with little trouble against their workers.

A TIME OF ACUTE POVERTY

To this time of strike organization there succeeded, for Place, a time of acute poverty. For eight months he could not obtain work of any kind. He had expended his small savings during the period of the strike and so was without resources. His only child had sickened of smallpox and died. He and his wife suffered every privation that comes from lack of food and adequate shelter. They had pawned all that they had to pawn, obtaining for this purpose the services of an old woman who lived in the same house; for, though they were actually enduring hunger, neither he nor she would go to the pawnbroker in person. When they could no longer find pledgable goods, the old woman guessing their state, informed the landlord of the house, and he offered them credit for everything he sold, whilst his wife almost forced them to accept bread, coals, soap and candles. "And at the end of our privation, notwithstanding we were only half fed on bread and water, with an occasional red herring, we were six pounds in debt to our landlord."

When it seemed that the boycott upon him would not be removed, Place decided to leave his trade, and sought employment as overseer of parish scavengers at eighteen shillings a week. He obtained the post, but a few days before he was expected to begin his duties, one of his former employers sent for him. He declined to go, suspecting that this was a trap, such as had already been laid for him, to obtain an admission from him of the existence of a trade club, in order to secure his prosecution under the Combination Laws. Mrs. Place, however, went in his stead, "and in a short time she returned and let fall from her apron as much work for me as she could bring away. She was unable to speak until she was relieved by a flood of tears." He and she set to work, laboring sixteen and sometimes eighteen hours a day. "We turned out of bed to work, and turned from our work to bed again." In a short time they were able to redeem their furniture and to purchase necessaries. They moved to a more convenient home, and so prosperous did they become that Place was able to assist his mother to some extent.

SELF-EDUCATION

During this terrible period of his life Place read a great many hard books, "many volumes in history, voyages and travels, politics, law and philosophy, Adam Smith and Locke, and especially Hume's Essays and Treatises..... I taught myself decimals, equations, the square, cube and biquadrate roots. I got some knowledge of logarithms and some of algebra. I readily got through a small school book of geometry, and having an odd volume, the first of Williamson's Euclid, I attacked it vigorously and perseveringly." Prior to this time he had read "the histories of Greece and Rome, and some translated works of Greek and Roman writers; Hume, Smollett, Fielding's novels and Robertson's works, some of Hume's Essays, some translations from French writers and much on geography, some books on anatomy and surgery, some relating to science and the arts, and many magazines. I had worked all the problems in the introduction to Guthrie's Geography, and had made some small progress in geometry." In addition he had read "Blackstone, Hale's 'Common Law,' several other law books, and much biography." He obtained these books partly through the good offices of an old woman who acted as caretaker of chambers in the Temple—she borrowed the books from the rooms she cleaned—and partly through hiring them from a book shop in Maiden Lane, Charing Cross, "leaving a small sum as deposit and paying a trifle for reading them."

After a few months of prosperity his work slackened, and again he found himself unemployed. He immediately set about reorganizing the Breeches Makers' Benefit Society, set it up in 1794 as a Tontine Sick Club, himself the secretary at a salary of £10 per annum, and was able to obtain in the spring of 1795,

41

D

without a strike the increase of wage which had unsuccessfully been demanded in 1793. This success, apparently, was too much for the members of the society. They seemed to imagine that their labor troubles were for ever at an end, and they dissolved the society, sharing the funds among the members. Place lost his post. For a time he was employed by other trade clubs to draft rules and articles, and was appointed secretary and organizer of the carpenters, plumbers, and other trade clubs. He was now twenty-three years of age.

THE STATE OF EUROPE

The history of the world at that time was one of change and revolution. Ancient institutions were toppling, and great traditions were dissolving. In America and in France, republics had been established. In England, the old order was speedily giving place to the new : the aristocrat and landed proprietor was collapsing before the plutocrat and factory owner. In Ireland, discontent was about to swell into rebellion. The naturalistic philosophers had dealt stout blows to religion and the divine right of kings—the whole social theory was being revised and restated. The spirit of Voltaire and Rousseau was abroad in England, preparing the way which later on was to be trodden by Byron and Shelley. Thomas Paine had lately published "The Rights of Man," the most famous of all the replies to Burke's "Reflections upon the French Revolution," and a million and a half copies had been sold in England alone. Later came the "Age of Reason," which, shattered Place's Christianity.

It was natural, therefore, that in the great recasting of the world's beliefs which then took place, Francis Place should turn his mind towards those who were identified with the building of a democracy in England. In 1794 he became a member of the London Corresponding Society—"the mother," as Burke called it, "of all the mischief." It was characteristic of Place that he joined the society at a time when many of its members had been frightened into resignation through the persecution of some of its officers. "Many persons, of whom I was one, considered it meritorious and the performance of a duty to become members now that it [the society] was threatened with violence." It seems incredible that this society, with mild intentions, should have so terrified the oligarchy as it apparently did. Its political program consisted of universal suffrage, annual parliaments, payment of members, and its object was to "correspond with other societies that might be formed having the same object in view, as well as with public-spirited individuals." The title of the society led many persons to believe that its function was to correspond with the Government of France : the state of the public mind at that time was so panicky that such correspondence was instinctively assumed to be of a treasonable character. The society, however, had no relationship with the French Government. Its constitution was framed for the purpose of enabling working class organizations throughout the country to communicate with each other by letter without violating the law against the federation of political bodies.

THE LONDON CORRESPONDING SOCIETY

In May, 1794, Thomas Hardy, the secretary and founder of the society, together with ten other persons, was arrested for high treason. Place became a member of one of the committees which were formed to arrange for the defence of the accused men. The result of the trial was that the prisoners were acquitted, and instantly there came a great accession to the membership of the society. Place became a person of consequence, generally taking the chair at committee meetings. He began to urge that method of political agitation which remained his method for the rest of his life, and which he practised with singular success. He opposed himself to those who were continually urging that public demonstrations should be held chiefly to scare the oligarchs into granting reforms. Place did not believe in the excessive susceptibility of the governing classes to terror. "I believed that ministers would go on until they brought the Government to a standstill—that was until they could carry it on no longer. It appeared to me that the only chance the people either had or could have for cheap and good government was in their being taught the advantages of representation, so as to lead them to desire a wholly representative government; so that whenever the conduct of ministers should produce a crisis, they should be qualified to support those who were the most likely to establish a cheap and simple sort of government. I therefore advised that the society should proceed as quietly and privately as possible." His advice at this date was disregarded, and the scarifying demonstrations were held; but the oligarchy, instead of frantically passing ameliorative Acts, promptly passed Treason and Sedition Bills, suspended Habeas Corpus, and clapped the agitators into gaol without trial. The effect of this was almost to destroy the society, the more timid members scurrying out of it in panic which they had hoped would fall upon the governing classes. It lived on in a state of depressed vitality, but Place, finding his advice several times foolishly disregarded, resigned from it, and in 1798, the year of the Irish rebellion, it died.

ATTEMPTS TO ESTABLISH A BUSINESS

While Place was engaged in these political adventures, he was also endeavoring to raise his status from that of a journeyman to that of an employer. He thought of a method of doing this which he calculated would take six years to execute, although, as the event showed, he was able to do it in four years. The success of the scheme depended upon patience, much knowledge of human nature, very hard work and an indomitable will. Place possessed all these qualities. He began to build up a connection by getting a few private customers, and then he set about obtaining credit from drapers and clothiers. "I knew that by purchasing materials at two or three shops, however small the quantities, and letting each of them know that I made purchases of others, each would sell to me at as low a price as he could, and each would after a time give me credit." He did this, and soon found, as he had anticipated, that offers of credit were made to him. "From this time I always bought on short credit; instead of paying for the goods, I put by the money, taking care always to pay for what I had before the term of credit expired. I thus established a character for punctuality and integrity . . . and, as I foresaw, I should if I could once take a shop, have credit for any amount whatever."

MISFORTUNE IN BUSINESS

Unfortunately, his fortune did not flourish as well at first as he had hoped. His charges were low and his customers were few, and some of them neglected to pay for the goods with which he supplier them. His family, which now consisted of himself, his wife, and two children, began to suffer hardship again, and his wife, whose nerve had been shattered in the bad time that succeeded the strike of the leather breeches makers, urged him to give up his hope of becoming a master and resume his occupation as a journeyman. He steadfastly refused to do this, insisting that he would work himself into a condition to become a master tradesman. During this period, one of "great privation," he displayed that immense strength of purpose which distinguished him always, and which, a little later than this, was to endure a greater trial still. Only a man of unbounded self-confidence would have faced the chilly, grey view which lay before Francis Place at that time. Only a man of unquenchable spirit would have thought, when he was half-starved, of learning French so that he might give his children "the best possible education which my circumstances could afford." He propped his French grammar before him while he worked, and learnt it by rote. He spent his evenings in reading Helvetius, Rousseau and Voltaire, and despite his acute poverty, men of advanced views began to seek him out in order that they might talk to him on the topics of the time.

His fortune improved a little, and in 1799 he and a fellow-workman entered into partnership and opened a tailor's shop at 29 Charing Cross. The stock was obtained on credit, and the joint cash funds of the partners on the opening day were one shilling and tenpence! In two years they were employing thirty-six men! It was now, when prosperity seemed to be leaping upon him, that Place suffered his greatest trial. His partner married a woman who could not agree with Place, and, apparently at her suggestion, and on the strength of the promise of a large loan, he forced the business into liquidation and bought the goodwill for himself. Poor Mrs. Place lost her spirit altogether. "She saw nothing before her but destruction. . . . . Industry was no use to us, integrity would not serve us, honesty would be of no avail. We had worked harder and done more than anybody else, and now we were to suffer more than anybody else." For the rest of her life she was haunted by the fear of poverty. But this sudden disaster did not destroy Francis Place. He convinced his creditors that he had been vilely served by his partner, and they offered him so much assistance that, in 1801, three months after he had first learnt of his partner's perfidy, he opened a finer and bigger shop on his own account at No. 16 Charing Cross. From this time onwards his affairs prospered, and in 1816 the net profits

45

for the year from his business were more than three thousand pounds. He retired from trade in 1817, his age being forty-six years, and devoted himself to politics.

Place had one very notable quality—the power to concentrate on a particular piece of work—and during the first five years that he was tenant of the shop in Charing Cross, he devoted himself entirely to the task of building up his business. The time, as has been said, was troublous, and the borough in which he lived, that of the City and Liberty of Westminster, was the vent of discontent. By arrangement, the two seats for the borough were shared by the Whigs and the Tories. Radical candidates sought election without success. At the end of five years' tenancy of his shop, Place began to relax his attention from business considerations and revived his interest in politics. At first he found his friends among the well-to-do Whig tradesmen, most of whom were electors of the borough and great admirers of Charles James Fox, Sheridan and Erskine. Place, who "never had any respect for Fox and Sheridan, and not much for Erskine," bantered his friends on their regard for the Whigs, "who cared little for the people further than they could be made to promote their own interests, whether those interests were popular or pecuniary." Indeed, his hatred of the Whigs was almost excessive. Always they were "the dirty Whigs," the sole difference between them and the Tories being that "the Tories would exalt the kingly powers that it might trample upon the aristocracy and the people, while the Whigs would establish an aristocratical oligarchy to trample on the king and the people." About this time Cobbett, for whom Place had very little respect, was endeavoring, in his *Political Register,* to revive the democratic movement, and seeing in the borough of Westminster a likely seat for a democratic representative, he wrote four "Letters to the Electors of Westminster," which were printed in his journal. The last of these letters was published just after Lord Percy, eldest son of the Duke of Northumberland, and "a very young man, without pretensions to talents of any kind," had, through a ministerial trick, been returned unopposed for the borough. The letter bitterly reproached the electors for allowing themselves to be hoodwinked as they had been, and it had considerable effect upon those who read it.

46

WESTMINSTER POLITICS

But the reproaches of Cobbett were not the only force which set going a movement among the electors to secure independent representation for Westminster. The conduct of the Duke of Northumberland during the sham election was one factor, Sir Francis Burdett was another. The Duke ordered his servants, clad in showy livery, to distribute bread and beer and cheese among a number of ruffians who congregated about his house. The servants tossed chunks of bread among these men and women, who were, of course, alleged to be the free and independent voters of Westminster. The spectacle of these people clawing at the bread and lapping up the beer, which had been upset from the barrels and was running through the gutters, filled the electors themselves with disgust. In 1807 Sir Francis Burdett, a very wealthy man, sick of the intrigues of parties, was nominated, almost against his desire, as a candidate for the borough, together with one James Paull, who had polled a respectable number of votes at a previous election. Place, who had begun to extend his circle of acquaintance in the district, took charge of the electoral arrangements, and, despite the fact that the two candidates quarrelled four days before the date of the poll and fought a duel in which they were both seriously wounded, managed to get Burdett elected. Paull's candidature had been dropped. For three weeks Place worked at the committee rooms from seven o'clock in the morning until twelve o'clock at night. The difficulties seemed almost insuperable, and the discouragements offered to the Radicals were enormous. They had decided not to have any "paid counsellors, attorneys, inspectors or canvassers, no bribing, no paying of rates, no treating, no cockades, no paid constables, excepting two to keep the committee-room doors." They simply informed the magistrates of what they were doing, and left the responsibility of keeping the peace to them.

Place had organized this election so remarkably that he was resorted to by all sorts of persons for advice in connection with demonstrations, and the Westminster Committee became the recognized political authority in the borough. Sir Francis Burdett, sincerely democratic, was not a very able man, and a few years later he allowed himself to be convinced that Place was a Government spy. The grounds for this charge were too flimsy to bear examination, but for nine years Place and Burdett did not speak; and, owing to the aspersions made upon him, Place withdrew from active association with his former friends, although he always gave his advice to them when they asked for it, which was frequently. What follows explains why.

IMPRISONMENT OF SIR FRANCIS BURDETT

It happened in the course of time that Burdett came into collision with the Government in defence of free speech. He had made a speech in the House of Commons protesting against the imprisonment of one John Gale Jones, who had been committed to Newgate for organizing a discussion at a debating society on the action of the Government in prohibiting strangers from the House during the debate on the Walcheren expedition. Burdett printed his speech in Cobbett's *Register,* and this act was held to be a breach of privilege. A motion to commit Burdett to the Tower was carried by a majority of 38, but Burdett, barricading himself in his house at Piccadilly, announced that he considered the Speaker's warrant to be illegal, and that he would resist its execution by force. The soldiers were called out, the mob became agitated, and the City authorities, who were antagonistic to the Government, tried, without success, to convince the Government that their conduct was illegal. A council of war, to which Place was invited, was held in Burdett house, a number of half-crazy people were present, one of whom had devised a plan for defending the house from the attack of the soldiery. Gunpowder mines were to be laid in front of the house, so that the attacking soldiers might easily be blown to a place where there is neither war nor rumors of war. The common sense of Place was obviously necessary to restrain these wild conspirators. "It will be easy enough," he said, "to clear the hall of constables and soldiers, to drive them into the street or to destroy them, but are you prepared to take the next step and go on?"

They were not prepared to take the next step; they knew that it was impossible for them to do so; and so the crazy scheme crumpled up. Place did not object to the proposal to resist the soldiers by force because it was a proposal to declare civil war, but because it was impossible for the rebellious Radicals to make any sort of a fight. "There was no organization and no arms, and to have resisted under such circumstances would have been madness." All they could do, he urged, with any hope of success was to use the police forces of the City against the Government. For various reasons, the City forces were unavailing, and Burdett was arrested and conveyed to the Tower. Whilst he was in prison, Place was called upon to serve on the jury which inquired into the circumstances in which Joseph Sellis, valet to the Duke of Cumberland, died.

CHARGED WITH TREACHERY

The duke was very unpopular with the populace, and most people desired that the jury should return a verdict to the effect that the valet had been murdered by his master. Place, having carefully investigated the evidence, came to the conclusion that Sellis died by his own hand, and succeeded in bringing the other jurymen to the same conclusion, although they were all prejudiced against the duke. It was because of his conduct on this occasion that Place was accused of being a Government spy, and through it, with the help of the malicious, he lost the friendship of Burdett. For ten years the word "spy" was the favorite taunt thrown at him by those whom he displeased.

The effect of this on his career was partly good and partly bad; bad, because it led to his abstention from movements in which he would have been of the greatest service; good, because the leisure he now had enabled him to get into contact with men who had other points of view than mere Radicalism. He became acquainted with Thomas Spence, the land nationalizer, and with Robert Owen. Spence was a very honest, very poor, and very single-minded man, who loved mankind in the abstract so passionately that when he contemplated mankind in the concrete he lost his temper. He had fixed his mind so completely on land nationalization that he could not see or think of anything else. He suffered very great privations in propagating his views, getting his living by trundling a barrow about London, from which he sold saloop and pamphlets denouncing landlords and their villainies. He was John the Baptist to Henry George. The nationalization of land meant to him the establishment of the kingdom of heaven on earth and the birth of a new race of men. The man who is optimistic about the future is invariably pessimistic about the present, and it was so with this poor Spence. No man loved humanity so purely as he, and no man lashed his fellows with his tongue so bitterly. He reviled the men about him because they

49

were not the men of his dream .... Contact with this one-idea'd man sharpened Place's belief that the men of the vision can only be brought to reality out of the flesh and blood of the men of fact.

ROBERT OWEN

Robert Owen, that curious compound of a man of vision and a man of affairs, came to Place in 1813 with his "New View of Society." He was "a man of kind manners and good intentions, of an imperturbable temper, and an enthusiastic desire to promote the happiness of mankind." Like all men who have discovered the secret of human ills, Owen was convinced that his project, so "simple, easy of adoption, and so plainly efficacious .... must be embraced by every thinking man the moment he was made to understand it." It is, perhaps, the fundamental defect of the idealist mind that it forgets that human nature is not a rigid, measurable thing, and that the charm of human beings is not in their resemblances, but in their differences. Owen looked upon the world and saw it peopled by millions of Robert Owens; and, since he knew what Robert Owen desired, he imagined that he also knew what all men needed and desired. Once, after he had seen Owen, Place wrote in his diary : "Mr. Owen this day has assured me, in the presence of more than thirty other persons, that within six months the whole state and condition of society in Great Britain will be changed, and all his views will be carried into effect."

Place also became acquainted with many of the Utilitarian philosophers. James Mill, the father of John Stuart, and Jeremy Bentham became his close friends, and from them he derived an amount of knowledge which he could not otherwise have obtained. James Mill was a man of notable austerity of manner, as those who have read John Stuart Mill's Autobiography will know. He must have been an uncomfortable sort of man to live with, for he could not, as Place could, comprehend the value of idleness. He saw the world as an enormous schoolroom, and all the men and women merely scholars, but he did not appear to see any place in which the knowledge when obtained would be used. Like St. Francis of Assisi, he despised every worldly thing; but, unlike St. Francis, he had no hope of a better place. He simply acquired knowledge for knowledge's sake. Whenever Place visited the Mills, he, like all who stayed with them, was put through his lessons as relentlessly as John Stuart and Willie and Clara Mill. For four hours every day he was compelled to grind at Latin, repeating the declensions afterwards to the inexorable Mill. Out of this tremendous industry, this search for knowledge, there came that spirit which tests and is not afraid to reject. The Utilitarians had for their watchword "the greatest happiness of the greatest number." James Mill did not believe in happiness at all, but he was prepared to make the best of a hopeless case, and so he and his friends set themselves to the task of delivering England from the mess in which they found her.

MALTHUSIANISM

Place saturated his mind with the writings of the political economists, and about this time he got the one bee which he ever had in his bonnet. He read Malthus's "Principle of Population," and became a Neo-Malthusian in theory, for in practice he had fifteen children. Until he died he believed that the redemption of the people from poverty could only be brought about by the limitation of families. Laws wisely administered might do much, but they would only be so much trifling with a great problem. It is astonishing, when one reflects upon the fact that he possessed rather more common sense than is generally given to men, that he should so easily have believed this economic fairy tale. But although he held this belief very firmly, he did not, as the one-idea'd do, preach it exclusively. He saw that Neo-Malthusian doctrines were not likely to impress ignorant and impoverished men, and he set about the work of creating an instructed and prosperous race. There was an enormous amount to be done. The Combination Laws were still in force, and these alone made it impossible for the working class to improve their status. The theory of individualism at that date had completely gone out of its mind. There were no trade unions, no Factory Acts, no Public Health Acts, no Education Acts, no Workmen's Compensation Acts; the Corn Laws were still unrepealed; the franchise was a limited one; the Poor Law was that of Elizabeth. The agricultural laborer was in a state of frightful demoralization, and the town laborer was little better. There was such a state of affairs in England as should have inspired any self-respecting deity to fury, and have reduced the most optimistic of men to a state of chronic

51

depression. The odd thing about human nature is that it never despairs, and although that terrible time in England seems to us, who stand at this distance from it, to have been one in which obstacles were piled so high in the way of the reformer that progress was almost impossible, the reformers of the day regarded them with as good heart as we regard the comparatively trifling obstacles that lie strewn about the field of endeavor to-day. If Carlyle, who came later, saw men as "mostly fools," Place saw them as "mostly ignorant," and so that this description might no longer be applicable to his countrymen he devoted himself to the business of education.

ELEMENTARY EDUCATION

It is commonly alleged by the Church educationists that the system of elementary education in England was started by members of the Established Church. "There is a sense," the *Church Times* says, "in which every Christian is a member of the Church of England . . . . but a Quaker is an unbaptized person, and therefore not a Christian at all." In 1798, a young Quaker, named Joseph Lancaster, began to teach poor boys in a shed adjoining his father's house in Borough Road. Lancaster was one of those men with whom Place frequently came in contact, a mixture of pure genius and pure folly. He could conceive big ideas, but he could not rear them after delivery. Place was the divinely-inspired foster-parent to the ideas of such men. He could not himself conceive large schemes, but he had the rare faculty of knowing a good idea when he saw it, and the still rarer faculty of being able to develop the idea and bring it to adult life. Lancaster was a wild creature, extraordinarily extravagant, somehow convinced that he had only to spend enough money for his difficulties to disappear. He was continually in danger of being committed to the debtors' prison. His proposal was to establish schools in which the pupils should be taught by older pupils— monitors. The whole education theory at that time, so far as working class children were concerned, was very hazy. The idea that the task might be undertaken by the State does not appear to have penetrated even Place's mind : he and his colleagues saw the Lancastrian schools resting for ever on a voluntary basis. In these circumstances, economy was essential. Subscriptions were not likely to be large or many, for a large number of influential persons were opposed to education for the working class. Lord Grosvenor, whom Place approached, "said he had a strong desire to assist the institution, but he had also some apprehension that the education the people were getting would make them discontented with the Government.... *we* must take care of ourselves." He did not subscribe. It must not be thought, however, that the necessity for economy was the cause of the monitorial system being employed. Place himself was of opinion that the teaching of children by children was a better way of educating them than having them taught by trained men and women. On this basis the schools were started after a great deal of wrangling between Lancaster and the trustees whom he had persuaded to provide the funds needed. In 1811 the "National Society for the Education of Poor Children in the Principles of the Established Church" was formed, and elementary education, so to speak, found its legs.

THE LANCASTRIAN SCHOOLS

The history of the Lancastrian schools is a saddening one. Lancaster quarrelled interminably, and finally he had to be pensioned off. The society was dissolved and a fresh one was formed, Place being a member of the committee. In drawing up the bye-laws of the new society he displayed his intense dislike of patronage of poor people. He deleted the words "poor" and "laboring poor" and any expression which "could give offence or hurt the feelings of anyone." he never at any time forgot that he, too, had suffered poverty; and even in connection with his fad, Neo-Malthusianism, he retained undiminished his loyalty to his class. "Mr. Malthus," he writes, concerning "Principle of Population," "denies to the unemployed workman the right to eat, but he allows the right to the unemployed rich man. He says, 'Every man may do as he will with his own,' and he expects to be able to satisfy the starving man with bare assertions of abstract rights. Mr. Malthus is not speaking of *legal right,* for, he says, the poor have a *legal right,* which is the very thing he proposes to destroy. It is an abstract right, which is denied to the poor man, but allowed to the rich; and this abstract, which has no meaning, although dignified with the title of the 'law of nature, which is the law of God,' is to be explained and taught to the poor, who are to be fully convinced."

Place worked with great assiduity for the success of the Lancastrian schools, and endeavored to start a series of higher schools on a similar basis, for which Jeremy Bentham devised a scheme of education. He mapped the whole of London into districts, in each of which there was to be a school to which poor parents could send their children on payment of a penny a week. This payment was to save pupils from the stigma of charity. But all his educational plans failed. The monitorial system was a bad one; Lancaster was plotting against Place; and, worst of all, the committee began to quarrel among themselves. Place was an atheist, and he made no secret of his disbelief in God. Lancaster wrote to members of the committee, alleging that Place secretly designed to remove the Bible from the schools, and succeeded in creating so much ferment that, although he personally was not discredited, Place found it no longer possible to work with his colleagues, and so he resigned his position.

JOSEPH HUME

By this time he was well acquainted with Joseph Hume, whom he supplied with facts and material for argument in favor of reforms in the House of Commons. The combination of talents that here took place was a remarkable one. Hume, a very sincere Radical, had enormous vitality and was absolutely impervious to discouragement. He could not be put out of countenance by any-one. Place was industrious and certain. He could draw up rules and schemes easily. When he presented a document to a mem-ber of Parliament, the member could be assured that it contained facts and not fancies. These two men in conjunction, the one in the House, the other outside, both of them the butts of the wealthy and the powerful, between them compelled the oligarchy to do their will. But Place was the greater man of the two. Hume had the sense to do what Place told him, though now and then, as in the case of the Combination Laws, he had to be urged some-what strenuously to action. When Hume had to speak in the House, he went as a matter of course to Place for instructions, and Place primed him so well that he always made a mark in the debates.

Reference has several times been made in this short sketch to the Combination Laws. During the eighteenth century there had been passed a series of statutes directed against combinations of journeymen in particular trades. The first of the series was an Act of 1721 "for regulating the journeymen tailors within the bills of mortality," and the last the General Act of 1799 "to prevent unlawful combinations of workmen." A unanimous refusal to work at reduced prices was regarded as sufficient evidence of unlawful combination, and the non-acceptance by an unemployed journeyman of work offered to him by an employer in his trade meant liability to undergo a long period of imprisonment or to be impressed into His Majesty's sea or land forces. These laws were the most serious obstacle that lay in the way of labor. So long as they were on the statute book the condition of the working class nearly approached that of slavery. It was to remove them from the statute books that Francis Place worked, and in 1825-5, working almost single handed, he managed to do it. "The Labor Question," wrote Mr. Gladstone in 1892, "may be said to have come into public view simultaneously with the repeal, between sixty and seventy years ago, of the Combination Laws, which had made it an offence for laboring men to unite for the purpose of procuring by joint action, through peaceful means, an augmentation of their wages. From this point progress began."

THE COMBINATION LAWS

In 1810, the *Times* prosecuted its journeymen compositors for belonging to a combination and taking part in a strike. This is the text of the sentence inflicted upon them by Sir John Sylvester (Bloody Black Jack), the Common Serjeant of London :

"Prisoners, you have been convicted of a most wicked conspiracy to injure the most vital interests of those very employers who gave you bread, with intent to impede and injure them in their business; and, indeed, as far as in you lay, to effect their ruin. The frequency of such crimes among men of your class of life, and their mischievous and dangerous tendency to ruin the fortunes of those employers which a principle of gratitude and self-interest should induce you to support, demand of the law that a severe example should be made of those persons who shall be convicted of such daring and flagitious combinations in defiance of public justice and in violation of public order. No symptom of

55

contrition on your part has appeared, no abatement of the combination in which you are accomplices has yet resulted from the example of your convictions."

Bloody Black Jack thereupon sentenced the prisoners, who had asked for higher wages, to terms of imprisonment varying from nine months to two years.

In the same year that this happened the master tailors tried to obtain an Act of Parliament to put down a combination of their workmen, and Place, who was a master tailor, was invited to join the committee. He refused to join the committee, but they elected him a member of it against his will. He attended one meeting and told the masters as plainly as possible why he would not join them, and why they ought to abandon their project. They declined to do this, and a committee was appointed by the House of Commons to take evidence. Place went before the committee and offered to give evidence, which was accepted, and succeeded in bringing to the ground the proposal to quash the union. He now began seriously to get the laws repealed. He could not hope for assistance from the workmen themselves, who had made up their minds that the laws were irrevocable. Whenever a dispute took place between employers and workmen, he interfered, "sometimes with the masters, sometimes with the men, very generally, as far as I could, by means of one or more of the newspapers, and sometimes by acting as a pacificator, always pushing for the one purpose, the repeal of the laws." He wrote letters to trade societies, sent articles to newspapers, interviewed employers and workmen, and collected as much evidence as possible to assist him in his purpose. He lent money to the proprietor of a small newspaper in order that he might propagate his views in it, and he had copies of the paper distributed among people who were likely to be affected by it. He induced Hume to take interest in the proposal, and in five years had worked up so much feeling on the subject that he began to think the repeal of the laws was now certain. He was too optimistic, however, and it was not until 1822 that Hume gave notice of his intention to bring in a Bill for that purpose. This Bill was mainly intended to be a demonstration. "I was therefore in no hurry to urge Mr. Hume to proceed beyond indicating his purpose. I supplied him with a considerable quantity of papers, printed and manuscript, relating

to the subject, advised him to examine them carefully, and promised my assistance to the greatest possible extent for the next
session. These papers were afterwards sent to Mr. McCulloch, at
Edinburgh, who was at this time editor of the *Scotsman* newspaper, and he made admirable use of them in that paper. This
gave a decided tone to several other country papers, and caused
the whole subject to be discussed in a way, and to an extent,
which it had never been before."

THE REPEAL OF THE COMBINATION LAWS

Unfortunately, a Mr. Peter Moore, member for Coventry, in
1823 produced a rival Bill, which so scared the House of Commons that when Hume introduced Place's measure in 1824 it
met with considerable opposition. In view of the temper of the
House, Place advised Hume to abandon the Bill and move for a
Select Committee to enquire into the working of the laws. The
timidity of the general body of the House spread to some of
Hume's supporters, who induced him to whittle the motion to
nothing. Place began to stir. He lectured Hume at great length,
wrote a letter to him to be shown to his wavering friends, and
drew up memoranda for Hume's own benefit. The upshot of the
affair was that Hume was bullied by Place into moving for the
committee, which was appointed. A great deal of publicity was
given to the fact that the committee was sitting, and delegates
from workmen's societies began to arrive in London from all parts
of the country. Place interviewed them all. "I heard the story
which everyone of these men had to tell. I examined and cross-
examined them, took down the leading particulars of each case,
and then arranged the matter as briefs for Mr. Hume, and, as
a rule, for guidance of the witnesses, a copy was given to each."
Place had to encounter great difficulties in preparing matter for
this committee. The members of the committee would not allow
him to assist Hume officially, and they professed great indignation at finding Hume's briefs made out in Place's handwriting.
They talked of calling him before them for tampering with the
witnesses, a course of action which would have pleased him
immensely, but, preserving their sanity, they did not do so. The
witnesses, too, were difficult. Many of them had pet theories of
their own to expound, and Place was hard put to it to induce
them to keep their theories to themselves. All of them expected

57

E

that wages would instantly rise when the Combination Laws were repealed. "Not one of them," says Place, "had any idea of the connection between wages and population." Presumably Place, who spent three months in arranging the affairs of this committee, did a little unobstrusive propaganda on Neo-Malthusianism on discovering this.

His tactics in connection with the Select Committee seem to have been extremely able. The mere secretarial work which he performed was enough to try the strength of several men; but, in addition to this, he found time to think out the best way of circumventing the upholders of the laws. He had to make it clear to his friends that speechmaking would be a mistake, and that instead of the committee presenting a report in the customary manner, it would be better to submit their recommendations at first in the shape of resolutions, and then, when argument had been expended and members of the House were tired of the subject, present the report.

This was done, and all went well until the Attorney-General persuaded Hume to allow a barrister, named Hamond, to draft the Bills. Hamond made a sad mess of the business, and the reformers were now in a difficulty. The Bills were not what they wanted, but if they were not careful they might lose even those. The difficulty was surmounted by Place, who simply redrafted the Bills as he desired them to be and said no more about it. Hamond, having received his fee, did not bother further, and in due course the Bills were passed through the Commons without anyone quite understanding what had happened, and, after a period of peril in the Lords, they became statutes. The Combination Laws were repealed and working men were free to combine for their own protection.

AFTER THE COMBINATION LAWS

Place, having soaked his mind in the economics of the time (he had too much respect for economists) naturally enough failed to appreciate the necessity for Trade Unions. He imagined that the repeal of the Combination Laws would make them unnecessary. "The combinations of workmen are but defensive measures resorted to for the purpose of counteracting the offensive ones of their masters. . . . Combinations will soon cease to exist. Men have been kept together for long periods only by the oppression of the laws. These being repealed, combinations will lose the matter which cements them into masses, and they will fall to pieces." He had not at that date discovered that the securing of victory is not nearly so important as the maintenance of victory. When the Combination Laws were repealed the country was enjoying great prosperity, and the freed workmen speedily set about demanding a more adequate share in it. Strikes broke out everywhere. A section of the employing class began to agitate for the re-enactment of the laws, and Place, fearful lest this should happen, urged the workmen to desist from striking. But the workmen were not going to be persuaded even by good friends like Place to desist from enforcing their demands. They were profoundly convinced that the law had been used for the purpose of keeping down wages, and they were determined to get them raised, particularly as the cost of living was rapidly increasing. In the cotton trade a great lock-out by the masters took place. The shipbuilders refused to confer with their workmen on the question of grievances, and issued a note to the effect that members of the Shipwrights' Union would not be employed by them. "The conduct of both the sailors and shipwrights was exemplary, no disorderly acts could be alleged against them. But as the shipping interest . . . had the ready ear of ministers, they most shamefully misrepresented the conduct of the men, and represented the consequences as likely to lead to the destruction of the commerce and shipping of the empire. Ministers were so ignorant as to be misled by these misrepresentations, and were mean and despicable enough to plot with these people against their workmen. The interest of the unprincipled proprietors of the *Times* newspaper was intimately connected with the 'shipping interest,' and it lent its services to their cause. It stuck at nothing in the way of false assertion and invective; it represented the conduct of Mr. Hume as mischievous in the extreme, and that of the working people all over the country as perfectly nefarious; and it urged ministers to re-enact the old laws, or to enact new ones, to bring the people into a state of miserable subjection." It will have been observed by those who read the press carefully during the Railway Strike of 1911 and the Coal Strike of 1912 that capitalist journalism has not changed its character.

ATTEMPT TO RE-ENACT THE COMBINATION LAWS

To this agitation there followed something which is one of the most discreditable of the many discreditable things that politicians have done. The shipbuilders, lying hard, induced Mr. Huskisson and Mr. (afterwards Sir Robert) Peel to give notice of their intention to re-enact the Combination Laws. Huskisson had already solemnly assured Hume that he had no intention whatever of doing this, and Hume, believing Huskisson to be a man of honor, had accepted his word, and so was unprepared to counter his motion for a committee. Fortunately, Huskisson had drafted his motion clumsily. He asked for a committee "to enquire *respecting the conduct of workmen*" Hume and Place were quick to see that such an enquiry could only be adequately conducted if the persons into whose conduct enquiry was to be made were given an opportunity of rebutting the charges made against them, and, to the astonishment and disgust of Huskisson, they demanded that the workmen should be brought before the committee and examined. Another factor in favour of Hume and Place was that the Easter holidays were approaching and the committee could not meet for at least a fortnight. Place used the time to great advantage. He wrote to the trade societies, urging them to send delegates and to collect money for the payment of parliamentary agents and expenses; he collected money himself; he wrote a pamphlet exposing Huskisson's speech, and had it carefully distributed. He and Hume "nobbled" the Attorney-General and succeeded in persuading him to refuse to draft Huskisson's Bill. They filled the passage leading to the committee room with workmen demanding to be examined. Place wrote letters here and letters there, put witnesses through their paces, interviewed members, induced witnesses to demand payment for their services, which had been refused, although it was made to employers without cavil, and annoyed the committee so intensely that they talked of having him brought to the bar of the Commons. He and Hume could not prevent a new measure from being passed, but they were able to mould it to so great an extent that it differed very slightly from the previous measure moved by Hume. In the Commons. during the committee stage, the ministers attacked them grossly. "Wallace gave loose to invective and was disgracefully abusive. Huskisson became enraged and most grossly insulted Sir Francis Burdett and Mr. Hobhouse. Mr. Peel stuck at nothing. He lied so openly, so grossly, so repeatedly, and so shamelessly, as even to astonish me, who always thought, and still do think, him a pitiful, shuffling fellow. He was repeatedly detected by Mr. Hume and as frequently exposed. Still he lied again without the least embarrassment and was never in the smallest degree abashed."

AGITATION FOR REFORM

The repeal of the Combination Laws was not the only service which Place rendered to the cause of democracy, but it was the greatest. He might then reasonably have desisted from his labors, for he was growing old, and had suffered a great loss in the death of his wife, but he was of that order of men for whom there is no rest in life. There was work still to be done which he, better than other men, could do. The entire system of Parliamentary representation needed reforming, and Place threw himself into this work with as much vigor as he had displayed over the Combination Laws.

George IV, a man of ungovernable temper, who was likely, said one of his tutors, to be "either the most polished gentleman or the most accomplished blackguard in Europe, possibly an admixture of both," died on January 26th, 1830. He was a god with clay feet, from the point of view of Whigs and Radicals; for his sympathy with Whiggery during the time that he was Prince of Wales was an affectation chiefly for the purpose of annoying his father. The movement for reform, begun in the reign of George III, was opposed, with the King's concurrence, by the ministers of George IV. A few months before he ascended the throne, the massacre of Peterloo took place. He opposed, on religious grounds, the passing of the Catholic Emancipation Bill until the Duke of Wellington informed him that either he would have to compromise with his religious conscience or make ready for civil war in Ireland. The King compromised. All compromise denotes friction and ill temper, and the circumstances of the time made it inevitable that the conduct of the State should be difficult. The Duke of Wellington, who as a politician lost the reputation he had gained as a soldier, was of the damn-your-eyes type of statesman, a type which, while picturesque, is unpleasant to live under. He rigidly opposed himself to any reform of the parliamentary system, and soon after the accession of William IV he was forced to resign the premiership. The state of Europe was again disturbed. The Three Days Revolution had taken place in Paris, and Louis Phillippe, a constitutional monarch, had supplanted Charles X, a despot. This change heartened the reformers in England. A little later came another revolution; Belgium broke away from Holland, but here there was less heartening for the reformers, who feared that the King's ministers, in consort with the governments of Prussia and Holland might make war on France. Had such an alliance been formed for such a purpose there might have been in England a revolution approaching in fearfulness that which took place in France in 1793. Place, indeed, was prepared for this to happen. In the towns the housekeepers were banding themselves together and threatening to refuse to pay taxes should war be declared. In the country the laborers were burning hayricks in thirteen counties. In London, workmen, stirred by Robert Owen and Thomas Hodgskin, the forerunner and inspirer of Karl Marx, were in that mood of sullenness which is the prelude to revolt. Reform had to be, and so the Duke went out of power and the Whigs, under Earl Grey, came in.

THE REFORM BILL

The Whigs, always valiant and progressive when the prospect of office was remote, were strangely reticent about their principles when the prospect of office was near. Place conceived it to be his duty to make them voluble again, and so he began once more his old task or organizing agitation. Letters were written here, there, and everywhere; deputations were arranged; public opinion was moulded through the press and from the platform; and at length backbone was put into ministers, who would much rather have been spineless. The Reform Bill was introduced into the House of Commons on March 1st, 1831. It was a better Bill than Place had expected. Its sponsors thought it was worse than he expected, and they were prepared for his rage; but while he proceeded to agitate for more, he was fairly content with what he had received. The Bill received a second reading on March 21st, by a majority of one, which meant that defeat in committee was certain. On April 19th and 21st the Government were defeated, and on April 22nd the King prorogued Parliament, which immediately dissolved. The new Parliament met on June

14th, having a majority of over a hundred in favor of the Bill, which was at once reintroduced. The Tories so successfully obstructed its passage through the Commons that it did not reach the Lords until September 21st. On October 8th the motion for the second reading in the Upper Chamber was rejected by a majority of forty-one. It was now that Place's fighting instinct was thoroughly aroused. On the day following the rejection of the Bill he organized a demonstration in its favor, which was held on October 13th, and was a great success. On Monday he attended four public meetings, and on Tuesday, hearing that the Whigs were likely to compromise over the Bill, he wrote a letter, which he hoped would be shown to the ministers, in which he hinted that a riot would probably take place. He addressed meetings, drew up a memorial to the ministers declaring that if the Bill were not passed in its original form "this country will inevitably be plunged into all the horrors of a violent revolution," and immediately took a deputation to see Lord Grey. The deputation was received by that lord at a quarter to eleven at night in a very hoity-toity manner. "Any disturbances would be put down by military force." Dissensions began to separate the reformers themselves. The middle class reformers were prepared to compromise on the Bill, they to be included in it, the working classes to be excluded from it. The fury of Place on this occasion was remarkable. He wrote to Grote, the historian, "they [the working-class] proved that they were ready, at any risk, and at any sacrifice, to stand by us. And then what did we do? We abandoned them, deserted, betrayed them, and shall have betrayed them again before three days have passed over our heads. . . . We, the dastardly, talking, swaggering dogs, will sneak away with our tails between our legs."

The amount of work he did was almost as great as he did when he organized the campaign for the repeal of the Combination Laws; and it was as effective, for the Government introduced a new Reform Bill which was as good as, if not better than, the old one. The troubles of the reformers were not yet over, for the Bill had to be forced through the Lords. Before the Bill reached that House there was an outbreak of cholera in England, which made political agitation almost impossible. "The King, under the influence of his wife, his sisters, and his illegitimate children," writes Mr. Graham Wallas, "was now nervous about the Bill,

and disinclined to secure ministers a majority by creating peers."
The Whigs were ignorant of this, although the Tories were
aware of it. On March 26th, 1832, the second Reform Bill was
introduced into the House of Lords. Place had drawn up a petition of the peers in favor of the Bill, and this petition, "quietly
offensive," was printed in many newspapers. Contrary to expecta-
tion, the Lords seemed willing to read the Bill a second time, and
this fact caused suspicion to grow in the minds of the reformers
that an intrigue to spoil the Bill was being carried on. Place discovered that the intrigue was to substitute a twenty pound franchise for the ten pound franchise in London. On April 17th the
Bill was read a second time by a majority of nine, but was
wrecked in committee, by a majority of thirty-five, on May 7th.
The King declined to create the peers demanded by Lord Grey,
who resigned, and the Duke of Wellington was called again to
power. This in itself was sufficient to inflame the people. A bishop
was mobbed in church and the King was hooted on Constitution
Hill. Queen Adelaide was publicly execrated. People made pre-
parations for the revolution which they felt to be at hand, and
military men set about drilling the reformers for the fight.

"GO FOR GOLD"

A far simpler means of breaking the opposition than that of
bloodshed was found by Place. He caused a number of bills to be
posted about the country which bore this legend : To stop the
Duke go for gold. The people were advised to draw their balances
from the Bank of England and to demand payment in gold. The
depletion of the reserve was not a thing to be contemplated by
the directors of the bank with equanimity. The King, a poor
creature, gave way, Lord Grey obtained his guarantees, and the
Bill was safe.

Its passage, however, made small difference to the working
class, in whose minds the doctrines of Robert Owen and Thomas
Hodgskin began to develop. A new word was added to the
language—Socialism—and in 1833 Owen, with others,
endeavored to form a national federation of trade unions. The
originators of the movement, which quickly attracted half a million members, proposed to begin their work by declaring a
general strike for an eight hours day on March 1st, 1834. This
strike, however, did not take place, the funds of the federation

having been wasted on a number of sectional strikes, and the movement almost died. On March 17th, 1834, six agricultural laborers were sentenced to seven years transportation for "administering illegal oaths" while forming a branch of the Grand National Trades Union. The declining movement was restored to strength, and strong efforts were made to secure the remission of this brutal sentence, but without success. There followed to this a period of industrial unrest, and then gradually the Grand National Trades Union drooped and died. But if the thing itself was dead, the discontent which caused it to be was still potent.

THE PASSING OF THE REFORM BILL

The enactment of the Reform Bill, after a discussion spread over a period of nearly a century, only added half a million persons to the list of electors. Almost the whole of the laboring class was still unenfranchised. On August 14th, 1834, destitution legally became a crime. The new Poor Law, with its principle of deterrence, was the instrument to this end. The Poor Law Commissioners asserted that, in the interests of the independent poor (a phrase without meaning), the condition of the pauper should be less eligible than that of the worst situated independent laborers, on the ground that if this were not so, there would probably cease to be any independent laborers. Two things were then operating on the working class mind: one was the treachery of the middle class, which, with the aid of the working class, obtained enfranchisement for itself, and then refused to assist the working class to similar political freedom; the other was the poverty brought about by the failure of the harvests and the depression of trade in 1837. Dear food, low wages, and scarcity of work made the difficulty of devising a condition of life for paupers which would be less eligible than that of the worst situated free laborer one which the administrators of the Poor Law could not surmount. They did their best, however, and the result was an agitation against the Poor Law, a demand for factory legislation and for political reform. Out of this discontent came Chartism.

CHARTISM

In 1838 Francis Place drew up the "People's Charter," in which were set forth the famous six points: Manhood Suffrage, Equal Electoral Districts, Vote by Ballot, Annual Parliaments, Abolition

65

of Property Qualification for Members of the House of Commons, and Payment of Members of Parliament for their services. The Chartist movement in England resembled the Fenian movement in Ireland, in that a great deal of fuss was made about nothing. The proposals contained in the "People's Charter," seem to us to be mild enough, but to the oligarchy of that time they seemed to denote the end of all things; and men went into the streets and fought with the soldiers for the sake of the Charter. In 1839 ten men were killed and many were wounded in Newport, Monmouthshire. Three of the leaders were sentenced to death, their punishment being afterwards commuted to transportation. In 1842 there were riots in the northern and midland parts of England, and in 1848 the Chartists scared the wits out of England with a proposal to hold a demonstration at Kennington Common, which demonstration turned out to be as futile as the Fenian invasion of Canada.

Francis Place had little to do with the Chartists. His habit of mind was different from that of Lovett, Vincent, Cleave, and the other leaders of the movement. He was a Malthusian economist, they were Socialists and angry class warriors; and so, although he respected them and maintained friendly relations with them, particularly with Lovett, his association with them was of small account. His chief work was to draft the Charter and to secure the commutation of the death sentences into sentences of transportation. They belonged to the order of pioneers; he belonged to the order of men who come after pioneers. But though he could not work easily with pioneers, he was fully conscious of their utility. "Such men," he wrote, "are always, and necessarily, ignorant of the best means of progressing towards the accomplishment of their purpose at a distant time, and can seldom be persuaded that the time for their accomplishment is distant. Few, indeed, such men would interfere at all unless they imagined that the change they desired was at hand. They may be considered as pioneers who, by their labors and their sacrifices, smooth the way for those who are to follow them. Never without such persons to move forward, and never but through their errors and misfortunes, would mankind have emerged from barbarism and gone on as they have done, slow and painful as their progress has been."

OLD AGE AND DEATH

Place was now an old man. Misfortune closed in on him towards the end of his life. He had married a second time and the marriage was unhappy. He separated from his wife. He lost some of his money; and then, last scene of all, paralysis fell upon him and his brain became affected. Death came to him quietly in the night, when no one was by. He passed out, almost forgotten. "Can death," wrote Marcus Aurelius, "be terrible to him to whom that only seems good which in the ordinary course of nature is seasonable; to him to whom, whether his actions be many or few, so they be all good, is all one; and who, whether he beholds the things of the world, being always the same, either for many years or for years only, is altogether indifferent?"

Francis Place was not of that order of democrats who believe that the common man knows more than the rare man. He had not the Chestertonian trust in instinct; he was an early Victorian Fabian. "We want in public men," he wrote, "dogged thinking, clear ideas, comprehensive views, and pertinacity, i.e., a good share of obstinacy or hardheadedness." Kind hearts might be more than coronets, but good brains were better than either. On the other hand, he knew enough of rare men to know that they were fallible. Politicians with careers to fashion and reformers who have gone mad on their theories, these were creatures against whom the common man must always be on his guard. He could not suffer fools gladly, but he was not that worst of fools, the fool who will not learn from fools. Spence and Owen were fools in his eyes because they allowed themselves to become obsessed with one idea, but he was not oblivious of the fact that that idea was of value. It was his fortune not to possess a sense of humor; he could not joke. No man who can see the ridiculous can possibly be a leader; no man with a sense of humor can ever head a revolution, for the absurdities of enthusiasm will stand up before him so prominently that he will not be able to see the goal towards which the enthusiasts are marching. Keir Hardie leads men; Bernard Shaw laughs at them. Although Place had spent so many years of his life in pulling strings and had frequently seen men's motives laid bare before him, he did not become cynical. "I take the past," he wrote to Lovett, "and comparing it with the present, see an immense change for the better." In the same letter he wrote: "I saw that to better the condition of others to any considerable extent was a long uphill piece of work; that my best efforts would produce very little effect. But I saw very distinctly that I could do nothing better, nothing indeed half so good." He was full of rare courage and rare faith. I have called him a Neo-Malthusian, although that term did not come into use until the time of Bradlaugh and Mrs. Besant, because his views were identical with those who were so named. He propagated his Neo-Malthusianism to his own detriment and loss. It was sufficient for him to believe in a thing to nerve himself to bring it to be; but he had to be convinced that the thing was worth while. He saw men as brains wasted. Great masses of people were born, passed through the world, and died without conferring any advantage on their fellows; not because they were indolent or indifferent, but solely because use was not made of them. It was his desire so to order the world that every man and woman in it could move easily to his or her place. That man is a democrat who believes in a world where the wise man may be wise and the fool may be foolish, and no one will call him out of his name or demand more from him than he can give; who believes in diversity rather than uniformity, knowing that it is the variations from type which make type tolerable. Fools and wise men have their place in the world; the one may be the inspiration of the other. Plato and Aristotle were the fulfilment of each other. Owen and Place made it possible for democracy to be in England.

> Bring me my bow of burning gold!
> Bring me my arrows of desire!
> Bring me my spear: O clouds unfold!
> Bring me my chariot of fire!
> I will not cease from mental fight,
> Nor shall my sword sleep in my hand,
> Till we have built Jerusalem
> In England's green and pleasant land.

So wrote William Blake. If Owen wielded the sword and stretched the bow of burning gold, Place forged the one and made the other. It was that men might know that Place worked without ceasing; he made mistakes, but he had the right vision, and in good time men came to know more than possibly he had expected. It is our vision that matters, not the mistakes we make.

We may go forth like Columbus, to discover a new way to the Indies, and fail in our endeavour. But what matter? We may discover the Americas.

4 B. L. Hutchins
ROBERT OWEN

I have never advocated the possibility of creating a physical and mental equality among the human race, knowing well that it is from our physical and mental varieties that the very essence of knowledge, wisdom, and happiness, or rational enjoyment is to arise. The equality which belongs to the new, true, and rational system of human existence is an equality of conditions or of surroundings which shall give to each, according to natural organization, an equal physical, intellectual, moral, spiritual, and practical treatment, training, education, position, employment according to age, and share in local and general government, when governing rationally shall be understood and applied to practice.—"Life of Robert Owen," by Himself, p. iii.

Robert Owen is a figure of great significance in the social history of the nineteenth century. It is easy to show the limitations of his educational theories; it is child's play to explode his particular form of Socialism; and it is not difficult to demonstrate that his style was ponderous and he himself something of a bore. Yet, when all these admissions have been made, "whatever his mistakes, Owen was a pathfinder."*

He was born into a time of crisis and convulsion,
> "Wandering between two worlds, one dead,
> The other powerless to be born."

The Industrial Revolution was ignored by some contemporary thinkers, and was a hopeless puzzle, a dark enigma, to others. It is Owen's glory that while still young, with little education, and all the cares of business and commercial responsibility on his shoulders, he saw his way to the solution of some of the most pressing social difficulties and anomalies, and put his ideas in practice in his own factory and schools with astonishing success.

* Helene Simon.

There are personalities, such as William Morris, or even Lord Shaftesbury, who in their different ways are more attractive, more affecting, more sympathetic, but the remarkable fact about Owen is that his ideas on social legislation were at once original and practical. Our factory legislation is still based upon his suggestions more than upon those of any other man; and if the unspeakable horrors of child labor under the early factory system have been mitigated, and the disgrace of England in this matter to a large extent removed, it should not be forgotten that Robert Owen showed the way.

Robert Owen was born in Newtown, Montgomeryshire, North Wales, on May 14th, 1771, and was baptized on June 12th following. His father, also a Robert Owen, was brought up to be a saddler, and probably an ironmonger also, the two trades being, in small towns, then often combined. The mother's name was Williams, and she belonged to a respectable family of farmers living near Newtown, where the couple settled on marriage. The elder Owen, in addition to his two trades, filled the office of postmaster, and had much of the management of parish affairs in his hands. There were seven children, of whom the subject of this memoir was the sixth. Two died young. The most characteristic of Owen's reminiscences of childhood is the incident, as related by him, of accidentally swallowing some scalding "flummery" or porridge when quite a little boy, which so damaged his stomach that he was always incapable of digesting any but the simplest food, and that in very small quantities. "This," he remarks, with an optimism all his own, "made me attend to the effects of different qualities of food on my changed constitution, and gave me the habit of close observation and of continual reflection; and I have always thought that this accident had a great influence in forming my character."

The boy attended the school of a Mr. Thicknesse, who appears to have had no very remarkable qualification for his office, but to have been on friendly terms with his pupil, whom (at the age of seven!) he associated with himself as assistant "usher." Owen was a voracious reader, and devoured all the books his father's friends in the town could lend him. Among these were "Robinson Crusoe," "Philip Quarle," "The Pilgrim's Progress," "Paradise

71

Lost," Richardson's and other standard novels. He also read, he says, "religious works of all parties," being a religiously inclined child; but this multifarious reading gave him cause for surprise in the immense hatred and opposition he found between members of different faiths, and also between the different sects of the Christian faith. These studies were diversified by games and dancing lessons, in all which amusements he records complacently that he excelled his companions, adding, rather comically, that "the contest for partners among the girls was often amusing, but sometimes really distressing." He also remarks in this connection that "the minds and feelings of young children are seldom duly considered, and that if adults would patiently encourage them to express candidly what they thought and felt, much suffering would be saved to the children and much useful knowledge in human nature would be gained by the adults." There is, perhaps, here a touch of over sentimentality; but, considering how brutal the treatment of children at this period frequently was, it is interesting to find a man who was himself so signally successful in the discipline and management of children, urging thoughtfulness and consideration upon the adult mind of his time.

APPRENTICESHIP

The experiences of this baby usher lasted two years. At ten years old, at his own earnest wish, he was sent to London, to be under the care of his elder brother, who, having worked with a saddler, had settled himself comfortably by marrying his master's widow and taking over the business. A situation was found for little Robert with a Mr. McGuffog, who had begun life with half a crown, which he laid out in the purchase of "some things for sale," for hawking in a basket. The basket had been exchanged for a pedlar's pack, and subsequently the pack for an establishment at Stamford, "for the sale of the best and finest articles of female wear." Robert was domesticated with the McGuffog family for some years, treated like their own child, "carefully initiated into the routine of the business, and instructed in its detail." "Many of the customers . . . were amongst the highest nobility in the kingdom, and often six or seven carriages belonging to them were at the same time in attendance at the premises." He recalls of his master and mistress that the husband belonged to the Church of Scotland, the wife to that of England; but so placable and tolerant were the two, that they went every Sunday first to the one church, afterwards to the other, and he "never knew a religious difference between them." This observation early inclined him to view dogmatic differences as unimportant.

After a few years he left these good friends, and took a place as assistant in an old-established house on Old London Bridge, Borough side. Being now arrived at the mature age of fifteen, he says, "My previous habits prepared me to take an efficient part in the retail division of the business of serving. I was lodged and boarded in the house and had a salary of twenty-five pounds a year, and I thought myself rich and independent. . . . . To the assistants in this busy establishment the duties were very onerous. They were up and had breakfasted and were dressed to receive customers in the shop at eight o'clock—and dressing then was no light matter. Boy as I was then, I had to wait my turn for the hairdresser to powder and pomatum and curl my hair, for I had two large curls on each side, and a stiff pigtail, and until all this was very nicely and systematically done, no one could think of appearing before a customer. Between eight and nine the shop began to fill with purchasers, and their number increased until it was crowded to excess, although a large apartment, and this continued until late in the evening, usually until ten or half past ten, during all the spring months. Dinner and tea were hastily taken —two or three, sometimes only one, escaping at a time to take what he or she could the most easily swallow, and returning to take the places of others who were serving. The only regular meals at this season were our breakfasts, except on Sundays, on which day a good dinner was always provided and was much enjoyed. But when the purchasers left at ten or half past ten . . . . a new part of the business began. The articles dealt in as haberdashery were innumerable, and these when exposed to the customers were tossed and tumbled and unfolded in the utmost confusion and disorder, and there was no time or space to put anything right and in order during the day. . . . . It was often two o'clock in the morning before the goods . . . . had been put in order. . . . . Frequently at two in the morning, after being actively engaged on foot all day from eight on the previous morning, I have scarcely been able with the aid of the bannisters to go upstairs to bed. And then I had but five hours for sleep." This strain and overwork seemed to Owen more than his constitution could bear, and he obtained another situation, in Manchester. Here he found good living, kind treatment, and reasonable hours of work. He received £40 a year, with board and lodging, and considered himself to be "overflowing with wealth."

IN BUSINESS AT EIGHTEEN

When he was eighteen years old, he heard from a mechanic who supplied the firm with wire bonnet frames that some extraordinary inventions were "beginning to be introduced in Manchester for spinning cotton by new and curious machinery." The maker of bonnet frames after a time succeeded in getting a sight of these machines at work, and told Owen "he was sure he could make and work them," if only he had capital. He thought that with a hundred pounds he could make a beginning, and offered Owen half profits and partnership if he would lend him that sum. Robert immediately wrote to his brother William in London to ask if he could make the advance required, which request was granted. Robert gave notice to his employer and told him he was going into business for himself. So far as we can learn from his autobiography, no one seems to have been particularly astonished at this lad of eighteen starting on his own account. Meantime a large workshop had been obtained, and about forty men set to work making machines, the necessary materials, wood, iron, and brass, being obtained on credit. Of this light-hearted pair of partners, one, Owen, "had not the slightest knowledge of this new machinery—had never seen it at work." The other, Jones, the mechanic partner, knew little about "book-keeping, finance matters, or the superintendence of men," and was without any idea how to conduct business on the scale now projected. Owen's experience in drapery establishments had given him some idea of business management. As he sagely remarks, he knew wages must be paid, and that if the men were not well looked after, the business must soon come to an end. He kept the accounts, made all the payments and received monies, and closely observed the work of the different departments, though at this time he did not really understand it. He managed to maintain order and regularity, and the concern did far better than he had expected. The firm made and sold mules for spinning cotton, and did a fair amount of trade, though as Robert confesses, the want of business capacity in his partner caused him some fear and trembling.* After some months of this, a man possessed of a moderate capital offered to join Jones and put some money into the business. They offered to buy out Robert Owen, and he separated very willingly from his partner. By arrangement with them he was to receive six mule machines for himself, three of which only were actually handed over, with a reel and a making-up machine.

At this time Arkwright was starting his great cotton-spinning mill, but the manufacture of British muslins was still in its infancy. Owen says that before 1780 or thereabouts no muslins were for sale but those made in the East Indies, but while he was apprenticed to McGuffog a man called Oldknow, of Stockport, in Cheshire, began to manufacture what he described as "British mull muslin." It was less than a yard wide, and was supplied to Mr. McGuffog for 9s. or 9s. 6d., and retailed by the latter to his customers at 10s. 6d. the yard. It was eagerly bought up by McGuffog's aristocratic customers at that price, and Oldknow could not make it rapidly enough. This incident no doubt helped Owen to realize that there were considerable possibilities in the new machines. Although employing only three hands he was able to make about £6 a week profit. A rich Manchester manufacturer called Drinkwater had also built a mill for finer spinning, and was filling it with machinery, but being entirely ignorant of cotton spinning, although a first-rate merchant, was somewhat at a loss to find an expert manager.

MANAGER OF A LARGE MILL

Owen, hearing of Drinkwater's dilemma, went to his counting house, and, inexperienced as he was, asked for the vacant situation. The great capitalist asked what salary the youth required, and was amazed at the cool reply, "Three hundred a year." His protest, however, being met by a demonstration that this surprising young man was already making that sum by his own business, Drinkwater agreed to take up Owen's references, and told him to call again. On the day appointed he agreed to the three hundred a year, and took over Owen's machinery at cost price.

Robert Owen was now installed as manager in authority over five hundred men, women, and children, and his predecessor

* Autobiography, p. 23 (Charles Knight Edn., 1971).

having already left, and his employer understanding nothing of the work, he entered upon his new duties and responsibilities without any instruction or explanation about anything. Much of the machinery was entirely new to him. He determined, however, to do the best he could, inspected everything very minutely, examined the drawings and calculations of the machinery left by Lee, was first in the mill in the morning, and locked up the premises at night. For six weeks he abstained from giving a single direct order, "saying merely yes or no to the questions of what was to be done or otherwise." At the end of that time he felt himself master of his position, was able to perceive the defects in the various processes, and the incorrectness of certain parts of the machinery, all then in a rude state, compared with later developments. Owen was able to greatly improve the quality of the manufacture, and appears to have been very successful in the management of the workpeople. Drinkwater, who cared nothing for personal supervision of his mill, was much pleased to find his responsibilities taken off his shoulders. He raised Owen's salary, and promised to take him into partnership in three years time.

LIFE AT MANCHESTER

The next three or four years were a time of mental growth and stimulus for this strange lad. He made friends among the staff at Manchester College, and joined in evening meetings for the discussion of "religion, morals, and other similar subjects." He met Coleridge, who had wished to discuss with him, and became a member of the celebrated "Lit. and Phil.," or the Literary and Philosophical Society of Manchester, which gave him an introduction to the leading professional men of the town, especially those of the medical profession. He was shortly afterwards invited to become a member of what he describes as a "club or committee" of this society, which included the celebrated Dr. Thomas Percival as its president, Dr. Ferriar, and others. Dr. Percival invited Owen to speak at a meeting, a suggestion which embarrassed and confused the young man, who succeeded only in stammering a few incoherent sentences. On a later occasion, however, Owen read a paper on the subject of fine cotton spinning. which was well received by the society; and his name appears in 1796 as a member of the Manchester Board of Health, a body formed by Dr. Percival to devise remedies for the evil and unhealthy conditions incidental to factory employment.

His connection with Mr. Drinkwater came to a sudden end. Oldknow proposed to marry Drinkwater's daughter, and wished to be taken into partnership. As he had the reputation of being a wealthy, rising man, Drinkwater was eager to accept him both as a son-in-law and a partner, and asked Owen to abandon the agreement for partnership and remain on as manager at an increased salary. Owen's pride was aroused by this rather shabby attempt to break the previous contract, and he at once resigned, not only the prospect of partnership, but also his existing situation. He received more than one offer of partnership from capitalists who doubtless knew of his technical knowledge and business capacity, and after declining one rather haughtily because its conditions seemed to him not sufficiently favorable, he accepted another, which was, in fact, less advantageous. He became managing director of the Chorlton Twist Company, and had to superintend the building of its new factory and the installation of the machinery.

MARRIAGE

In the course of a business visit to Glasgow, where his firm had many customers, Owen made the acquaintance of Miss Dale, destined later on to become his wife. Her father was David Dale, owner of the New Lanark Mills, a man of great wealth, and at that time probably the leading merchant in Glasgow. Not only was his worldly position greatly superior to Owen's but there was a further obstacle to be overcome in his religious opinions. Dale was an extremely pious and narrow-minded Nonconformist; Owen was already a Freethinker, taught by determinism that a man's religious beliefs were irrevocably fixed by his antecedents and circumstances, and therefore could be the subject neither of blame nor praise. Having discovered that the young lady was not unresponsive to his affection, but that her father was unlikely to receive him favorably, Owen determined nevertheless to obtain an introduction to Dale, and, with his usual curious mixture of simplicity and audacity, conceived the idea of calling on him with a proposal to purchase the mills. Dale was somewhat astonished by such a proposal from so young a man, but advised him to journey to New Lanark and inspect them. The previous

77

negotiations that had been going on between the young people subsequently came to Dale's ears, and at first displeased him. Owen was a stranger, an Englishman, and unknown to him. Owen, however, was backed up by his partners, John Barton and John Atkinson, who arrived at Glasgow to go into the matter in person. The upshot of the matter was that their offer was accepted by Dale, who eventually consented to the marriage of Owen and his daughter. In 1798 or '99 (the dates are somewhat confused in the Autobiography) Owen found himself at twenty-eight manager and part proprietor of the New Lanark Mills and a married man.

AT NEW LANARK

This event forms the turning point in Owen's career. His extraordinarily rapid success in winning an assured position at an early age was no doubt due in part only to his own ability, since some part of it can be accounted for by the peculiar circumstances of the time, the introduction and development of steam power and machinery having made it possible to obtain profits on a startling scale. But Owen was a junior partner, and his own capital was but small. His first concern was to secure an ample dividend for the firm, this being the necessary condition of liberty to carry out the measures of reform in the works that he was already considering in his own mind. An isolated remark in the Autobiography (which is written in a rambling and unsystematic manner) gives the clue to his cogitations. Early in the time of his association with Drinkwater he "noticed the great attention given to the dead machinery, and the neglect and disregard of the living machinery," or, in plainer language, of the workers employed. Owen's peculiar power of detachment from the merely personal aspect of his affairs preserved him from the egotistic optimism characteristic of many manufacturers of that date, who, having greatly increased their own wealth through the Industrial Revolution, could not see its attendant evils. He had associated with Dr. Percival in Manchester, and had heard of the diseases and other terrible evils that were caused by the herding of pauper apprentices in insanitary dens in the neighbourhood of the mills. In some of the mills, especially those in secluded valleys removed from any check of public opinion, little children were made to work night and day, in heated rooms, uncleansed and unventilated, with little or no provision for teaching, care, or education. In the worst cases there were cruel beatings and other brutal punishments, and in most, probably, little thought for means of safeguard against and prevention of terrible accidents from machinery. Owen's intention was "not to be a mere manager of cotton mills, as such mills were at this time generally managed, but to ... change the conditions of the people, who were surrounded by circumstances having an injurious influence upon the character of the entire population of New Lanark."

THE MILLS

A considerable amount of information as to the state of these mills before Owen took them in hand is accessible, but it is not all unanimous. Owen, in his Autobiography, paints a gloomy picture; while visitors, who made excursions to New Lanark, professed themselves impressed by Mr. Dale's liberality to the factory children and his zeal for their morals and education. The discrepancy of evidence is, however, more apparent than real. According to the standard of those days the New Lanark Mills were models. They were kept much cleaner and were far better ventilated than the ordinary cotton mill, and the pauper children, whom Mr. Dale was obliged to obtain from a distance, were, as Owen himself told Sir Robert Peel's Committee in 1816, well fed and cared for. But, in spite of these advantages, Owen, who made himself intimately acquainted with the condition of the operatives, found much that was objectionable. Five hundred children were employed, who had been taken from poorhouses, chiefly from Edinburgh, and these children were mostly between the ages of five and eight years old. The reason such young children were taken was that Mr. Dale could not get them older. If he did not take them at this early age, they were not to be had at all. The hours of work were thirteen a day (sometimes more), including meal times, for which intervals, amounting to an hour and a half in all, were allowed. Owen found that, in spite of the good food and relatively good care enjoyed by the children when out of the mills, the long hours of work had stunted their growth and, in some cases, deformed their limbs. Although a good teacher, according to the ideas of the time, had been engaged, the children made very slow progress, even in learning the alphabet. These facts convinced Owen that the children were injured by being

79

taken into the mills at so early an age and by being made to work for so many hours, and as soon as he could make arrangements, he put an end to the system, discontinued the employment of pauper children, refused to engage any child under ten years old, and reduced the hours of work to twelve daily, of which one and a quarter were given to rest and meals. He would have preferred to raise the age of full time employment to twelve years and to reduce the hours of work still further, but, being more or less in his partners' hands, he was compelled to initiate these reforms gradually. He soon, however, arrived at a conviction, based on the experience gained by watching his own factory at work, that no loss need be incurred, either in home or foreign trade, by reducing work to about ten hours employment daily. The improvement in health and energy resulting from increased leisure was so remarkable as to convince him that more consideration for the operatives, more attention given to their conditions of work generally, especially shorter hours, so far from increasing expenses, would tend to promote efficiency, and as he also pointed out, would effect a great improvement in the health of operatives, both young and old, and also improve their education, and tend to diminish the poor rates of the country.*

It is, indeed, hardly credible that the schooling which was supposed to be given to the children after their seven o'clock supper till nine, could have been of much use after so many hours at work in the mill. Owen's view was that "this kind of instruction, when the strength of the children was exhausted, only tormented them, without doing any real good; for I found that none of them understood anything they attempted to read, and many of them fell asleep during the school hours."

THE VILLAGE

Owen also did a great deal to improve the village houses and streets, and build new houses to receive new families to supply the place of the paupers, and to re-arrange the interior of the mills, and replace the old machinery by new.

"The houses contained at that time no more than one apartment, few exceeded a single storey in height, and a dunghill in

* See Parliamentary Papers, 1816, Vol. III, Peel's Committee, Evidence of Robert Owen.

front of each seems to have been considered by the then inmates as a necessary appendage to their humble dwelling." Owen rebuilt or improved the houses, and had the streets daily swept and cleansed and refuse removed by men employed for the purpose. The next difficulty was to induce habits of domestic cleanliness, which at first Owen tried to achieve by means of lectures and persuasive talks. Finding more urgent measures were necessary, he called a public meeting and advised the people to appoint a committee from amongst themselves to inspect the houses in the village and report as to cleanliness in a book kept for the purpose. This suggestion at first nearly produced a revolution among the women, but it is stated nevertheless that the measure was put in operation, by Owen's orders, in so conciliatory a manner that hostility soon subsided.* Stores were opened to supply the people with food, clothing, milk, fuel, etc., at cost price. Previously the credit system prevailed, and all the retail shops could sell spirits. The quality of the goods was most inferior, and the charges high to cover risk. The result of this change saved the people twenty-five per cent. in their expenses, besides giving them the best, instead of very inferior, articles.†

It is, however, in his plans for mental and moral improvement that Owen is seen at his most characteristic and singular aspect. The factory population of that date, it must be remembered, was usually imported away from its own place of abode. Prejudice against cotton mills was very strong among the laboring classes of Scotland, who disliked the close confinement and long hours of labor incidental to factory life. The people working at New Lanark had "been collected from anywhere and anyhow, for it was then most difficult to induce any sober welldoing family to leave their home to go into cotton mills as then conducted."

* "Owen at New Lanark." By One formerly a Teacher at New Lanark. Manchester. 1839. Pp. 4, 5.

† There are risks in connection with shops run by employers for profit which are now well known, and have been the occasion of many Truck Acts; but in this case the profits of the stores were not taken by Owen, but were used for the benefit of the workpeople themselves and for the upkeep of the schools, the scheme resembling a consumers' co-operative store rather than a shop for private profit. Compare Report of Peel's Committee, Robert Owen's evidence, p. 22.

It is evident that the factory population thus recruited might not be altogether easy people to deal with. Owen says that he had at first "every bad habit and practice of the people to overcome." Drinking, immorality, and theft were general; and Dale, who had given but little time to personal supervision of the mills, had been freely plundered. But Owen was not disheartened. In a curious passage he shows his views on the subject of human nature and his characteristic confidence that with his methods all would be well. "There were two ways before me by which to govern the population. First, by contending against the people, who had to contend against the evil conditions by which, through ignorance, they were surrounded; and in this case I should have had continually to find fault with all, and to keep them in a state of constant ill will and irritation, to have many of them tried for theft, to have some imprisoned and transported, and at that period to have others condemned to death; for in some cases I detected thefts to a large amount, there being no check upon any of their proceedings. This was the course which had ever been the practice of society. Or, secondly, I had to consider these unfortunately placed people as they really were, the creatures of ignorance and vicious circumstances, who were made to be what they were by the evil conditions which had been made to surround them, and for which alone society, if any party, should be made responsible. And instead of tormenting the individuals, imprisoning and transporting some, hanging others, and keeping the population in a state of constant irrational excitement, I had to change these evil conditions for good ones, and thus, in the due order of nature, according to its unchanging laws, to supersede the inferior and bad characters, created by inferior and bad conditions, by superior and good characters, to be created by superior and good conditions." Success in this great undertaking could only be obtained by the knowledge "that the character of each of our race is formed by God or nature and by society, and that it is impossible that any human being could or can form his own qualities or character."

Owen drew up a set of rules to be observed by the inhabitants of New Lanark for the maintenance of cleanliness, order and good behavior. Every house was to be cleaned at least once a week and whitewashed at least once a year by the tenant; the tenants were further required, in rotation, to provide for cleaning the public stairs, and sweeping the roadway in front of their dwellings, and were forbidden to throw ashes and dirty water into the streets, or to keep cattle, swine, poultry or dogs in the houses. There were provisions for the prevention of trespass and damage to the company's fences and other property. A rather extreme view of authority inspired a rule requiring all doors to be closed at 10.30, and no one to be abroad after that hour without permission. Temperance in the use of liquors was enjoined. Toleration was urged upon the members of different religious sects and the whole village was advised "to the utmost of their power as far as is consistent with their duty to God and society, to endeavor both by word and deed to make everyone happy with whom they have any intercourse."

'THE SILENT MONITOR'

A singular device was adopted by Owen as an aid to enforcing good behavior in the mills, punishment of any kind being contrary to his principles. A four-sided piece of wood, the sides colored black, blue, yellow, and white, was suspended near each of the factory workers. The side turned to the front told the conduct of that person during the previous day, the four colours being taken as by degrees of comparison, black representing of course bad, blue indifferent, yellow good, and white excellent. There was also a system of registering marks for conduct. The superintendent of each department had to place these "silent monitors" every day, and the master placed those for the superintendent. Anyone who thought himself treated unjustly by the superintendent had the right of complaining to Owen, but such complaints very rarely occurred. With his usual simplicity, Owen attributes much of his success to this quaint little device, which probably, apart from his own character and influence, and the beneficial measures introduced, would have had but little effect. His humanity to the people is illustrated by the fact that at one time, when owing to trade conditions the mills were at a standstill for several months, he expended £7,000 in wages rather than turn the people adrift.

FINANCIAL SUCCESS

As a matter of business, the mills were highly successful. From 1799 to 1809, over and above interest on capital at five per cent., a dividend of £60,000 was cleared, which, however, includes the £7,000 spent on payment of wages as just indicated. Owen's partners, however, in spite of this financial success, took alarm at his schemes for social betterment. They came down from London and Manchester to inspect what had been done, expressed themselves highly pleased, listened to his plans, but eventually presented him with a silver salver bearing a laudatory inscription, and decided they could go no further with him. Owen offered to buy the mills off them for £84,000, and they gladly consented. A second partnership, formed to purchase the mills, resulted again in strain and tension. Owen then drew up a pamphlet describing his work at New Lanark, and the efforts he had made and hoped still to make for furthering the cause of education and improving the position of the people concerned, and making an appeal to benevolent and wealthy men to join him in partnership and purchase the business, not only for the sake of the immediate good of the employees, but in order to set up a model of what a manufacturing community might be. Among those who responded to the invitation were Jeremy Bentham, the philosopher, and William Allen, the Quaker and philanthropist. When Owen had completed his arrangements for taking over the business, and returned to New Lanark, the work-people were so overjoyed to see him that they took the horses out of the carriage and drew him in it home, in spite of his expostulations.

On balancing the accounts of the four years partnership now dissolved, it was found that after allowing five per cent. for the capital employed, the concern showed a net profit of £160,000.

A NEW VIEW OF SOCIETY

Owen came before the world as an educational reformer in 1813, when he published his "New View of Society : or, Essays on the Principle of the Formation of the Human Character." Education in England, as most people know, was grossly neglected at this time, especially in regard to the children of the working class. The grammar schools endowed by mediæval piety were appropriated to the instruction of middle-class children, and the charity schools founded in the eighteenth century were, though numerous, utterly inadequate for the needs of a growing industrial society, nor was the education offered in those schools planned on lines that could by any stretch of imagination be

84

called liberal. William Allen, Owen's partner, estimated the number of children in London who were wholly without education at over 100,000. From the very beginning of the nineteenth century education was already a battlefield. The Liberal Nonconformists, led by Lancaster, and the Church party, inspired by Dr. Bell, were each responsible for plans for cheap popular education. Owen gave generous assistance to both, but in the schools he established at New Lanark he went beyond either. The schemes of Bell and Lancaster were little but plans for economising the teacher, that is to say, by setting the older children to teach the younger. Owen distrusted the system of teaching by rote, and laid great stress on the personality of the teacher and the individual attention given to children.

A building was erected at New Lanark, to be used exclusively for school classes, lectures, music and recreation. There were two schoolrooms, one hung round with pictures of animals, shells, minerals, etc., and with large maps. Dancing and singing lessons were given, and the younger classes were taught reading, natural history, and geography. Both boys and girls were drilled, formed in divisions led by young drummers and fifers, and became very expert and perfect in their exercises. The children all wore white garments, given them by Owen, tunics for the boys, frocks for the girls, which were changed three times a week.

Before the shortening of the hours of work, the average attendance at the evening schools was less than 100 a night; but after the reduction on January 1, 1816, the attendance rose rapidly, and was 380 in January, 386 in February, and 396 in March.

The basic principle of Owen's educational system was that man is before all things a social and gregarious being, from which it follows that the happiness of the individual is most intimately bound up with that of the community of which he is a member. The practical corollary of this principle was the exclusion of all artificial rewards or punishments. No child got a prize for industry and good conduct, none was punished for idleness and disobedience, Owen holding the belief that such incentives are bad for the character, introduce false ideals and erroneous notions, and generally leave the will weak and unfortified against temptation when the artificial stimulus is removed. The scholars were taught to feel that the best incentive to industry is the pleasure of learning, and the best reward for kindliness and good behavior the friendly feeling of companionship set up. Instead of being scolded or punished for being untruthful or disobliging, the children at New Lanark were taught that sincerity and good fellowship are the means to a happy life.* A child who did wrong was considered to deserve pity rather than blame. Owen's son, Dale, who was a convinced believer in his father's system, points out that though children educated on the old-fashioned method, "over-awed by the fear of punishment and stimulated by the hope of reward," might appear very diligent and submissive while the teacher's eye is on them, habits formed by mere mechanical inducements would not be rooted in the character, not to mention that obstinacy and wilfulness may even be fostered by feeling there is something courageous and independent in thus rejecting baits offered to their lower nature and daring to choose the more perilous path. However that may be, there is a general testimony of those who visited the schools that the children were singularly gentle, happy looking, and well behaved; which, indeed is markedly the case in a school of the present day, run on similar principles, and known to the writer.

METHODS OF EDUCATION

As regards the teaching itself, every effort was made to make every subject attractive and interesting; to teach as much as possible by conversation and by maps, pictures, and natural objects; and not to weary the children's attention. A special feature of the system was the lecture on natural science, geography, or history, which would be illustrated, as the subject might permit, by maps, pictures, diagrams, etc., and, as occasion might serve, made to convey a moral lesson. Thus a geography lesson would be combined with descriptive detail and made to illustrate Robert Owen's favorite thesis that character is the product of circumstances. These lessons, the value of which obviously would depend mainly on the teacher's personality, seem to have given immense pleasure to the children, and to have greatly interested strangers, who were now visiting New Lanark in increasing numbers.

Instead of reading in a mechanical fashion or learning mere words by rote, the children were questioned on what they read,

* R. Dale Owen, "System of Education at New Lanark," 1824, p. 13.

and encouraged to discuss, ask questions, or find illustrations of what they read. Thus the habit was formed of endeavoring to understand what is read or heard, instead of conning a mere jingle and patter of unmeaning words, which, it is to be feared, make up the idea of "lessons" to many hapless little scholars even up till now. On this point Dale Owen asks pertinently whether a chemist, being anxious that a child should be able to trace and understand some valuable and important deductions, which with great study and investigation he had derived from certain chemical facts, would act wisely in insisting that the child should at once commit to memory and implicity believe these deductions? The answer is obvious; that any wise man would first store a child's mind with facts and elementary knowledge, and only gradually, as judgment and intelligence became matured, make him acquainted with theory and principle.*

In the training both of the character and of the intelligence, the aim of the school was to awaken the will and observation in the child to act and reflect for himself, rather than drive him by mere mechanical compulsion.

Many were the distinguished strangers who at this time made a pilgrimage to New Lanark. Griscom, an American Professor of Chemistry and Natural Philosophy, visited Owen in the course of a tour, and was most favorably impressed with the school. He records that the children appeared perfectly happy and fearless, and would take Owen by the hand or the coat to attract his attention. The Duke of Kent (father of Queen Victoria) was deeply interested in Owen's experiments, and sent his physician to visit and report upon New Lanark. Many others—statesmen, philanthropists, reformers, and humanitarians, enthusiasts of all kinds —also found their way to the factory and school.

CONDITION OF THE PEOPLE

About 1815 Owen began to turn his attention to measures of a public character which should improve the condition of the operatives employed in the now rapidly increasing textile industry. He visited many mills in various parts of the country, and was much struck by the wonderful machines employed in these factories and the improvements that were constantly being made

---

* "System of Education at New Lanark," p. 55.

in them. But he was also painfully impressed, as he had been years before, by the deteriorating effects on young people of the conditions of employment. He saw that the workers were almost literally slaves of the new mechanical powers, and later on he asserted that the white slavery of English manufactories under unrestricted competition was worse than the black slavery he had seen in the West Indies and the United States, where the slaves were better cared for in regard to food, clothing, and conditions as to health than were the oppressed and degraded children and workpeople in the factories of Great Britain. It is true that some of the worst evils were tending to disappear, e.g., with the introduction of steam power night work was considerably discontinued; and as employers were no longer obliged to place their factories in out of the way spots for water power, the need for employing parish apprentices had therefore largely ceased. The factories were placed in populous centres and to some extent at least under the check of public opinion; whilst the children were living at home with their parents, under more human and natural conditions than the unhappy apprentices who had been lodged at the mills. It also appears that the factories of the new type were larger and better kept than the old, and the operatives of a higher social grade. But, in spite of these influences, which made for good, the evidence before Peel's Committee shows that conditions were still very bad. Children were employed at a very early age, and for terribly long hours. Even the better class manufacturers usually kept the mill open for thirteen hours a day, and allowed an hour off for dinner, breakfast and tea being brought to the children in the mill and snatched at intervals, the machinery going all the time. Sometimes even a dinner interval was not given, and some mills were kept going for fifteen or even sixteen hours a day. Many of the children had to attend for several hours on Sunday to clean the machinery. It was asserted by the manufacturers that these long hours did not really mean the same duration of actual work; that the children were merely in attendance to watch the machines and piece the broken threads, no physical exertion being required. This description conveniently ignored the fact that the children had practically to stand the whole time, and the bad effects of such long standing and confinement were heightened by the close and heated atmosphere. The finer qualities of yarn, at all events, needed a warm atmosphere, and in many factories the temperature, summer and winter, was kept up to about eighty degrees. Sir Robert Peel told the House of Commons that he employed nearly a thousand children in his cotton mill, and was seldom able to visit it, owing to press of engagements; but whenever he could go and see the works, he was struck with "the uniform appearance of bad health and, in many cases, stunted growth of the children. The hours of labor were regulated by the interest of the overseer, whose remuneration depending on the quantity of work done, he was often induced to make the poor children work excessive hours and to stop their complaints by trifling bribes."

FACTORY CHILDREN

In 1815 Owen called a meeting of Scottish manufacturers, to be held in the Tontine, Glasgow, to consider, first, the necessity and policy of asking the Government, then under Lord Liverpool's administration, to remit the heavy duty then paid on the importation of cotton; and, secondly, to consider measures to improve the condition of children and others employed in textile mills. The first proposal, to remit the import duty on raw material, was carried unanimously. He then proposed a string of resolutions for improving the condition of the workers. In the course of his remarks he pointed out that the cotton manufacture, vast as were its profits, was not an unmixed benefit to the nation, but, under existing conditions, was destructive of the "health, morals, and social comforts" of the mass of the people engaged in it. He urged those present not to forget the interests of those by whom their profits were made, and suggested a Factory Act. Not one person in the meeting would second the motion. Subsequently Owen published a pamphlet,* dedicated significantly "to the British Legislature," in which he described the position of children under the manufacturing system, and suggested a remedy. "The children now find they must labor incessantly for their bare subsistence. They have not been used to innocent, healthy, and rational amusements. They are not permitted the requisite time, if they had been previously accustomed to enjoy them. . . . Such a system of training cannot be expected to pro-

---

* "Observations on the Effect of the Manufacturing System." London. 1815.

duce any other than a population weak in bodily and mental faculties, and with habits generally destructive of their own comfort, of the wellbeing of those around them, and strongly calculated to subdue all the social affections. Man so circumstanced sees all around him hurrying forward, at a mail coach speed, to acquire individual wealth, regardless of him, his comforts, his wants, or even his sufferings, except by way of degrading parish charity, fitted only to steel the heart of man against his fellows or to form the tyrant and the slave. . . . The employer regards the employed as mere instruments of gain."

The legislative measure he suggested was to limit the hours of labor in factories to twelve per day, including one and a half for meals; to prohibit employment of children under ten in factories; to require that employment of children from ten to twelve should be for half time only; and that no children should be admitted to work in factories at all until they could read and write, understand elementary arithmetic, and, in the case of girls, sew and make their clothes. The arguments used by Owen in support of this suggested measure are such as have been amply confirmed by the experience of those in touch with industry; but they were then new and startling, and, it is to be feared, even at the present day are unfamiliar to many of the dwellers in Suburbia. In regard to the objection then commonly raised that the quantity produced would be decreased by shorter hours, he explained that by making the proposed Factory Act uniform over the United Kingdom, any increase of cost, supposing such to ensue, would be borne by the consumers, not by the manufacturers; but he doubted much whether any manufactory, arranged so as to occupy the hands twelve hours a day, would not produce its fabric nearly, if not altogether, as cheap as those in which work was prolonged to fourteen or fifteen hours a day. Even should this view not prove to be entirely justified, the improved health and comfort of the operative population and the diminution of poor rates would amply compensate the country for a fractional addition to the prime cost of any commodity. "In a national view, the labor which is exerted twelve hours a day will be obtained more economically than if stretched to a longer period. . . . Since the general introduction of expensive machinery human nature has been forced far beyond its average strength, and much, very much, private misery and public injury are the consequence."

THE HUMAN MACHINERY

In an address to the superintendents of manufactories, written about the end of 1813, Owen thus voices his appeal for the operatives : —

"Experience has shown you the difference of the results between mechanism which is neat, clean, well arranged, and always in a high state of repair; and that which is allowed to be dirty, in disorder, without the means of preventing unnecessary friction, and which therefore becomes and works much out of repair. In the first case the whole economy and management are good; every operation proceeds with ease, order, and success. In the last the reverse must follow, and a scene be presented of counteraction, confusion, and dissatisfaction among all the agents and instruments interested or occupied in the general process, which cannot fail to create great loss.

"If, then, the care as to the state of your inanimate machines can produce such beneficial results, what may not be expected if you devote equal attention to your vital machines, which are far more wonderfully constructed? When you shall acquire a right knowledge of these, of their curious mechanism, of their self-adjusting powers; when the proper mainspring shall be applied to their varied movements—you will become conscious of their real value, and you will readily be induced to turn your thoughts more frequently from your inanimate to your living machines; you will discover that the latter may be easily trained and directed to procure a large increase of pecuniary gain, while you may also derive from them high and substantial gratification.

"Will you then continue to expend large sums of money to procure the best devised mechanism of wood, brass, or iron; to retain it in perfect repair; to provide the best substance for the prevention of unnecessary friction, and to save it from falling into premature decay? Will you also devote years of intense application to understand the connection of the various parts of these lifeless machines, to improve their effective powers, and to calculate with mathematical precision all their minute and combined movements? . . . . Will you not afford some of your attention to consider whether a portion of your time and capital would not be more advantageously applied to improve your living machines? . . . Far more attention has been given to perfect the raw materials of wood and metals than those of body and mind . . . . . Man, even as an instrument for the creation of wealth, may be greatly improved. . . . . You may not only partially improve these living instruments, but learn how to impart to them such excellence as shall make them infinitely surpass those of the present and all former times."*

In the course of this campaign for the remission of the cotton duties and for the regulation of child labor, Owen sent copies of his proposals to the members of both Houses of Parliament, and went up to interview members of the Government. In regard to the first proposal he met with a favorable reception from Vansittart, the Chancellor of the Exchequer, but his efforts on behalf of the children were not so immediately fruitful, although they excited considerable interest and sympathy in the minds of some. Sir Robert Peel was asked to take charge of Owen's draft Bill. The choice was an appropriate one, the Act of 1802, for regulating the conditions of pauper apprentices in cotton and woollen mills, having been due to the same statesman's initiative. This Act, the only Factory Act then on the statute book, had become out of date owing to technical and economical changes which had caused the employment of pauper apprentices to be largely discontinued. The new Bill was more comprehensive, and applied to all children in mills and factories. Its main provisions were that no child should be employed in a mill or factory below the age of ten; that no person under eighteen should be employed for more than twelve and a half hours per day, of which only ten were to be given to work, half an hour to instruction, leaving two hours for rest and meal times. The justices were empowered to appoint duly qualified inspectors and to pay them for their services. It was explicitly provided that these inspectors were not to be interested or in any way connected with the mills and manufactories they were to inspect, and they were given full powers to enter the mills for purposes of inspection at any time of day they chose.

It is interesting in considering this Bill to recall that the institution of factory inspectors was not effected till 1833, the ten hours

* Appendix B, Autobiography, p. 259.

day did not become law till 1847, and the prohibition of work under ten years old did not come into force until the year 1874.

PEEL'S COMMITTEE

Nothing more was done in 1815, the Bill having been introduced and published as a tentative measure to evoke discussion and criticism. In 1816, however, Sir Robert Peel returned to the subject, and moved for the appointment of a committee to take evidence and report upon the state of children employed in manufactories. Some of the evidence given before this committee by Owen has already been quoted above. Perhaps the most remarkable point is the hostility shown by some members of the committee to Owen's ideas and proposals, which, so far as the Factory Bill went, would nowadays be considered very mild. When he said he thought it unnecessary for children under ten to be employed in any regular work, and considered instruction and education at that age were enough exertion, he was asked by some moralist, whose name is unfortunately not handed down to fame, "Would there not be a danger of their acquiring by that time (*ten years old*) vicious habits for want of regular occupation?" and replied that his own experience led him, on the contrary, to find that habits were good in proportion to instruction. When he was pressed to explain his contention that a reduction of hours had resulted in a greater proportional output, he showed that a larger quantity might be produced by greater attention or by preventing breakage, and by not losing any time in beginning or leaving work. This evidently surprised some of the committee, who appeared incredulous that he, "as an experienced cotton spinner, or a spinner of any kind," could think that machines could produce a greater quantity save by the quickening of their movement. Owen again repeated that greater attention by the workpeople in avoiding breakage or waste of time might increase output, and that in his experience the shorter hours work did result in closer attention.*

* The present writer has been told the same by several manufacturers. One of these remarked that "in nine hours the girls had done all the work it was in them to do," and that the attention could not be satisfactorily maintained longer. Another remarked that overtime in the evening generally meant bad work next morning. See also instances described in "History of Factory Legislation," Hutchins and Harrison, Chapter VII.

THE FACTORY ACT, 1819

The Factory Bill was delayed for some reason till 1818, when Sir Robert Peel introduced it again. The second reading was carried in the Commons by ninety-one to twenty-six, but the Bill was again delayed by the action of the House of Lords, who professed themselves not satisfied that the need for any such legislation had been demonstrated. They appointed a committee of their own, which took evidence during 1818 and 1819. A great deal of evidence was produced, which was intended to show that factories were ideally healthy and the death-rate much below that in ordinary places; that England's place in the markets of the world would be endangered; that wages must be reduced in a proportion equal to or greater than the proposed reduction of hours; that the morals of the "lower orders" must be deteriorated by so much free time. Doctors were found to testify, e.g., that it need not hurt a child to work at night, or to stand twelve hours a day at work, or to eat their meals while so standing! The evidence of 1816, however, had not been forgotten, and other evidence was produced before the Lords' Committee which amply proved the conditions to be highly injurious to the children's health. The Bill became law in the summer of 1819, but, in order to conciliate the millowners and the House of Lords, the original provisions were deprived of much that was valuable. Woollen, flax, and other mills were omitted, the Act applying to cotton only; the age limit for child labor was fixed at nine years instead of ten; the hours of labor were to be twelve instead of ten or ten and a half hours. Worst of all, the provisions for inspection in Owen's draft was deleted and nothing was put in its place, the supervision of factories being left, as before, in the hands of the justices, although it was perfectly well known that they had not enforced the Act of 1802.

Owen's direct influence on the development of English factory legislation thus suffered a check. The fact nevertheless remains that the Act of 1819, mutilated and imperfect as it was, was the first real recognition of responsibility by the State for industrial conditions. The Act of 1802 had been merely an extension of the State's care for Poor Law children; the Act of 1819 recognized the employed child as such. It was not until 1833 that an effective measure was placed upon the statute book, and the guidance of this movement had long before this passed out of Owen's hands. But he it was who first compelled the State to recognize the changes made by the growth and concentration of capital; he it was who tried practical experiments in the way of shorter hours and improved conditions; and, much as he had done himself as a model employer, it was he who recognized the fact that, under the conditions of modern industry, State intervention was necessary, because the forces of competition are too much for the manufacturer, single and unaided, to resist, save in especially favorable circumstances.

INTERNATIONAL AGITATION

Owen was also fully conscious that in years to come the problem of social reform would have to be faced internationally. In 1818 he addressed a memorial, on behalf of the working classes, "to the Allied Powers assembled in Congress at Aix-la-Chapelle." This document is characterized by extraordinary optimism and a pathetic conviction that society was, in actual fact, moving rapidly to a state of harmony and co-operation. It also shows a curious ignorance of recent history in assuming that child labor was a recent introduction, whereas we know now from other sources that child labor had been general, and in some cases excessive, in textile industry carried on under the domestic system. In spite of these misconceptions; the document makes some valuable and important points. It shows that by the introduction of machinery and the factory system an enormous increase in productive power had been achieved. By the aid of science Great Britain could now produce many times as much wealth in a given time as she could previously. This surplus of wealth might be either wasted in war, dissipated in competition with the nations, or applied directly to improve her own population. Moreover, the existing productive power was but trifling compared with that which might be obtained in the future. Capital and industry were unemployed or misapplied which might be used to create more wealth. "Already," said Owen, "with a population under twenty millions, and a manual power not exceeding six millions,* with the aid of new power, undirected, except by a blind private interest, she

---

* This figure is arrived at by comparison with the era before machinery. The exact figure is unimportant. The increase of productive power is an undoubted fact.

supplied her own demand, and overstocks with her manufacturers all the markets in the world to which her commerce is admitted. She is now using every exertion to open new markets, even in the most distant regions; and she could soon, by the help of science, supply the wants of another world equally populous with the earth. . . . The grand question now to be solved is, not how a sufficiency of wealth may be produced, but how the excess of riches which may be most easily created may be generally distributed throughout society advantageously for all, and without prematurely disturbing the existing institutions or arrangements in any country." Owen's estimates were based on manufacturing industry, and he did not give sufficient weight to the consideration that mechanical science was not likely (so far as we can see) to effect so rapid and startling an increase in the production of food or other necessaries obtained from the soil itself.* The really important point made by Owen here and elsewhere is his insistence on the problem of distribution. It is still the case that much wealth which might be used to enrich life is squandered in the war of armaments and the war of competition. There is no way of avoiding that destructive waste save by co-operation and mutual control.

Owen died in 1858. It might seem that his life was a failure, his immediate efforts having been sorely disappointed over the Factory Act of 1819, and his wonderful forecasts of universal peace and prosperity having been sadly falsified by events. But the real results of Owen's work are to be seen in the long series of factory legislation, which, slowly and imperfectly, it is true, has yet built up a system of protection for the worker, and in the efforts which, in the twentieth century, have at last achieved some beginnings of success for international regulation of labor. In 1900 the "Union Internationale pour la Protection légale des Travailleurs" was formed. Through its initiative, influence, and suggestion, conventions have already been accepted by a large number of the leading Powers, under which the night work of women is forbidden and the use of white phosphorus, a deadly poison, formerly employed in matchmaking with great dangers to the workers, is prohibited. Other measures with regard to the night work of boys and the control of other industrial poisons are

* Podmore, I, p. 261.

being considered. This is a work which is as yet in its infancy, but is likely to be fraught with great results in the future.

CONCLUSION

It is difficult in a few words to sum up the singular career and personality of Robert Owen. The so-called "usher" of seven, the boy who, with powdered hair, waited on his master's customers in the old warehouse on London Bridge, has a curious old world air, which clings to him even when a dozen years later finds him face to face with the intricate problems of the modern industrial world. It will not have escaped readers of the extracts given above from Robert Owen's works that he wrote a painfully long winded style, and that his thought is often uncritical and obscure. In a candid passage his son, R. Dale Owen, reminds us that Owen was without any real educational or scientific training. As a child he managed to read a good many books, but had neither time nor opportunity to be a student. "In this way he worked out his problems for human improvement to great disadvantage, missing a thousand things that great minds had thought and said before his time, and often mistaking ideas that were truly his own for novelties that no human being had heretofore given to the world."*

Owen's personal temper and character appear to have been of unusual sweetness. His "ruling passion," his son records, "was the love of his kind, individually and collectively." An old friend said of Owen, jokingly, that "if he had seven thousand children instead of seven, he would love them all devotedly." He was, in fact, to his own children a most affectionate and careful parent, but had none of the selfish narrowness that sometimes goes with strong domestic instincts. The whole human race was to him the subject of warm, even indulgent, affection. He simply brushed aside the impression then general that the best way to manage children was to bully them, and the best way to get work out of factory operatives was to keep them incessantly at it. He did not believe in sin and wickedness, and saw in the sinner only the victim of untoward circumstances. He was sometimes misled by the illusion, characteristic of many eighteenth century thinkers, that the human race, if surrounded by a healthy and comfortable

* "Threading My Way," p. 66 *et seq.*

environment, and properly instructed in the advantages of social, as opposed to anti-social, conduct, must inevitably go right of itself, and he left out of account the whole array of inherited weaknesses of character and constitution, the strength of passions (which probably his own temperament left him unaware of), and the temptation of greed and tyranny offered by almost any known form of organized social life. It is easy to indicate the limitations of his thought. The fact remains that wthin those limiits there is an immensely fruitful field for the application of his ideas, as he proved by the almost startling results of his training and influence on a set of operatives and their children who were by no means picked members of society to start with.

The importance of Owen's life and teaching does not lie in his social philosophy, which was crude and already somewhat out of date, but in the practical success of his experiments as a model employer, and in his flashes of social intuition, which made him see, as by inspiration, the needs of his time. Leslie Stephen said of him that he was "one of those intolerable bores who are of the salt of the earth," but it is evident that he must have possessed a large measure of the undefinable attribute known as "personal magnetism." Thus we find him achieving an entrance into good posts early in life with little aid from capital or influence, able to control and manage workpeople in the factory, to banish drunkenness and disorder, to win the affection of the children in the schools, to persuade the teachers to adopt his new and unfamiliar methods, and to excite the active sympathy and interest of men, like the Duke of Kent, greatly above him in social station. Owen could see and act far better than he could think, and his views have been justified by events. His Life, by Frank Podmore, is a great book, one of the most fascinating of English biographies, but perhaps even Mr. Podmore hardly does justice to the clearness of Owen's vision in the human side of economics. Owen found the politicians and economists obsessed by a mechanical conception of industry. An hour's work was an hour's work, and in the debates and pamphlets of the time there is an almost entire omission of any reference to the personality of the worker, or to the possible effect of his health, strength, and efficiency on the output. Manual labor was then taken as a constant quantity, the only means of augmenting the output being by increasing the hours or by improving the machinery. Later economists have given more attention to the personality of the operative, and modern scientific investigation has shewn that Owen's conception of industry is a true one, solidly based on the facts of life. There is much evidence now accessible to show how eminently susceptible to influences the human worker is, and how shortsighted it is to regard him or her as a mere pair of hands. Better food, better air, more rest, teaching, and recreation, improve the human machine, even regarding him merely as a machine. From the point of view of the State or the community it is hardly necessary to say the case is tenfold stronger. The State can by no means afford to have its citizens, actual or potential, endangered by unhealthy, dangerous, or demoralizing conditions of work. This statement is becoming almost a truism now, though its full implications have not yet been adopted as part of practical politics. But the measure of recognition it has obtained, both at home and abroad, is a measure of the greatness of Robert Owen, the pathfinder of social legislation, who had a vision for the realities of modern industrial life when they were as yet dim, strange, and unknown to his contemporaries. No one has yet done so much as he did to show that man must be the master of the machine if he is not to be its slave.

5 L. Barbara Hammond
WILLIAM LOVETT

William Lovett was born at Newlyn, a mile from Penzance, in the year 1800. His father, a Yorkshireman, captain of a small trading vessel, was drowned before his birth. His mother a Cornishwoman, left to her own resources, supported herself, the child and her own mother by hawking fish and doing various odd jobs in Penzance. As a child Lovett showed no signs of the passion for learning that marked him in later life, for no dame's school in the town could succeed in teaching him to read, though he consented finally to learn his alphabet from his great grandmother, an old lady of 80. Later on he learnt at school "to write tolerably well, and to know a little of arithmetic and the catechism, and this formed the extent of my scholastic acquirements." His mother, an ardent methodist, was kind and indulgent except where religious duties were concerned. The Sundays of his childhood were long remembered by Lovett with horror— three services at chapel, "the reading of texts, prayers and portions of Scripture" in between the services filled up the gloomy day. One Sunday when the boy played truant and ran off to play with other boys on the sands he was unlucky enough to sprain an ankle. His mother concerned for his body, but even more concerned for his immortal soul, pronounced it a judgment on him for breaking the Sabbath, but nevertheless sent for the doctor.

When he was about thirteen Lovett was apprenticed for seven years to learn ropemaking. During his apprenticeship he led a hard life, for his mother made a second and unhappy marriage, and he and his grandmother lived together on the five shillings a week he was paid, helped out by what little she could earn in the fishing season. His work was laborious and involved carrying great weights and, what he minded more, the walking along

100

lonely roads by night, for the terror of his early childhood, the cry, "The press gang is coming," was now succeeded by an over-whelming fear of ghosts and goblins that lasted till London life made him a sceptic. Fond though he was of reading, he had noth-ing to read except "the Bible, and Prayer and hymn book, and a few religious tracts, together with fragments of an old magazine," and occasionally a nonsensical pamphlet about "giants, spirits, goblins, and supernatural horrors." There was no bookshop in the town and no opportunity for intellectual improvement, but the future writer of manifestoes and addresses found some scope for his gifts in composing love letters for his young neighbours. His leisure was busily spent in making "gimcracks of every kind," boxes, birdcages, a machine for spinning twine, a turning lathe and so on, and he was allowed to play about and pick things up in the shop of a friendly carpenter, a privilege that ultimately proved of great importance, for at the end of his apprenticeship he found himself, at the age of 20, master of a skilled trade in which there was no work. Chains had begun to supersede ropes, and, except for a few weeks in the winter, there was nothing in Penzance for a ropemaker to do. For one season Lovett tried a fisherman's life; the opening was promising, for he had the offer of succeeding to the fishing business of a great uncle, but he could not overcome his sea-sickness, which attacked him even before he got on board at the mere thought of the "short cross loping waves," and so when the season was over he renounced all thoughts of becoming a fisherman, and obtained work at a neighbouring carpenter's. But the regular apprenticed carpenters of Penzance objected, and he had to leave. In despair of obtain-ing employment of any kind at home, he determined to try his fortune in London. By making a lady's workbox with secret drawers and a pair of tea caddies he raised about 50s.; another workbox paid for part of his passage money on a small trading steamer, and he found himself in London in 1821, aged twenty-one, with 30s. and some letters of introduction to ropeworks in his pocket.

EARLY STRUGGLES IN LONDON

In London the prospects of work seemed at first no brighter than in Penzance. The ropeyards needed no hands, and attempts to obtain employment in the company of some carpenters from the

101

country were no more successful. His sailor's dress, as worn by
the young men of Penzance, told against him. For weeks he was
reduced to a penny loaf a day and a drink at the pump. Then he
got one or two odd carpentering jobs, but when these were finished
and the money they brought exhausted, the half-starved youth
determined, in spite of sea-sickness, to take a situation as ropemaker on board an Indiaman. Before finally engaging himself he
went to see his carpenter friend from Penzance, who, after failing
in business, had come to London and obtained work in a
carpenter's shop in Somers Town. This friend's master, seeing
probably a chance of cheap labour, agreed to take Lovett on as
well, and for several months employed him making furniture.
Though the pay was poor, Lovett managed to provide himself
with more conventional clothes and a few tools. Soon, however,
the pay ceased altogether, and the master after being sent to the
Fleet Prison for debt, and persuading his workmen to finish their
work on the understanding that it would be paid for when sold,
turned out to be a thorough rogue, and they never received a
halfpenny of the six or seven pounds due to each of the three.
Lovett was again in low water; he lived in a damp unhealthy
back kitchen and fell seriously ill. When he recovered he tried in
vain to earn a living by making and selling small bits of furniture,
and when this failed decided to try his luck as a cabinet maker,
in which line he had now some experience. He was fortunate
enough to be given a job at a small repairing shop, where he met
a Scotchman, David Todd by name, "one of the most intelligent,
kindhearted, and best disposed men I ever met with." Todd
urged Lovett to join the Cabinet Makers' Society, but the Society
very naturally rejected him as he had not served the five years
required by their rules. Todd then procured him a situation at a
small cabinet maker's for twelve months at a guinea a week.
Though it was not a Society shop, his fellow workmen threatened
to oust him because he had not been apprenticed. Lovett thereupon called a meeting and put his case before them, and they
agreed to let him stop on, charging him heavily for help in different parts of the work. Once started as a cabinet maker Lovett
succeeded in getting employment at different shops, and after he
had served the required five years was admitted a member of the
Cabinet Makers' Society, of which he afterwards became President.

INTELLECTUAL DEVELOPMENT

When Lovett first came to town he was too much absorbed in attempts to earn his bread to have much leisure or energy for other things, though a fellow lodger, a kind old schoolmaster, helped him during this time by correcting his "provincialisms and bad English," and by advising the study of Lindley Murray's Grammar, a book which became his pocket companion. His first real intellectual awakening came after he was in regular work, when he was introduced by chance to a small society called "The Liberals," composed mostly of working men, who had a circulating library, and met twice a week in Gerrard Street for discussion. Lovett had never officially joined the Methodist connection, though for a short time under the influence of some female preachers he had become a "converted member" of an obscure sect called the Bryanites; but when he came to London he still thought that impromptu speaking, which he had never heard except in the pulpit, was a "kind of inspiration from God." To his astonishment, at the meetings of "The Liberals" he found the members making speeches, and good speeches, about the soul. He was at once fired by the desire to defend Christianity, and, with the help of David Todd, became a member of the society in order to study for this purpose. Political questions were also discussed at the meetings and roused his interest. "In short, my mind seemed to be awakened to a new mental existence; new feelings, hopes and aspirations sprang up within me, and every spare moment was devoted to the acquisition of some kind of useful knowledge. I now joined several other associations in its pursuit, and for a number of years seldom took a meal without a book of some description beside me." The youth who had often wondered in vain in Cornwall about "the causes of day and night, the seasons and the common phenomena of nature," joined the Mechanics' Institute, and was soon discussing scientific theories. On other evenings he would attend the debates in coffee houses and listen to the heroes of past campaigns, such as Gale Jones and Richard Carlile. The vicissitudes of his love affair with his future wife stimulated his intellectual pursuits. She was a lady's maid, and he first saw her in Marylebone Church. He managed to make her acquaintance, and all went well till she asked him to take the sacrament with her. Lovett, whose religious views had been considerably affected by a year or two of London,

103

explained that this was impossible for him. She then decided that she could not marry him and they parted, she returning with her mistress to the continent, he endeavouring to drown his grief in associations "literary scientific, political." "And this means," he wrote later, "of diverting the mind from the object that preys upon it, I would venture to recommend to all those who may experience a similar heartrending disappointment." He resigned himself to a bachelor's life, but unnecessarily, for a year later the young lady relented, and after some "controversial correspondence" on the subject of the sacrament they were married on June 3, 1826, the various associations were given up, and for a time Lovett led a purely domestic life, devoting himself to his wife and interesting her in all his pursuits. He was firmly convinced that much of the unhappiness and failure of working class life came from the men's habit of expecting their women to be on a lower level of intelligence and omitting to share their intellectual interests with them. In his own case the opposite policy brought great happiness. "My wife's appreciation," he wrote later, "of my humble exertions has ever been the chief hope to cheer, and best aid to sustain me." All through his long life he retained the enthusiastic feminism of his early days. In 1856 he published a poem, written in 1842, called "Woman's Mission," of which the sentiments, though not perhaps the verse, are admirable. One stanza runs : —

> "Would man in lovely woman ever find
> His best adviser, lover, truest friend.
>
> .   .   .   .   .   .
>
> He must at once his gothic laws annul,
> Fling back her dower, strive only for her love,
> And proudly raise her up all rights to share."

OWENISM AND POLITICS

Lovett's studies in London led him to become an ardent Owenite. The accumulation of property in the hands of individuals seemed to him to be the root of all evil : community of property the key to human happiness. Owen and his followers were flooding the world with schemes for the regeneration of mankind. Of one of these, the first London Co-operative Trading Association, founded during Owen's absence in America, Lovett became storekeeper in 1828. For two years after his marriage in 1826 he had been in good work at his trade; he had then made an unfortunate venture in a pastrycook's business. On getting rid of his business, though not his debts, he accepted the storekeeper's post, at some financial sacrifice, but in the belief that "the gradual accumulation of capital by these means would enable the working classes to form themselves into joint stock associations of labour, by which (with industry, skill, and knowledge) they might ultimately have the trade, manufactures and commerce of the country in their own hands." But so far was the London Trading Association from fulfilling these expectations that it could not even pay Lovett's salary, and in a few months his wife was asked to take his place at half his pay. Lovett went back to his trade with his optimism undaunted, for he became hon. secretary of the British Association for Promoting Co-operative Knowledge. But these various co-operative societies only lasted three or four years, failing, according to Lovett, from want of custom, want of legal security, and from the over-strong meat provided in Owen's Sunday morning lectures, which alarmed "the religious portion of their members."

Lovett's Owenism did not prevent him from being critical of Owen the man and autocrat, or from taking part in Radical campaigns. Amongst these was the "Unstamped Agitation," described by him afterwards as "one of the most important political movements that I was ever associated with." At that time every newspaper was bound by law to have a 4d. stamp on it. Henry Hetherington, the protagonist of the movement, started publication in 1830, in defiance of the law, of an unstamped paper called the *Poor Man's Guardian*. The Stamp Office soon proceeded against the publisher and the booksellers who sold it; volunteers then came forward for the work of distribution, some for love, others for the reward of a stock of papers and £1 a month during imprisonment. A "Victim Fund" was started for the sufferers, and Lovett became secretary of the Committee of Management. The campaign lasted five years. Over 500 persons in different parts of England suffered imprisonment. Hetherington himself when not in prison was "on the run," and his business was nearly ruined. In 1836, in consequence of the agitation, the 4d. stamp was reduced to 1d. Curiously enough, the *Poor Man's Guardian*, over which the battle had been fought, was finally declared by Lord Lyndhurst to be a strictly legal publication.

105

H

In the years before the passing of the famous Reform Bill of 1832 there were three schools of opinion amongst advanced working class thinkers about the question of reform. First, there were Owen and his followers, who despised political action, believing that mankind would be saved by other means. Secondly, there was the group of Radicals, who believed that universal suffrage (by which they meant, as a rule, adult male suffrage), and nothing less than universal suffrage, was the necessary preliminary to all social improvement. This school was joined by many Owenites, who came to believe that democracy must precede communism, and gradually dropped their communistic dreams. Thirdly, there were the Radicals like Francis Place, who believed in taking the Bill as it stood, or with such amendments as were possible, and treating it as an instalment of a larger measure.

Lovett belonged to the second group. His conversion from Owenism to political reform was no doubt hastened by his acquaintance with Henry Hunt, the veteran reformer, whom he first met about 1828. For some years he continued working for the two movements side by side : one day he would be discussing the founding of an incipient community on the plan of Mr. Thompson, of Cork; another day he would be helping to found the Metropolitan Political Union, to obtain effectual and radical reform in the Commons. Not content with these activities, he became "greatly interested in the temperance question," and in 1829 drew up a petition for the opening of the British Museum on Sundays. "Your petitioners," ran the opening sentence, "consider that one of the principal causes of drunkenness and dissipation on the Sabbath is the want of recreation and amusement." All the time, too, he was working at his trade of cabinet making. By 1831 his Radical convictions were so strong that on being drawn for the Militia he refused to serve or to pay for a substitute on the ground that he was unrepresented in Parliament. The authorities seized his little stock of household furniture, which his wife suffered to go "without a murmur"; but the protest had its effect, for discussion on the subject in the House of Commons and fear of an epidemic of "the no-vote no-musket plan" brought the balloting system to an end. Lovett had become a public character.

THE REFORM BILL

In 1831 Lovett joined the newly founded National Union of the Working Classes and Others, which amongst other objects such as "the repeal of all bad laws," aimed at "an effectual reform of the Commons House of Parliament." When the Whig Reform Bill was produced Lovett and Watson drew up a declaration of the principles of the National Union, headed by a quotation from Thales, calling for nothing less than adult male suffrage, voting by ballot, the abolition of property qualification for Members of Parliament, and annual Parliaments, thus comprising four of the six points of the future Charter. The National Union was an active body; besides holding many small meetings for discussion under class leaders, it held public meetings, of which those at the Blackfriars Rotunda were the most important, and from these meetings its adherents were often called "Rotundanists." It attracted some violent spirits: "could the violence and folly of the hot-brained few," wrote Lovett later, "have been restrained, a far larger amount of good might have been effected. But, as in almost all associations that I have ever been connected with, our best efforts were more frequently directed to the prevention of evil by persons of this description than in devising every means and in seeking every opportunity for the carrying out of our objects." But whilst Lovett was blaming the "hot-brained few," Place was blaming Lovett and his friends. Place and those who thought with him formed a society called the National Political Union, with the object of supporting the Whigs in carrying their Reform Bill. They were bitterly opposed by the Rotundanists, who objected to being made the "tools" of the middle classes. Both sides tried to mobilise working class opinion. Lovett moved a universal suffrage amendment at the first public meeting of the National Political Union, but it was drowned by the "noise and clamour" of the opposing side, though a later proposal that half the Council should consist of working men was carried. The Rotundanists, however, found themselves pitted against a past master of strategy and intrigue in Place, who managed to secure for the Council the election of "respectable" working men untainted with Rotunda heresy.

Another blow to the Rotundanists was the proclamation of their proposed public meeting to ratify the declaration drawn up by Lovett and Watson. In vain, Lovett, Watson and the secretary waited on Lord Melbourne to assure him of their peaceable intentions. Lord Melbourne, receiving them with a barrier of chairs in front of him and a posse of police in the next room, assured them that their meeting was illegal, and that attendance at it would be high treason. The meeting was abandoned.

It cannot be said that the National Union of the Working Classes, or Rotundanists, were conciliatory in their methods. When the Government ordered a general fast for the cholera in March, 1832, the National Union, on the grounds that the cholera was largely due to underfeeding, decided to celebrate the day by providing a good dinner for their members, to be preceded by an orderly procession through the streets, headed by Lovett, Watson and Hetherington. The police interfered with the procession, using their bludgeons freely, and a few days later Lovett, Watson and the veteran and violent Benbow were arrested and charged with having "made a great riot, tumult and disturbance . . . . and caused great terror and alarm." All three were triumphantly acquitted by the jury, but Lovett and Watson withdrew from the Committee of the National Union as a protest against what they considered Benbow's unscrupulous conduct in connection with the expenses of the trial.

In spite of the efforts of the Rotundanists, the Reform Bill was passed in June, 1832. The National Union of the Working Classes and Others continued to exist for a time, but Lovett took little part in its activities, though a police spy did his best to entrap him into attending a meeting of whose objects he disapproved. The agitation for the "unstamped press" was absorbing his energies.

The twenties, thirties and forties of last century produced a bewildering procession of organisations and associations. The National Union of the Working Classes and Others was succeeded by the remarkable though short-lived movement known as the Grand National Trades Union of 1833-1834, a movement due largely to the reaction amongst the working classes against political intervention after the Reform Bill, and described by Mr. Hovell as "militant Owenism." The object of the Grand National was to obtain better conditions of life by means of combinations and strikes. Lovett joined it, and tried in vain to make it declare in favour of universal suffrage. By the end of 1834, after a series of unsuccessful strikes, it was dead.

In 1834 Lovett left his trade and made a second venture in business. He opened the premises of one of the defunct Co-operative Stores as a coffee house. Its conversation room and debates were well attended, but its financial side was a failure. After struggling with it for two years at a loss, Lovett gave it up. Opposite the coffee house was a school for poor music boys, opened by Mazzini, with whom Lovett became acquainted.

LONDON WORKING MEN'S ASSOCIATION

It was in the year 1836 that Lovett did the most important work of his life, the founding of the London Working Men's Association. What kind of a man was he at this time? Place, a critical friend, described him as "a tall, thin, rather melancholy man, in ill-health, to which he has long been subject; at times he is somewhat hypochondriacal; his is a spirit misplaced." To his upright character and to his gentleness, all his contemporaries bear witness. Place wrote to Lovett urging him to overcome his melancholy, and to be less troubled by the miseries of mankind. "When youth and strength and flow of spirits," answered Lovett, "have been wasted in unrequited toil and poverty, and when after years of great physical and mental exertions, after a life of sobriety and industry, you find yourself losing your physical energies (so necessary for those who have to depend on their labour), and getting more and more involved in difficulties inextricable, and having the cares of a family in whose welfare is your highest hope, you need not be surprised if my tone and manner correspond with my situation. Perhaps the scenes I have had to encounter in my journey may have increased my sympathies for my fellow men; and while I believe with you that this is the best world of which I have any hope, yet when I feel conscious of how much could be done to make it a comparative paradise of happiness instead of the hell of toil, of poverty and crime we find it, I cannot help lamenting that the wise and intelligent few do not carry their views of reformation beyond making comfortable slaves of the many to pamper and support the few." Lovett had only one child, a daughter, a second daughter having died in infancy.

Fifteen years experience of London life and political campaigns had brought a certain disillusionment. He no longer pictured his fellow workmen as waiting eagerly for opportunities of study and regeneration. They were more inclined "to croak over their grievances with maudlin brains, and to form and strengthen their appetites for drink amid the fumes of the tap room" than to put Lindley Murray's grammar in their pockets. But their shortcomings were due to the "circumstances and constitution of society, and not to the organisation of man." Salvation, he felt convinced, must come not from above, but from the workers themselves. They must cease to look up to leaders, they must educate themselves. He complained that "a lord, an M.P., or an esquire was a leading requisite to secure a full attendance and attention from them on all public occasions"; this must cease, and they must develop "discrimination and independent spirit in the management of their political affairs." With this object the London Working Men's Association was started. Its membership was confined "as far as practicable" to the working classes : it aimed at mental improvement as well as at equal political and social rights. The ideal of the founders was expressed in an address as follows: "Imagine the honest, sober and reflecting portion of every town and village in the kingdom linked together as a band of brothers, honestly resolved to investigate all subjects connected with their interests, and to prepare their minds to combat with the errors and enemies of society—setting an example of propriety to their neighbours, and enjoying even in poverty a happy home." Political rights were not to be aimed at as an end in themselves; "when we contend for an equality of political rights, it is not in order to lop off an unjust tax or useless pension, or to get a transfer of wealth, power or influence for a party; but to be able to probe our social evils to their source, and to apply effective remedies to prevent, instead of unjust laws to punish."

The London Working Men's Association exercised an influence on public affairs out of all proportion to its membership. Quality, not quantity, was aimed at. Between its foundation in June, 1836, and 1839 only 279 members were admitted, in addition to some 35 honorary members. But missionaries were sent into the country, and a hundred and fifty kindred associations sprang up elsewhere. Lovett, who was secretary of the London Association, found full scope for his passion for drafting addresses and manifestoes. Attention was not confined to domestic affairs, urgent though these might have seemed; the importance of international affairs was fully recognised. The workers of Belgium were sympathised with over the persecution of Jacob Katz; in the course of an exhaustive view of foreign politics the working classes of Europe, and especially the Polish people, were assured that it is "the ignorance of our brethren which generates and fosters the despot"; the Canadians were encouraged in their opposition to Whig coercion : "It gives us great pleasure to learn, friends, that you are not so easily scared *by proclamation law*—by the decree of a junta against a whole nation. Surely you know and feel, though Governor Gosford may not, that 'A NATION NEVER CAN REBEL' "; the Americans were congratulated on their republican institutions and on the heights of political liberty to which they had attained, but were asked the searching question, "Why, after sixty years of freedom, have you not progressed further?"

A long address on education, a subject dear to Lovett's heart contained a scheme of schools of various grades to be provided by public money and managed by local school committees elected by universal suffrage, and ended with an appeal to Christians to rise above sectarian jealousies in the matter of religious education. An address on "The Rotten House of Commons" gave a scathing description of the personnel of the existing House, and urged on working men the duty of demanding equal political and social rights so that they might send working class representatives to Parliament.

THE CHARTER

But the most important work of the Association was the preparation of the Charter, with its famous six points. At a public meeting at the Crown and Anchor in the Strand, on February 28, 1837, a petition to Parliament was adopted embodying the six points : (1) universal suffrage, (2) the ballot, (3) payment of members, (4) annual Parliaments, (5) equal electoral districts, (6) the abolition of property qualifications for M.P.s

The petition was entrusted to Roebuck for presentation, and he suggested enlisting the support of other Radical M.P.s. A joint meeting of eight members of Parliament and various members of the Working Men's Association accordingly took place. The Radical members of Parliament, fresh from the chilly atmosphere of the House, showed little enthusiasm, and were taken severely to task by Lovett, who charged them with thinking more of their

111

seats than of their principles. O'Connell retorted that Lovett was impracticable. The result of this and of a later meeting was the formation of a committee, consisting of six members of Parliament and six members of the Working Men's Association, to draw up a Bill embodying the six points, to be known as "the People's Charter."

This committee was hardly appointed when William IV died, Parliament was dissolved, and the members disappeared to their constituencies. The business of drawing up the Bill was in consequence postponed for several months. Lovett's pen was busy in the interval with an Address to Reformers on the elections and with an Address to Victoria on her accession. This latter Address the Association proposed to present in person by a deputation of six, but they were deterred by the necessity of appearing in Court dress. "With every respect for those forms which make personal cleanliness and respectful behaviour necessary qualifications to approach her Majesty, we have neither the means nor the inclination to indulge in such absurdities as dress swords, coats and wigs," wrote Lovett to Lord John Russell. If Victoria ever read the Address she must have been somewhat bewildered by the exhortation contained in it to distrust alike Whigs and Tories, who "have for many years past succeeded in making Royalty a mere puppet of their will," and to instruct her Ministers to prepare a Bill for universal suffrage.

When Parliament reassembled the committee of twelve appointed Roebuck and Lovett to draw up the proposed Charter. Roebuck was too busy with Canadian affairs to help, so the task fell to Lovett. In such leisure as his trade left him he compiled a rough draft which he then submitted to Place, who suggested alterations. In the first draft of the Bill provision was made for women's suffrage, but it was afterwards decided to omit this on the ground that it would "retard the measure," a decision that Lovett regretted. In a composite document the question of authorship is a nice one, and both Place and Lovett afterwards claimed to have composed the Charter. Place's were not the only amendments, and the physical work of writing and rewriting the document several times—no light task—was Lovett's. It was finally published in May, 1838, accompanied by an address composed by Lovett, in which he characteristically dwelt on self-government as a means to "enlightenment." "When a knowledge of their rights and duties shall have taught the people that their own vices and ignorance are the chief instruments by which they are bowed to the dust, titles, privileges and wealth will lose their potency to enslave them."

The Charter itself had nothing simple or popular about it except its name. It was a long and complicated Bill entering into the minutest details about arrangements for registration and elections. Never has so dull a document had such sensational effects. Within twelve months over a million persons had signed a petition in its favour, and the middle classes were quaking at the very name of Chartism.

The Charter was published at a crucial moment, and succeeded in focussing heterogeneous movements of discontent. (1) The Birmingham Political Union, which had done yeoman service for the Reform Bill of 1832, had lately been revived under the leadership of Attwood, described by Disraeli as "a provincial banker labouring under a financial monomania." Attwood's panacea for the ills of society was the creation of unlimited paper money, but he and his followers were ready to press for suffrage reform as a means to this end. The Birmingham Association drew up what came to be known as the National Petition, and the Working Men's Association agreed to adopt it as the petition for the Charter. It was from the Birmingham Association, too, that the suggestion came of a General Convention of the Industrious Classes, which was to create and extend public opinion in favour of the principles of the People's Charter, and present the monster petition to Parliament. It was decided to hold the General Convention next year, and meanwhile to procure signatures for the Petition.

(2)The agitation in the North in favour of Factory Reform and against the new Poor Law was also all swept into the stream of Chartism. The audiences which had acquired the habit of being lashed into frenzy by Oastler, Stephens, and O'Connor had now a fresh object for excitement and enthusiasm. The Charter was to be the cure for economic evils. "Universal Suffrage," said Stephens, "is a knife and fork question, a bread and cheese question." "Six months after the Charter is passed," declared O'Connor, "every man, woman and child in the country will be well fed, well housed, and well clothed." "The furious appeals to the passions of the multitude"; "the violent ravings about

113

physical force," as Lovett called them, were now transferred to the Chartist campaign. Henceforth, though Lovett and his friends may have launched the boat, the new crew controlled her course. The *Northern Star,* O'Connor's organ, which shrieked out denunciations week after week, was a brilliant success with a huge circulation, "a melancholy tribute," it has been called, "to the low intelligence of its readers." (Hovell, The Chartist Movement). On the other hand, the *Charter,* started in London by the intellectuals of the movement, was a dismal failure and died early, leaving debts behind it.

No two men could have been more antagonistic to each other than Lovett and Fergus O'Connor, who now began to plan an important part in the Chartist agitation; O'Connor, the born demagogue with his unscrupulous appeals to the emotions; Lovett, the composer of innumerable addresses directed to the reason of his fellow men. "We are of opinions," wrote Lovett, "that whatever is gained in England by force, by force must be sustained : but whatever springs from knowledge and justice will sustain itself." O'Connor preferred to rouse his audiences by vague threats of "fleshing swords to the hilts," though when opportunity offered he showed no disposition to draw the sword from the scabbard. The two men had already had a bitter encounter over the Committee on the Combination Act, a Parliamentary Committee appointed early in 1838 largely as the result of attacks on Trade Unions by Daniel O'Connell. O'Connor falsely accused Lovett and the Working Men's Association of engineering the appointment of the Committee out of hostility to Trade Unions. In reality, Lovett had been appointed by the Trade Unions to watch over their interests in connection with it. In his answer to O'Connor's attack, he showed that it was not only the Northern demagogues who could use vituperation. "You tell the country," he wrote, "that you alone have organised the Radicals of London"—and tell the Londoners the wonders your genius has performed in the country. You carry your fame about with you on all occasions to sink all other topics in the shade—you are the great "I AM" of politics, the great personification of Radicalism—Fergus O'Connor."

THE CONVENTION

To avoid prosecution under the infamous Six Acts of 1819, it was necessary to elect the delegates for the proposed Convention at public meetings. These meetings gave ample opportunity for the mob orators of the North to exercise their gifts. At the London meeting the speakers were specially warned by the Working Men's Association, but warned in vain, so far as O'Connor was concerned, to avoid "every abusive or violent expression which may tend to injure our glorious cause." The moderates were already suffering for the ebullitions of the physical force party in the alienation of middle class opinion. "But the meeting of the Convention," wrote Lovett afterwards, "was now fast approaching, and so strong was the hope reposed in that meeting by the Chartist body, that the great majority of them manifested the strongest desire to sacrifice their peculiar feelings and convictions for the sake of union. A few hot-brained enthusiasts, however, were not so patriotic; union was naught with them compared with their own blustering harangues about arming and fighting; these and their daily invectives against everything bearing the resemblance of moderation, preparedness, or intellectual and moral effort, served to create constant irritation in our ranks, and ultimately to cause distrust and disunion."

The Convention met in London on February 4, 1839. It was composed of 53 delegates, a few of whom never sat. It met in an atmosphere of wild hopefulness combined with a certain vagueness as to its objects. Lovett was appointed secretary, a post from which O'Connor, who was not present at the election, tried in vain to oust him. His literary facility and business-like ways made him the obvious choice. As the first business of the Convention was to promote the Petition, missionaries were sent out to procure signatures from districts hitherto untouched. In the meantime the Convention showed an unlimited capacity for discussion of topics like "the suffering in the manufacturing districts," "the new Rural Police Bill," "the factory system." Outside, its supporters grew restive; one association declared "that if the Convention did its duty the Charter would be the law of the land in less than a month." Inside, O'Connor and his party became so violent in their language and methods that in March the Birmingham delegates and others of the moderate party seceded from the Convention. By May 6 the great National Petition was ready to be taken to Attwood for presentation to Parliament. It contained 1,283,000 signatures, was nearly three miles long, and was escorted to his house by the members of the Convention, marching two by two.

The presentation of the Petition was postponed by the dissolution of Parliament, and meanwhile the Convention on May 13th moved to Birmingham, in hopes of securing immunity from arrest and more sympathetic surroundings. The question of what was to be done if Parliament rejected the Petition became acute, for rejection seemed only too probable. Discussion of this question produced the famous "Manifesto of Ulterior Measures," drawn up by Lovett from notes of the conclusions arrived at in an unofficial meeting of delegates, and formally ratified by the Convention after they reached Birmingham. The manifesto contains probably the most violent language that Lovett ever penned. "I believe that I did an act of folly in being a party to some of its provisions," he wrote in later life. Ignorance of the world outside London and close association with men who claimed to speak for multitudes ready to rise seem to have made him for a time almost a convert to physical force. At any rate, he pressed for the adoption of the manifesto on the grounds that the Convention ought to give a lead to its followers. (Hovell, p. 149.) "Shall it be said, fellow-countrymen," runs the manifesto, "that four millions of men, capable of bearing arms, and defending their country against every foreign assailant, allowed a few domestic oppressors to enslave and degrade them?" "We solemnly believe that the Radical Reformers are the only restraining power that prevents the execution of an outraged people's vengeance." "We have resolved to obtain our rights, 'peaceably if we may, forcibly if we must'; but woe to those who begin the warfare with the millions, or who forcibly restrain their peaceful agitation for justice—at one signal they will be enlightened to their error, and in one brief contest their power will be destroyed." After these threats the methods suggested for enforcing the people's will read rather like an anti-climax. "Simultaneous public meetings" are to be asked if they are prepared (1) to draw out their money from the banks, (2) to convert their paper money into gold, (3) to give effect to the proposed "sacred month," that is, to have a general strike and to "go dry" for a month. They are further asked (4) whether "they have prepared themselves with the arms of freemen" according to their old constitutional rights, (5) whether they will provide themselves with Chartist candidates at the next election and treat them as M.P.s if elected by show of hands, and (6) deal exclusively with Chartists, and finally (7 and 8) work for the Charter and obey the Convention.

A few days after adopting the manifesto, the Convention adjourned till July 1st, and the "simultaneous meetings" were held during Whitsuntide. Thanks to the wisdom of General Charles James Napier, who had been in command of the Northern district, the demonstrations were peaceful. The Convention had tried to leave the decision as to "ulterior measures" to the people, but when it met again it was clear that the "simultaneous meetings" had given no lead. What was to be done? Were the "arms of freemen" to be used or only kept in the background? How were the workers to be supported during the "sacred month"? Lovett proposed that as a preliminary test one or two trades should be called on to stop work and a fund be raised to support them. Benbow, one of the wilder spirits, talked of "the cattle upon a thousand hills" as the best strike fund. The aim of the Convention was described by a Scottish delegate : "We must shake our oppressors well over hell's mouth, but we must not let them drop in." Whilst plans for the shaking were being discussed, a serious blow was dealt at the Convention by the arrest of Lovett.

During the agitation for the Reform Bill of 1832 Birmingham reformers had been in the habit of meeting in the Bull Ring. When the Chartist agitation began the Bull Ring was again used as a place of meeting. These Chartist meetings were prohibited by the magistrates, some of them ex-reformers of 1832. The Chartists took no notice of the prohibition or of the spasmodic arrests, and continued to meet. The Birmingham authorities thereupon sent for police from London, who proceeded on their arrival to attack a peaceful crowd in the Bull Ring. The crowd, exasperated, tore up the railings from a neighbouring churchyard, and ugly retaliation on the police was only prevented by the intervention of two members of the Convention, Dr. Taylor and Dr. McDouall. Dr. Taylor was arrested by the police. Next morning the Convention received an appeal from some of the frequenters of the Bull Ring. Lovett, whose personal courage never failed, drew up three resolutions condemning the police, which the Convention passed unanimously, ordering them to be

117

placarded throught the town. The first and strongest resolution declared "that a wanton, flagrant, and unjust outrage has been made upon the people of Birmingham by a bloodthirsty and unconstitutional force from London." "Characteristically enough, Lovett insisted that his own signature alone should be attached, so that the Convention should run no risk. Characteristically enough, the Convention was quite willing to sacrifice him." (Hovell, p. 157.) On July 6th, when the placards appeared, Lovett and Collins, who had taken the draft to the printers were both arrested.

Lovett and Collins were committed for trial at the next assizes, and though bail was fixed at £1,000 each, the magistrates made great difficulties about their sureties, and detained them in prison for nine days. During those nine days they were subjected to great indignities, which Lovett made the subject of a petition to both Houses of Parliament. Stripping, dirt, infection were among the things complained of, and the House of Lords was moved to merriment by the idea of Lovett's hair being cropped by a common felon, merriment that Brougham very properly rebuked. On the day on which the two prisoners were released on bail, there was another more serious riot in the Bull Ring, the culmination of a succession of collisions between police and people. Shops were burnt and the military called in, and though Lovett and Collins had nothing to do with the affair, the weapons used by the rioters were produced, to their prejudice, at their trial.

Two days before the riot, on July 12th, the long-expected debate on the Petition had taken place in the House of Commons. Attwood, supported by Fielden, proposed that it should be taken into consideration. Forty-six members only voted for him, 235 voted against him. The Petition's parliamentary career was over.

The later history of the Convention, from which Lovett was, of course, absent, is soon told. They reassembled in London, and blew hot and blew cold about "ulterior measures." August 12th was fixed on as the day for beginning the "sacred month," but further enquiries showed that most of the would-be strikers had no work to strike against. The "sacred month" was abandoned, and after some futile recriminations the Convention was dissolved on September 6th, 1839.

A successful popular agitation in England uses physical force as an ally in the background, but is careful not to produce the ally for too close an inspection. The more violent Chartists made the mistake of parading their ally till his weakness was apparent to everyone. The abortive rising in November at Newport, when twenty-eight soldiers successfully routed what was called a Chartist army, was a final proof of the futility of their threats. One after another the leaders had been clapped into prison, and the first Chartist agitation had collapsed.

TRIAL AND IMPRISONMENT

On August 6th Lovett was tried before Mr. Justice Littledale, at the Warwick Assizes, for publishing a "false, malicious, scandalous and seditious libel" on the police. Four persons had previously been condemned to death for the second Bull Ring riot (the death sentence was afterwards commuted to imprisonment through the exertions of Joseph Sturge), and Collins had been tried and found guilty the day before. Collins was defended by counsel, Sergeant Goulbourne, a Tory, who, to Lovett's disgust, regarded it as "a glorious opportunity of having a slap at the Whigs." Lovett defended himself in an able speech, pleading justification, and appealing to public opinion. The resolutions, he argued, were true and not malicious, they were public censure of a public act. "My lord, it is for directing public attention to a flagrant and unjust attack upon public liberty that I am brought as a criminal before you." His condemnation was a foregone conclusion; two of his jury had been heard to wish that all Chartists were hanged. He and Collins were sentenced to twelve months imprisonment in the county gaol.

During his imprisonment Lovett suffered severely, both physically and mentally. A diet of gruel with blackbeetles in it disgusted him with his food and gastric trouble set in. The society of companions, one of whom planned the robbery of his own mother and the division of the spoils with a fellow prisoner shortly to be released, whilst another described how he had thrown down a woman and kicked her on the face and eyes, was torture to a sensitive man. The chaplain and the doctor seem to have been caricatures of their type in fiction, the former consigning men to the refractory cell for coughing in chapel, the latter depriving the prisoners of half their scanty allowance of meat because it made the soup too rich. None of the ordinary privileges of political

119

prisoners were granted the two Chartists. Application to the visiting magistrates was referred to the Secretary of State : application to the Secretary of State was referred to the visiting magistrates. It was with the latter that the power really lay, but Lovett and Collins had prejudiced their case by exposing the way in which they had been treated before trial, an exposure which had obliged the magistrates to provide sheets and more hygienic bathing arrangements. Ultimately, though other privileges were withheld, pen, ink, and paper were given to the two prisoners, and Lovett, with the help of Collins, set about writing a book called "Chartism, or a New Organisation of the People." Lovett and Collins were offered the remission of the last three months of their sentence if they would be bound for good behaviour for a year. This they refused to accept, considering it to be an admission of past guilt. By the end of their year the portly Collins had become a thin man, and the thin Lovett a weak emaciated wreck.

Lovett and Collins were released in July, 1840. Lovett was too ill to attend most of the festivities arranged in their honour, and after one public dinner in London set off for Cornwall in hopes of regaining his health. Funds for the journey to Cornwall were provided by friends, who had also supported Lovett's wife and daughter whilst he was in prison. It would be interesting to know whether his Chartism or his scepticism about the supernatural excited more surprise in his native place, where his visit was preceded by that of a ghost, who walked about without a head. After some months of rest he returned to town, and being still too weak to work at his trade, opened a small bookseller's shop in Tottenham Court Road— his third venture in business, and, like the other two, unsuccessful.

KNOWLEDGE CHARTISM

Lovett's views on policy had undergone some modification after his experiences in the Convention and his imprisonment. Now, as always, an enlightened people was his ideal, and the enactment of the Six Points the means to that end and not an end in itself. But the Six Points seemed more difficult to achieve than in the early days of the Convention, and he began to lay greater stress on a preliminary enlightenment of the people as the means by which the Charter itself would be won. The Charter itself when won would in its turn be the means to "political and social reform."

It was the same idea of education at which the Working Men's Association had aimed, but Lovett had now given up the idea of a purely working class movement, and appealed to "the wise and good" of all classes to unite and to "labour and reason together to work out the social and political regeneration of man." They must "redeem by reason what had been lost by madness and folly," and the middle classes must not stand "apart from the name and principles of the Charter" because of "the intolerant and mischievous conduct" of certain Chartists. The workers, whilst "labouring to obtain the Charter," should be "instructing themselves, so as to realise all its advantages when obtained," and no longer "be engaged, as reformers have heretofore been, in periodically arousing the public mind to the highest state of excitement, suddenly to sink into apathy, *with* or *without* the attainment of their object. . . ."

This ideal was to take practical shape in a "National Association of the United Kingdom for Promoting the Political and Social Improvement of the People." This Association was to work for the Charter, and it was also to subsidise missionaries, circulating libraries, tracts, public halls and schools—a vast programme wth an Owenite ring about it. As for funds, Lovett suggested that if each signatory to the petition for the Charter gave a penny a week, this would bring in £256,000 a year, of which £240,000 could be used for the erection of 80 halls or schools at £3,000 each, and the rest be spent on the libraries, missionaries, tracts, &c.

Lovett had outlined this scheme with Collins' help in the thesis on "Chartism" that he wrote in jail and smuggled out to Place, with the request that it should be published on the day of his release. Place, thinking the scheme grandiose and impracticable, threw cold water on it, and hence publication was delayed—a delay that Lovett resented bitterly. After his release he and Collins published the book, following it up in March, 1841, with an address setting out the plan for the National Association. Many leading Chartists signed this address, but when the plan came under the ban of O'Connor, who attacked it with virulence in the *Northern Star,* some of the signatories withdrew their signature: the second edition of the book failed to sell, and by the time the National Association actually came into being, in October, 1841, the scheme was foredoomed to failure. O'Connor, as an ally, might have made success impossible, but as an enemy he made success equally impossible.

Working class support, such as it was, lay behind O'Connor and the National Charter Association, a body formed in July, 1841, in Manchester, to restart the agitation after its ignominious collapse. This body Lovett refused to join, though he disclaimed all hostility to it. Its illegal constitution was given as the reason for his refusal, and by the time the constitution had been amended his relations with O'Connor were too bitter to make co-operation between the two men possible.

COMPLETE SUFFRAGE MOVEMENT

As his scheme fell flat, so far as working class support went, Lovett was driven more and more to the middle classes, and he took a prominent part in the attempt in 1842 to amalgamate the middle class and the working class movements for suffrage reform, known as the Complete Suffrage Union, and associated with the name of Joseph Sturge of Birmingham. Lovett, unlike O'Connor, was a Free Trader, but he thought the suffrage more important than the repeal of the Corn Laws, which were "only one of the effects of the great cause we are seeking to remove." Hence he resented the anti-Corn Law agitation as side-tracking enthusiasm for the Charter. Sturge, who belonged to the anti-Corn Law League, came to a similar conclusion, and in April, 1842, he organised a conference in Birmingham of middle-class democrats, including John Bright, drawn largely from the ranks of the anti-Corn Law League, together with working class representatives such as Lovett and Collins. To everyone's surprise, complete unanimity was reached on the Six Points, and the substance of the Charter was adopted, though its name was studiously avoided. Its name had now too many sinister associations for the middle class delegates to allow its use. Lovett pleaded hard for a motion that the actual Charter should be considered at a future meeting, but the question was shelved, the Conference agreeing to a resolution that "any documents which embody the necessary details" should be considered. Meanwhile, on Lovett's motion, the Complete Suffrage Union was formed.

The future looking promising enough for the new body. Local

associations sprang up : a petition promoted by the Union was discussed in Parliament, and though it obtained only 67 votes as against 226, all the Radicals and Free Traders voted for it, including Cobden, and, of course, Bright. But, again, O'Connor's ban was on the project, and he threatened to swamp the coming Conference. To checkmate him, and to keep discussion off the tabooed subject of the Charter, the middle-class members of the Council resorted to what seemed to Lovett a piece of sharp practice. They drafted a new Bill, called the Bill of Rights, containing the Six Points, but avoiding the name of Charter, and this Bill they presented to the Conference as the basis of discussion. This rejection of the actual Charter, the symbol for which men had fought and suffered and died, roused Lovett's indignation, and drove him to make common cause with O'Connor. He proposed a motion, seconded by O'Connor, that the People's Charter should be discussed. It was carried by 193 to 94, but the middle classes thereupon withdrew from the Conference and co-operation was at an end. Lovett's lip was said to have "curled in scorn," whilst O'Connor poured flattery on his ally. It was the only occasion after the 1839 Convention on which the two men worked together, and their co-operation did not outlast the day.

Whilst Lovett was working for the Complete Suffrage project, the National Charter Association had occupied itself in promoting another monster petition to Parliament. This second petition, six miles in length, with over three million signatures, was presented in the House of Commons in May, 1842. The activities of its "physical force" members, which usually found scope only in breaking up meetings of the anti-Corn Law League and other societies, a policy abhorred by Lovett, were given a real opportunity in the summer of 1842, when a series of strikes spread through the North and the Midlands. It was a chance for the Chartists to dominate the situation. An attempt was made to call on the workers to remain on strike till the Charter was won, but not only was the response half-hearted, but the "physical force" Chartists themselves were in two minds about it; O'Connor disavowed the action, and the Government promptly packed away most of the leaders in prison. Lovett, during the strike, had issued a characteristic address urging the strikers to avoid violence.

One more effort was made to close up the ranks and produce co-operation between Lovett and O'Connor. When O'Connor diverted the Chartist agitation to his ill-fated land scheme, Lovett was asked, in 1843, to become its secretary. He refused, and published his letter of refusal, with its bitter indictment of O'Connor and of this mischief he had done. "Previous to his notorious career there was something pure and intellectual in our agitation. There was a reciprocity of generous sentiment, a tolerant spirit of investigation, an ardent aspiration for all that can improve and dignify humanity, which awakened the hopes of all good men, and which even our enemies respected. He came among us to blight those feelings, to wither those hopes...... By his great professions, by trickery and deceit, he got the aid of the working classes to establish an organ to promulgate their principles, which he soon converted into an instrument for destroying everything intellectual and moral in our movement."

Lovett made a last effort in 1845 to induce the Chartists to change their ways, and to eschew "violence and folly." "Be assured," he wrote, "that those who flatter your prejudices, commend your ignorance, and administer to your vices, are not your friends. 'Unwashed faces, unshorn chins' and dirty habits will in nowise prepare you for your political or social equality with the decent portion of your brethren..... Empty boastings, abusive language and contempt for all mental and moral qualifications will rather retard than promote your freedom." Using his favourite phrase about a combination of "the wise and good," he urged them once more "to rise into vitality and strength." But his appeal fell on deaf ears. After the failure of the Complete Suffrage agitation, Lovett had, in fact, become a publicist and not a politician. He continued to compose addresses, including appeals to the working classes of France and America against war, and could organise a successful meeting of protest in 1844 against the reception in England of that "active, scheming, wily tyrant," Nicholas of Russia, but he had no following, and the societies he tried to found, such as "The General Association of Progress" and the "People's League" were failures. After 1846 he became for a time publisher of *Howitt's Journal*, which he used as a vehicle for fresh manifestoes.

Henceforth his main work in life was as an educationalist, fostering those "mental and moral qualifications" which he felt to be the basis of all improvement. The National Association, though it failed to fulfil the dreams of the writer of "Chartism," and sometimes seemed to exist only to afford him a platform from which to address the public, had managed in 1842 to open one, though only one, of the proposed National Halls. The hall was in Holborn, where a music hall now stands. It started in debt, and it remained in debt, and much of a testimonial of £140 given to Lovett by friends in 1848 went in payments connected with it; but, though a constant source of pecuniary worry, it gave opportunities for educational experiments; a Sunday school was opened there in 1843, at which Lovett taught; and in 1848 a regular day school was started under Lovett's superintendence. Later on, in 1851, he began to do most of the teaching himself.

It cannot be said that he was a disappointed man. Few men who have led movements have cared less for leadership. His denunciations of the evils done by relying on leaders were sincere. He neither possessed nor desired the gift of swaying multitudes. That one man should influence others, except by helping them to use their own reason, seemed to him a vicious thing. The work of education was congenial to him—his whole life had been an attempt to help the working classes to educate themselves—and he threw himself with as much zest into writing elementary school books on anatomy and physiology as he had shown for his studies in his early twenties. At the age of sixty-four he was engaged on a text book about vertebrated animals, but found the subject so important that he "determined to treat of the invertebrated animals also." Nor can a man be called disillusioned who, after Lovett's experiences, could at the age of fifty-six seriously send a petition to the House of Commons, urging the need for a higher intellectual and moral standard for members of Parliament, to be obtained by a compulsory examination for all candidates, or could advocate that the clergy should be turned into an instrument of progress by inducing them to teach elementary astronomy on Sundays. But he was a sad man, as, indeed, he had always been, and it was a sombre old age. The closing of the National Hall, and, in consequence, of his school in 1857, was a heavy blow. He taught elementary science at other schools afterwards, and continued writing text books, which sometimes found and sometimes did not find a publisher, but he could not support himself, and was forced to accept help from a generous friend. "Such kindness, indeed," he wrote, "has been rarely witnessed towards a stranger as that which I have received from my noble-hearted friend. But while I know that all this kindness is extended towards me freely and ungrudgingly, it does, however, jar upon my feelings to think that, after all my struggles, all my industry, and, I may add, all my temperance and frugality, I cannot earn or live upon my own bread in my old age."

As an old man he lived with his devoted wife and his grand-daughter, the only child of his daughter, and wrote his "Life and Struggles," a book in which he strung together the addresses and manifestoes of his earlier days, adding long comments on later events. He died on August 8th, 1877, aged seventy-seven, and was buried at Highgate.

6 G. D. H. Cole
JAMES KEIR HARDIE

In 1893, James Keir Hardie presided over the conference which brought the Independent Labour Party into being : in 1900 he saw the victory of his ideas further celebrated in the creation of the Labour Representation Committee, which became the Labour Party and chose him as its first leader in Parliament after the General Election of 1906. The name of Keir Hardie stands in the history of the British working class for the thing of which these several events were the practical manifestation—the development of a working class party based directly upon the organised workers, and standing for a policy of practical Socialism directly related to immediate working-class needs and demands. In creating this party Keir Hardie's foremost task was to draw the active section of the working class away from Liberalism, and to persuade it of the need for a policy of independence in politics as well as in industrial affairs. His great battles were fought against the older Trade Union leaders who believed in the 'Lib-Lab' alliance, and stood at most for the improvement of labour conditions inside the framework of the capitalist system. But, in order to realise his ideals, he was driven to wage war also on a second front—against those Socialists who stood for the creation of an out-and-out Socialist Party, asserting the necessity of a complete break not merely with the Liberal Party, but with all forms of compromise with capitalism. Hardie was as much a Socialist as Hyndman, and as fully convinced of the necessity of overthrowing the capitalist order; but he disbelieved in the possibility of building in Great Britain an effective class-war party on strictly Marxian lines, and insisted that no Socialist Party worthy of the name could be created unless the Trade Unions could be induced to take part in it. In order to secure Trade

127

Union participation he was ready to compromise—to accept much less than a fully Socialist programme, provided that he could ensure that the new party should be founded on a basis of strict independence of Toryism and Liberalism alike. He had his way; and, whereas in most of the continental countries there developed Social Democratic Parties which professed strict adherence to Marxian doctrine, there was created in Great Britain a 'Labour Alliance'—a federal union of Socialists and Trade Unionists which, beginning without any defined policy at all beyond independence of the older political parties, came gradually to accept Socialism as its objective, but did not therewith cease to make the achievement of social reforms its primary immediate concern.

Whether this policy of Hardie's was good or bad is open to dispute. But it is beyond question that it was the only policy on which it was possible at the time to base any considerable political movement of the British working class. The older 'Lib-Lab' policy had manifestly exhausted its usefulness : appropriate to the stage at which Trade Unionism meant little more than a movement peculiar to certain limited groups of skilled workers, it had become inapplicable as soon as there had begun a stirring among the masses of less skilled labourers—a movement symbolised in the famous Dock Strike of 1889. On the other hand, Marxism, as embodied in Hyndman's Social Democratic Federation, had entirely failed to catch the imagination of the awakening masses, and was anathema, not merely to the old 'Lib-Lab' leaders but to the main body of their Trade Union followers as well.

British Marxism, represented by the SDF, failed, not so much because it was too revolutionary as because its approach was alien to the ideas and prejudices of the general mass of organised workers. In the 1880's, when Hardie began his campaign for an Independent Labour Party, religion had a deep hold on the main body of the miners and skilled workers who made up the Trade Union movement. They were Nonconformists, devout attendants at chapel, nurtured on the Bible, and most easily moved by Scriptural phrases and by ethical appeals. To wean them from Liberalism, which had also its strongholds in the chapels, required the presentation of Socialism as an ethical gospel. On no other terms would they have responded; and no leader who had not been like-minded with themselves could have appealed to them with any hope of success. Keir Hardie was like-minded with them. Like most of the 'Lib-Lab' leaders, he learnt the arts of oratory as a lay preacher and a temperance lecturer. Unlike his predecessors he realised that the principles of the Sermon on the Mount would never be put into practice by a Liberal party led, financed and controlled by capitalist advocates and interests, and that the simple claim of the workers for measures of social justice —the eight hours' day, the legal minimum wage, and the 'right to work'—could be made the basis of a practical political programme only by a predominantly working-class party which would put these things first, and demand them in the name of Christian morality and common human decency of man to man.

There was no hypocrisy in Hardie's attempt to create a Labour Party on this essentially ethical basis. That was how he felt himself: he wanted Socialism because he wanted social justice, and not social justice because he believed in Socialism as an historic necessity or a rational theory. He had a mind which generalised only on a basis of practical experience: he was never a theorist, and never burdened himself with more theories than he could put to practical use. He saw misery, and wanted passionately to cure it—and to cure it soon. He revolted against Liberalism because it offered no cure, and he rejected dogmatic Socialism because he was not prepared to wait for alleviation until after 'the revolution'. He therefore appealed to the workers to follow his middle way; and, for good or ill, they followed him, and the British Labour Party was born. In telling his story I shall be narrating the history of this birth.

CHILD

James Keir Hardie was born at Laighbrannock, near Holytown, Lanarkshire, in a one-room, mud-floor, thatched cottage, on August 15, 1856. His father, a ship's carpenter, was mostly away at sea, and his mother lived there with his grandmother, Mary Keir, and went out to work as a farm servant both before and after his birth. He was the eldest son, and soon there were six brothers and two sisters to keep him company. His grandfather had died of cholera in 1836, under circumstances which had left hard memories behind. His infancy and childhood were full of hardships, which made permanent marks upon his mind. He

129

knew dire poverty at first hand; and he never forgot what it meant.

Hardie had almost no schooling before he was sent out to work. He was doing odd jobs when he was six, and worked regularly from the age of seven. At that stage his family moved to Glasgow, where his father got a job ashore as a joiner in Napier's Shipbuilding Yard. The boy was employed in turn by the Anchor Line as a messenger, by a baker, in a brassfinishing shop, by a firm of lithographers, and then again by a baker. He was in this last job when the great Clyde lock-out of 1866 took place. His father was out with the rest, and strike pay fell to 2/- and 1/6 a week. The household lived largely on the boy's wages of 3/6 a week—for a day of twelve and a half hours.

There was fever in his home—one of his brothers died of it—and his mother was ill and near her time. Hardie was twice late at the baker's. On the second occasion, without giving him a chance to explain, his employer discharged him. He described the event many years later, and the description helps to show how, without eloquence, he was able to move large masses of his fellow-men.

> It was the last week in the year. Father had been away for two or three days in search of work. Towards the end of the week, having been up most of the night, I got to the shop fifteen minutes late, and was told by the young lady in charge that if it occurred again I should be "punished". I made no reply. I couldn't. I felt like crying. Next morning the same thing happened—I could tell why, but that is neither here nor there. It was a very wet morning, and I reached the shop drenched to the skin, barefooted and hungry. There had not been a crust of bread in the house that morning.
>
> But that was pay-day, and I was filled with hope. "You are wanted upstairs by the master," said the girl behind the counter, and my heart almost stopped beating. Outside the dining-room a servant bade me wait till "master had finished prayers". (He was much noted for his piety.) At length the girl opened the door, and the sight of that room is fresh in my memory even as I write, nearly fifty years after. Round a great mahogany table sat the members of the family, with the father at the top. In front of him was a very wonderful-looking coffee boiler, in the great glass bowl of which the coffee was bubbling. The table was loaded with dainties. My master looked at me over his glasses, and said, in quite a pleasant tone of voice : "Boy, this is the second morning you have been

late, and my customers leave me if they are kept waiting for
their hot breakfast rolls. I therefore dismiss you, and, to make
you more careful in the future, I have decided to fine you a
week's wages. And now you may go!"

I wanted to speak and explain about my home, and I mut-
tered out something to explain why I was late, but the servant
took me by the arm and led me downstairs. As I passed
through the shop the girl in charge gave me a roll and said
a kind word. I knew my mother was waiting for my wages.
As the afternoon was drawing to a close I returned home,
and told her what had happened. It seemed to be the last
blow. The roll was still under my vest, but soaked with rain.
That night the baby was born, and the sun rose on the first
of January, 1867, over a home in which there was neither
fire nor food, though, fortunately, help came before the day
had reached its noon. But the memory of those early days
abides with me, and makes me doubt the sincerity of those
who make pretence in their prayers. For such things still
abound in our midst.[1]

PIT BOY

This incident happened on New Year's Eve, 1866. Hardie's
next job was heating rivets in Thompson's shipyard at 4/6 a
week. But soon his father got work as a joiner in an ironworks,
and the family moved to Quarter, in the colliery area. In 1867,
at the age of ten, Keir Hardie went to work in the mines, at first
as a pit-pony boy and latter in various jobs till he became a skilled
coal-hewer before he was twenty. Most of this period he spent
in the pits; but in the course of it he worked for two years as a
quarryman.

Soon after he went down the pit, his father lost his job and
returned to the sea. His mother then joined his grandmother at
Newarthill, quite near his birthplace. From this point he set
seriously to work to educate himself after his day's labour in the
pit. His mother had already taught him to read, but not to write;
and now, at the night school at Holytown, he settled down
seriously to learn. He learnt to write well, and to write shorthand
—which stood him in good stead later in his journalistic work.
He became an assiduous reader of all manner of books, from
treatises on mining to poetry and history, and to the Bible, which

[1] *Merthyr Pioneer*, 2/1/1915

had a powerful influence on his writing and speaking throughout his life.

Hardie's early experiences as a pit-boy included a narrow escape from death, which also left its mark upon his mind.

For several years as a lad I rarely saw daylight during the winter months. Down the pit by six in the morning, and not leaving it again until half-past five meant not seeing the sun, and even on Sunday I had at that time to spend four hours down below. Such an experience does not develop the sunny side of one's being. But the Muirkirk accident set my mind back to an incident of the long ago. I would be about twelve at the time, and was a pony driver. We were working at nights, and some thirty men were employed, I being the only boy. It was dreary work. The pit was very old and very wet. To this day the dreary, monotonous drip, drip, drip of the water on every side is quite fresh in my ears. My pony was a little shaggy Highlander, appropriately named Donald— strong and obstinate, like the race among whom he had been reared. We were great friends, and drank cold tea from the same tin flask, sip about. I have to confess that betimes his old reiving propensities overcame his loyalty, and on these occasions, should opportunity offer, he would steal the tea-flask from where it was kept, extract the cork, and empty it of its contents with, I doubt not, all the satisfaction which stolen sweets never failed to afford. One night, just after mid-night hour, when the weird noises of the pit are always at their height, Donald and I were jogging along, when the voice of Rab Mair, the big, genial fireman, came reverberating out of the gloom, his little lamp shining like a star in the blackness. "Run into the dook and warn the men to come at once; the shank's closin'." I did not stay on the order of my going. The shank closing! The shank is the shaft by which entrance and egress to the pit is obtained. It was the only outlet. Should it close in we were entombed, and what that might mean I did not care to think. In a very short time all the men were at the pit bottom, only to find that already they were too late. We were seventy fathoms from the daisies, and the weary rocks, tired of hanging in mid air, seemed bent on settling down into some semblance of solidarity. For once in a way the drip of water could not be heard. The timber props were creaking and bursting all around us; whilst the strong rocks were groaning and cracking and roaring as they were settling down. As man after man rushed to the bottom breathless and alarmed, they were met with the news that already the cage, by which men and materials are taken to the surface, was "stuck in the shank". The sides of the shaft had so far come together that the cage had no longer a free passage and was held fast some fathoms above us. We were prisoners.

I can recall every detail of the scene. The men gathered in groups, each with his little lamp on his bonnet, their blackened, serious faces, discussing what should be done. The roaring and crackling, as if of artillery, went on overhead, and gloom began to settle on every countenance. Some of the more susceptible were crying, and I remember two by themselves who were praying and crossing themselves. Rab Mair remained cool and strong, and did his best to keep up the spirits of his fellow-prisoners. By and by I began to feel sleepy, and made my way to the stables, whither Donald had already gone. By this time it was evident the worst of the crisis was over; the noise overhead was subsiding and the drip of water was again to be heard. But the shaft was closed. We were prisoners indeed. After cleaning Donald down, I gave him a feed of corn, put some hay in his manger, and rolling myself in this, kissed him, as was our wont, and then went off to sleep. A boy of twelve will sleep when there is nothing to do, even if he be cooped in a trap. How long I slept I have no means now of knowing. It was Rab Mair's voice—swearing, if the truth must be told—and some vigorous punches from his fist which brought me back to consciousness.

The engineman, on finding the cages stuck fast in the shaft, and hearing the signals from below, knew there was something wrong, and raised an alarm. In a short time the news spread, and soon the bulk of the people were at the pit, my mother among the rest. Volunteers were plentiful, and soon some brave fellows had been lowered by an improvised kettle into the shaft, where they soon discovered what was amiss. Cold chisels, picks, and saws were requisitioned, and the imprisoned cage cut free and allowed to drop in pieces to the bottom, after which the kettle—a bucket used by pit sinkers, and narrower than the cage—was used to bring the imprisoned men to the surface. But where was the trapper? Everyone had seen him in the bottom, and perhaps in the excitement of the moment no one would have missed him had there not been a mother there waiting for him. And so Rab Mair and two companions had to descend into the depths again and search. For a time their searching was in vain, until Rab bethought him of Donald's crib, and there sure enough I was, sound asleep. Rab pretended to be angry—but he wasn't. I think the reception at the top was the most trying part of the affair. At least, it was the only part when I cried.[1]

[1] *The Labour Leader,* 26/3/1898.

YOUTH

Hardie grew from boyhood to adolescence, facing such risks as these, improving his knowledge at the night school, and gradually developing a point of view of his own. His parents, during their residence at Glasgow, had become strong Radicals and Republicans, Secularists and regular readers of Charles Bradlaugh's *National Reformer,* and vigorous critics of all the religious sects. Young Hardie, however, differed from his parents in these matters. Like most of the active spirits among the miners of those days he became religious. He attached himself in due course to the Morrisonians—the Evangelical Union, which followed the teachings of Dr James Morrison, expelled for heresy from the United Presbyterian Church. Morrison was a keen opponent of predestination. He preached that all men could be saved if they would, and that their salvation depended not upon God but upon themselves. This doctrine suited Hardie, and with it he combined a strong belief in temperance. At Holytown he joined the Good Templars, at the age of seventeen, and came into contact with Dr G. B. Clark, the editor of *The Good Templar,* who was thereafter his close friend all his life. Dr Clark had been connected with Marx's International Working Men's Association, and was the advocate of the Highland crofters, who were presently to elect him to the House of Commons as MP for Caithness. He furnished Hardie with his first introduction to Socialist ideas; but at that time there was no Socialist movement, and the Radicals who were inclined to Socialism still sought to achieve their immediate objects by working with the advanced wing of the Liberals. Hardie became a regular speaker for the Good Templars, a lay preacher for the Evangelical Union, and before long a worker for the advanced Liberalism represented in Lanarkshire by Eugene Wason. Meanwhile, his household moved yet again—to Low Waters, near Hamilton, where his mother supplemented his earnings by opening a small grocer's shop.

TRADE UNIONIST

The early 'seventies had been a great time of prosperity for the mining industry; but from the middle of the decade prosperity was passing into depression, which became profound in the bad year, 1879. Hardie had before this begun his efforts to reorganise the Lanarkshire Miners' Union, which had fallen to pieces in the

134

depression after the great years in the 'sixties and early 'seventies when Alexander Macdonald had created a powerful miners' movement both in Scotland and throughout the English coalfields. In the spring of 1879 the colliery owners demanded further wage-reductions, on top of those exacted during the previous years. The result was a revival of Trade Unionism; but Keir Hardie, regarded already as a dangerous agitator, was discharged from the pit with his two brothers who were working there, on account of his efforts to organise the miners, and found himself victimised and boycotted throughout the Lanarkshire coalfield. His mother was at this time running her grocer's shop, with miners for her principal customers; and Keir Hardie opened a tobacconist's and stationer's shop beside hers while he continued his efforts at organisation. He also made his first sally into journalism, by getting himself made local correspondent for the *Glasgow Weekly News,* and earning a few shillings here and there by contributions, in both prose and verse, to other newspapers.

In July 1879 his efforts caused him to be appointed as unpaid secretary to the Hamilton Miners, who were taking the lead in the attempt to form a wider Union. Alexander Macdonald came to Low Waters to address a series of meetings, and Hardie took the chair for him. At this stage, trade was so bad that strike action seemed to be out of the question, and the policy advocated by the leaders was that of voluntary restriction of output by the miners in the hope of keeping up the price of coal—a policy which had a long history behind it. Low as earnings were, the miners cooperated to share out the available work, while they attempted to group their scattered lodges into a wider Union in the hope of offering more effective resistance to the repeated demands for wage reductions.

At the end of July Hardie went from Hamilton as delegate to a National Conference of the Scottish Miners, and thence he returned to be appointed as agent by the men at Hamilton, who, in spite of bad trade, were getting ready for a struggle with the owners. In October 1879, at a further Conference, he was made National Secretary of the Scottish Miners—not of their Union, for that did not exist, but with a mission to organise a national Union or Federation if he could. Thus, at the age of twenty-three, he found himself at the head of the miners' movement in

Scotland—already victimised as an agitator, and compelled to earn his living outside the pits as best he might.

In the following year, 1880, trade having slightly improved, the miner's movement in Lanarkshire came to a head. There were strikes, widespread but not general, against the intolerable conditions that prevailed; and Hardie found himself the leader of a campaign in which he could see no hope of success. He went into Ayrshire in order to prevent the importation of blacklegs to break the strike, and thus became well known to the Ayrshire miners. Meanwhile, his and his mother's private affairs went from bad to worse. The grocer's shop supplied goods on credit to the strikers, and the debts were mostly never paid. The embryonic Lanarkshire Union broke up as the strikers were forced back to work by sheer starvation, and Hardie was nearly starved out with them. In the meantime, he had added to his responsibilities by marriage. At the age of twenty-three, he married Lily Wilson of Hamilton, who thereafter shared his troubles with an unfailing heart.

After the collapse of the strikes and of the Union, Hardie's position in Lanarkshire became impossible, and early in 1881 he removed his household to Old Cumnock, in Ayrshire, in response to a request from the Ayrshire Miners to undertake the task of reorganising their disbanded County Union. He was to be paid for this work, but his pay was precarious as well as small, and depended on his own success as an organiser. He could not have lived at all, unless he had been able to eke out from other sources the income which he received from the miners. He began to write as a local correspondent for two Ayrshire papers—the Liberal *Ardrossan and Saltcoats Herald,* and its subsidiary, the *Cumnock News,* of which in the following year he became virtually editor and manager on an exiguous salary.

Meanwhile the Ayrshire miners, on the strength of better trade and some improvement in Union organisation, had demanded a wage increase, and had struck for it in October 1881, over nearly the whole county. The strike lasted into the depth of winter; and as the funds were low Hardie was ceaselessly active in organising soup kitchens, begging for gifts of potatoes and other food from the farmers, and trying to keep the men's spirits up through the prolonged struggle. At length the miners were too weak to struggle any longer; but they went back to work solid, as they had come out, and before long the wage increase they had demanded was granted as trade continued to improve. Hardie had become meanwhile the unquestioned leader of the Ayrshire Miners' Union, which emerged from the struggle intact; and when the strike was over, he set to work to reorganise the Union on a more lasting basis, with the help of Alexander Barrowman and of James Neil, flute-player and song-maker, who had been the pioneer of the Union before Hardie came to settle in Old Cumnock.

FROM LIBERAL—

In this year of the Ayrshire strike, Hardie's first son, James, was born. Hardie took up actively in his new home his work for the Good Templars and his preaching for the Evangelical Union; and in the following year, having seen his way to a modest income from journalism, he resigned his irregularly paid office of secretary to the Ayrshire Miners' Union, and became its unpaid President, without relaxing his efforts on its behalf.

At this time Socialism, in Great Britain, was practically non-existent. The memory of Marx's International had died out; and Hyndman's Democratic Federation, organised in 1881, had not yet adopted a socialist name or programme. Dr Clark and others were agitating among the crofters for land reform; and the Irish Land League, founded in 1879, was influencing opinion in both England and Scotland. Hardie's awakening was greatly stimulated in 1884 by a visit from Henry George, who spent two days lecturing in Ayrshire, mainly in his company. He and George argued; and Hardie was already insisting that George's panacea, the Single Tax on land, was not enough. Hardie wanted a legal eight hours' day for the miners, and other industrial legislation which George regarded as unwarranted interference with individual liberty. But there was in Hardie's retorts to Henry George no consciousness of Socialism, of which he had barely heard. He was a Radical and a Republican, demanding that the State should intervene to protect the miners' lives, but working still inside the Liberal Party, and writing for Liberal newspapers with no consciousness that the gulf between his creed and that of Liberalism was too wide to be bridged.

His introduction to Socialism as a movement began in the following year, 1885, when James Patrick, who had come under

137

K

the influence of the Social Democratic Federation in London, paid a visit to James Neil at Old Cumnock. Neil had read Owen's writings, and he became promptly a convert to the newer Socialist ideas. Hardie was slower to respond; but the breach between his views and those of Liberalism widened steadily as he found the main body of Liberals strongly opposed to his demands for the legal eight hours' day and an improved safety code for the miners. In 1886 he ceased to edit *The Cumnock News,* while continuing to contribute regularly both to it and to *The Ardrossan and Saltcoats Herald,* in which, in addition to his work as local reporter, he wrote of mining conditions under his pen name, 'The Trapper'.

In 1886 the Ayrshire Miners' Union was again reorganised, and Hardie agreed to become its Organising Secretary at a salary of £75 a year. Out of this reorganisation sprang a renewed attempt to get all the Scottish miners into a single body; and soon Hardie took on in addition the office of Secretary to a Scottish Miners' Federation which loosely joined together the various county Unions. The Ayrshire miners then pressed him to stand for Parliament as their candidate, for the North Ayrshire Division; and his adoption led to the final severance of his relations with the two Liberal papers for which he had worked continuously since 1882.

—TO INDEPENDENT LABOUR

But in the meantime Hardie had decided to launch out with a paper of his own. In January 1887 he produced the first number of *The Miner,* a monthly journal in which, beginning chiefly with mining questions, he gradually widened his appeal to include a demand for a Radical political programme based on the needs of the workers. He had found the Liberals determined to oppose his candidature in North Ayrshire; and the colliery disaster at Udston, in Lanarkshire, in May 1887, had made him more determined than ever to go to all lengths in pressing the miners' claims for legislative protection. The foundations of Hardie's demand for an independent Labour political movement were laid at this time. He was shaking himself free of Liberalism, and beginning to form in his mind the conception of a Socialism which would appeal directly and plainly to the ordinary working people.

138

Hardie's position as Secretary of the Ayrshire Miners' Union and of the embryonic Scottish Miners' Federation made him, for the first time, something of a figure in the national world of Labour; and in 1887 he paid his first visit to London, where he met both Eleanor Marx, Karl Marx's daughter, and Friedrich Engels, both of whom had quarrelled with the Social Democratic Federation, and were urging the need for a body more in touch with the Trade Unions and more capable of moving the main body of the British working classes. Hardie was deeply influenced by these contacts, his first glimpses of the wider world of Socialism; and he came back to Scotland determined to work for an independent Labour movement, which should cut clear of the ideas of orthodox Liberalism. By July 1887 he was strongly attacking, in *The Miner,* the Liberal-Labour leaders who still dominated the national miners' movement and the Trades Union Congress. Thomas Burt and Ben Pickard, 'Lib-Lab' M.P.s and leaders among the English miners, had just contributed to a volume entitled *The New Liberal Programme,* and had cautiously proclaimed themselves as desiring 'to establish such restrictions on the hours of labour as may on enquiry be found judicious'.

Hardie retorted :

> I wish to ask the miners of this country if this is what they [Burt and Pickard] received votes for. Have we grievances as a class? If we have, have we sufficient intelligence to state what these grievances are, and what would constitute a remedy? If we have these, why do we not make our demands clear and intelligible, and place them before our fellow-electors all over Great Britain? Oh, because, say some, we might thereby injure the prospects of our Party, and besides, we would be considered extreme men. Party be hanged ! We are miners first, and partisans next; at least, if we follow the examples of our "superiors" the landlords and their allies, we ought to be. I have contempt for the men who, knowing what should be done, are yet afraid to proclaim it from the house-tops if need be. It is the half-heartedness of the present leaders which keeps our cause from progressing. If respectability be maintained by silence regarding the suffering of the people, then away with it. We want none of it. If it be not possible for Parliament so to legislate as to enable our honest, temperate, and industrious workman to spend his working days in plenty, and his old age in comfort, then Parliament is rather a hindrance than a help.

The Trades Union Congress Labour Electoral Committee[1] has just issued an address to the Labour Party of the United Kingdom and Ireland. I am extremely pleased to learn that there is a Labour Party in the United Kingdom, but should be better pleased to see some fruits of its existence. I turn to the manifesto issued by this body and find out what the programme of this body is, and find it summed up in these words : 'To promote the return of working men to Parliament'. Now undoubtedly, this is a very good object. But what difference will it make to me that I have a working man representing me in Parliament if he is a dumb dog who dare not bark, and will follow the leader under any circumstances? There is something even more desirable than the return of working men to Parliament, and that is to give working men a definite programme to fight for when they get there, and to warn them that if they haven't the courage to stand up in the House of Commons and say what they would say in a miners' meeting, they must make room for someone else who will.[2]

Here, quite unequivocally, is the demand for an independent Labour movement, with a clear political programme of its own. The demand is not for Socialism, but for a Labour programme which is evidently meant to consist of immediate and practical reforms. But the appeal to the workers to cut clear of the existing parties and make a party and a programme of their own is quite unqualified. In *The Miner,* during its first year, Hardie was already proclaiming forcibly the gospel of Independent Labour Representation to which he was to devote the rest of his life.

Throughout the year 1887 Hardie was busy with the attempt to put the Scottish Miners' Federation on its feet. He toured the coalfield areas, organising and speaking; and he also made with other leaders of the Scottish miners—Chisholm Robertson of Stirlingshire, Robert Brown of the Lothians, and John Weir of Fifeshire—visits to London in connection with the Mines Regulation Bill which the newly enfranchised miners were pressing hard upon the Government. He also first appeared in 1887 as a

[1] This was the body through which the Trade Unions were seeking, in the eighteen eighties, to secure the return of working men to Parliament under the auspices of local Liberal and Radical Associations in the industrial districts.

[2] *The Miner,* 1887.

delegate at the Trades Union Congress, and leapt into prominence there by delivering a frontal attack on Henry Broadhurst and the other "Lib-Lab" leaders, both for their supineness in pressing working-class claims and for their support at elections of 'sweating' employers who belonged to the Liberal Party. It was at this Congress that the Parliamentary Committee met defeat over the question of holding an International Labour Congress in London. The Committee had disobeyed the instructions of the 1886 Trades Union Congress to summon this gathering, on the plea that there were no true working-class movements in the continental countries; but in 1887 it was again ordered to convene the meeting, which was duly held the following year.

PARLIAMENTARY CANDIDATE

The Trades Union Congress of 1887 was also largely concerned with the question of Labour representation. The Congress of 1886 had set up the Labour Electoral Committee; and under the auspices of this body local Labour Electoral Associations had been set up in many parts of the country, and were endeavouring to promote the return of working men to serve on local governing bodies as well as in Parliament. The 1887 Congress allowed the L E C to become a separate organisation, under the name of the Labour Electoral Association; but Hardie's demand that the Trade Unionists should severe their connection with the existing parties, and establish an independent party of their own, backed by the entire strength of the Trade Union movement, met with little response. The L E A, under the leadership of T. R. Threlfall, sought to achieve its objects by persuading local Liberal and Radical Associations to adopt a few working men as candidates here and there, and rejected altogether any policy which threatened to involve it in serious conflict with the Liberal party machine.

This was the situation when, in March 1888, Stephen Mason, an advanced Liberal M P who had given steady support to the claims of the miners, retired for reasons of health from his seat in Mid-Lanark. Hardie, who had been responsible for organising the miners in the division before his removal to Ayrshire, was asked by them to become their candidate; and the question at once arose whether the Liberals would support him and under what auspices he was to run. In *The Miner* he declared his willingness to stand, and added that in his opinion the seat should be fought by a Labour candidate, whatever the attitude of the Liberals might be. "Better split the party now," he wrote, "if there is to be a split, than at a general election; and if the Labour Party can only make their power felt now, terms will not be wanting when the general election comes."

From this it will be seen that Hardie did not exclude the notion of being adopted by the Liberals, despite his advice to the Trades Union Congress a few months before. Difficult negotiations followed, including the complications introduced by the arrival on the scene of T. R. Threlfall, of the LEA, who, having come to speak on Hardie's behalf, proceeded to arrange with the Liberals for his withdrawal, on condition that a suitable constituency should be found for him elsewhere at the next general election. The Liberals offered Hardie, if he would withdraw, both payment of his election expenses at the general election, and a salary if he were returned to Parliament. Hardie indignantly rejected the offer, and continued his campaign without the backing of the L E A, though some of its leading members, especially Henry Hyde Champion, continued to give him their support.

Hardie's votes numbered 617, against 3,847 for the Liberal and 2,917 for the Conservative. But the contest produced important results; for it led directly to the formation of the Scottish Labour Party later in the same year. This body, mooted at a conference in May and definitely launched in August, had Keir Hardie for its secretary, and for its President R. B. Cunninghame Graham, who had been elected as a Radical in 1886 for the neighbouring division of North-West Lanark, and had by now thrown in his lot with the Socialists. Dr G. B. Clark, who had been elected for Caithness as a crofters' candidate in 1885 (and continued to hold the seat till 1900) was a Vice-President. The Scottish Labour Party adopted an advanced programme, including public ownership of banks and transport, as well as measures of social legislation; and it set out to organise the Scottish Labour movement on a basis of political independence.

INTERNATIONALIST

Invigorated by success in forming the Scottish Labour Party, Hardie proceeded to the Trades Union Congress at Bradford, where he renewed his attacks on the "Lib-Lab" leaders and his

142

demand for an independent party on a national basis, and also took the principal part in the debate on the legal eight hours day. In November, he was a delegate to the International Labour Congress, which the reluctant Parliamentary Committee had been compelled to convene; and he there first came into contact with the leaders of continental Socialism—Liebknecht and Bebel of the German Social Democratic Party, Anseele from Belgium, and many others, as well as with some noted figures in English Socialism, such as John Burns and Annie Besant. He moved at the Congress a resolution, which was not carried, calling for an international organisation of the Trade Union movement, based on national and international Unions for each trade, and on a system of federated General Trade Unions Councils governed by a triennial International Conference—in effect pretty much the scheme of organisation which was adopted by the International Federation of Trade Unions 13 years later.

This year, 1888, saw Hardie fairly launched on his career as a national leader. In conformity with this development, at the end of the year he dropped *The Miner* and replaced it by *The Labour Leader,* which was meant to be the national mouthpiece of the movement for an independent Labour Party.

In 1889 Hardie was a delegate at the Paris Conference, convened by the continental Marxists, which formed the Second International. His fellow-delegates were Cunninghame Graham, who with him represented the Scottish Labour Party, and William Morris, from the Socialist League. The main body of British delegates, including those of the Social Democratic Federation and the Fabian Society as well as the Trade Unionists, attended the rival Conference called by the French "Possibilists" —and moderate wing of French Socialism. Here again Hardie fraternised with the continental Socialist leaders, with marked consequences on the development of his ideas. He became both a convinced Socialist—albeit never fundamentally a Marxist, for his Socialism continued to be essentially ethical in its foundations —and a strong believer in internationalism and in working-class unity against capitalism and war.

Cunninghame Graham has described Hardie as he was at about this stage of his career.

> He was then about thirty years of age, I should judge, but old for his age. His hair was already becoming thin at the

top of the head, and receding from the temples. His eyes were not very strong. At first sight he struck you as a remarkable man. There was an air of great benevolence about him, but his face showed the kind of appearance of one who has worked hard and suffered, possibly from inadequate nourishment in his youth. He was active and alert, though not athletic. Still, he appears to be full of energy, and, as subsequent events proved, he had an enormous power of resistance against long, hard and continual work. I should judge him to have been of a very nervous and high-strung temperament. At that time, and I believe up to the end of his life, he was an almost ceaseless smoker. . . . He was a very strict teetotaller and remained so to the end, but he was not a bigot on the subject and was tolerant of faults in the weaker brethren. Nothing in his address or speech showed his want of education in his youth. His accent was Ayrshire. I think he took pride in it in his ordinary conversation. He could, however, to a great extent throw his accent aside, but not entirely. When roused or excited in public or private speech it was always perceptible. His voice was high pitched but sonorous and very far-carrying at that time. He never used notes at that time, and I think never prepared a speech, leaving all to the inspiration of the moment. This suited his natural, unforced method of speaking admirably. He had all the charm and some of the defects of his system.

. . . His chief merits as a speaker were, in my opinion, his homeliness, directness and sincerity; and his demerits were a tendency to redundancy and length, and a total lack of humour, very rare in an Ayrshire Scot. This was to me curious, as he had a considerable vein of pathos. . . . Hardie's dress at this time was almost always a navy blue serge suit with a hard bowler hat. His hair was never worn long, and his beard was well-trimmed and curly. Later on, to the regret of the "judicious", he affected a different style of dressing entirely foreign to his custom when a little-known man. He was then, and I believe always, an extremely abstemious eater, and in the long peregrinations about the mining villages of Lanarkshire and Ayrshire . . . in rain and wind, and now and then in snow, an oatcake, a scone, a bit of a kebbuck of cheese always contented him. He would then sit by the fireside in the cottage in the mining row, and light up his corncob pipe and talk of the future of the Labour Party, which in those days seemed to the miners a mere fairy-tale. Now and then I have seen him take the baby from the miner's wife, and dandle it on his knee while she prepared tea. He had the faculty of attracting children to him, and most certainly he "forbade them not". They would come round him in the miners' cottages and lean against him for the first few minutes. One felt he was a "family man" and so, I suppose did the children.

This description bears the impress of truth. It is like the later Hardie, except that, by the time I knew him, he had certainly developed a sense of humour which he did not reveal to Cunninghame Graham. It should be added that, in finding the cause of temperance, Hardie had early found religion as well. His parents were Bradlaughites; but there is a manuscript book of his, written in 1884, in which he records as follows : "Brought up an atheist, converted to Christianity in 1878—that is, at the age of about 22." This conversion lasted. Hardie soon ceased to care, if he ever cared, for the doctrines of any Church; but he continued for the rest of his life to use the Christian ethic as his sheet-anchor. His pamphlet, *Can a Man be a Christian on a Pound a Week?*, is an excellent illustration of his application of his religion to politics and to Socialism.

1889 was the year of the great dock strike, which gave the signal for a widespread uprising of the less skilled workers, and made possible the creation of an extensive Socialist movement. But at the Trade Union Congress of that year the "Lib-Lab's" successfully routed the Socialists for the last time. The following year, the "New Unionists" came in full force, and carried a resolution in favour of the legal eight hours day—the test question of the time. Henry Broadhurst resigned from the secretaryship. But the Congress was not yet ripe for Socialism. Hardie, John Burns and James Macdonald, of the Tailors, the leading spokesmen in favour of Socialism, were voted down by 263 votes to 55.

MEMBER FOR THE UNEMPLOYED

Hardie was looking for a constituency which he could hope to win as an independent Labour candidate. He fixed on South West Ham, which had been won by the Lib-Lab, Joseph Leicester, in 1885, but lost in the election of the following year. Leicester was still in the field; but Hardie, invited by the local Socialists, elbowed him aside, and from 1890 began to nurse the constituency as far as he could spare time from his other work. The Ayrshire miners had promised to pay his salary if he were elected to Parliament. Up to the end of 1891 he retained his close connection with the Scottish miners; but by that time he was so deeply immersed in his work for *The Labour Leader*—then still a monthly—and in his propaganda throughout the country for the creation of a Labour Party, that he felt compelled to resign his position as President of the Ayrshire Miners' Union. Thereafter, he devoted himself entirely to political and Socialist work, though he still kept up his connection with the Trades Union Congress as a delegate of the Scottish Miners.

At South West Ham he had to face the prospect of further Liberal opposition after Joseph Leicester had been disposed of. But the Liberals decided in the end not to fight him, but instead to approach him with an offer of financial help. His answer to Schnadhorst, the famous Liberal organiser, was that he wanted no help "except to keep out of our way : we will do all that is needed there without your aid." When the election came, Hardie was able to make good his words. He was elected in 1892 by 5,268 votes to 4,036 for his Tory opponent. The same general election brought in John Burns for Battersea and James Havelock Wilson, the seamen's leader, for Middlesbrough—both regarded at the time as Independent Labour MPs. But Wilson soon reverted to Liberalism; and when Hardie offered to regard Burns as his leader in an Independent Labour group, the offer was not accepted. Burns was already at loggerheads with his fellow-Socialists : he was beginning the political journey which was to carry him, during the next decade, into the Government as a Liberal Cabinet Minister.

The story of Hardie's triumphal entry into the House of Commons has been often, and variously, told. He is said to have been escorted to the House by a brass band, and to have taken his seat ostentatiously arrayed in a cloth cap and workmen's clothes. The brass band has been disputed; but the cloth cap is authentic, and I fancy Cunninghame Graham is right in believing that Hardie deliberately adopted a style of dress which was not his usual go-to-meeting garb. He meant to look, as well as to be, unlike the familiar "Lib-Labs", with their frock-coats and top hats; and I think he was egged on by some of his East End supporters into making a somewhat flamboyant demonstration.

In the House of Commons, Keir Hardie speedily earned himself a nickname—"The Member for the Unemployed". But before I come to his work in Parliament, it will be best to carry

146

on rather further the record of his efforts to create a Labour Party in the country.

THE ILP

Hardie's own *Labour Leader* was not yet much of a power; and H. H. Champion's *Labour Elector,* first published in 1888 and designed to push the Labour Electoral Association towards an independent policy, had perished in 1890. From that year, one of the leading journals devoted to the cause of independent Labour politics was Joseph Burgess's *Workman's Times,* which provided through its local editions the means of stimulating local organisation and of keeping the advocates of independent Labour representation in touch with one another. It was due to Burgess's efforts almost as much as to Hardie's that in 1891 local Labour Leagues and Labour Parties began to be set up in a number of areas, and that some of the local Labour Electoral Associations founded by the "Lib-Labs" and some of the Trades Councils showed signs of rallying to the cause of independent Labour representation.

In 1891 the new movement was reinforced by a more powerful recruit—Robert Blatchford's *Clarion*—which, published at first in Manchester, rapidly became well-known all over the country as by far the most effective Socialist journal that had ever been produced. Blatchford and his friend, Alexander Thompson, threw up well-paid posts on *The Sunday Chronicle* in order to start a paper in which they would be free to speak the whole of their minds; and when Blatchford's *Merrie England* appeared in book form in 1894, after running serially in *The Clarion,* the new movement was armed with a perfect piece of simple propagandist literature calculated to make converts even faster than the speaking tours of Hardie, Tom Mann, and the other platform protagonists of Socialism.

But before *Merrie England* appeared an attempt had been made to consolidate on a national basis the now numerous local societies which stood for the cause of independent Labour. At Bradford, which shared with Manchester the claim to be the centre of the growing agitation, 124 delegates, mostly from the North of England and from industrial Scotland, met in January 1893 under Keir Hardie's chairmanship and founded the Independent Labour Party.

In the meantime, Keir Hardie had been pursuing his efforts at the Trades Union Congress and by speaking tours about the country. At the Congress of 1891 he moved a resolution in favour of a levy of 1d on all Trades Union members for the purpose of establishing a parliamentary fund for the support of candidates accepting the Labour programme and endorsed by approved Labour organisations. This was defeated by 200 votes to 93; but in 1892 Hardie succeeded in carrying an amendment instructing the Parliamentary Committee to prepare a scheme of Labour representation; and in 1893 Tillett on behalf of the Committee actually produced a scheme for a levy in support of independent Labour candidates. This was approved in principle; but Hardie's amendment for the setting up of a separate Labour Party was beaten by 119 votes to 96. Nothing came of Tillett's scheme; for the Trade Unions made no response to the lukewarm suggestion of the Parliamentary Committee that they should subscribe to a political fund, and thereafter Hardie, having ceased to be connected officially with the Trade Union movement, transferred his main activities to the building up of the ILP outside Congress, though he continued to advocate the "Labour Alliance"—that is, the creation of an independent party based on cooperation between the Trade Unions and the Socialist societies—and his lieutenants carried on in subsequent Congresses the fight which he had began.

In the meantime, Hardie's principal activity had been tranferred to the Independent Labour Party. The Conference which created the ILP was preceded by meetings of delegates sympathetic to the cause which Hardie convened at the Trades Union Congresses of 1891 and 1892. Having failed to persuade the Trades Union Congress immediately to establish a Labour Party on an independent basis, Hardie determined to create, as the forerunner of a mass party of the working classes, a society or federation which should bring together the Scottish Labour Party and the already numerous local Leagues and Parties which had come into existence in various parts of England. The ILP was founded at Bradford, under Hardie's chairmanship, as a federation of these local bodies; but during its first year of existence it became in effect a national society with branches based on individual membership, all accepting an evolutionary Socialist programme. It was hoped at first that both the Fabian Society and the local Fabian Societies which had sprung up in many areas, and also most of the local branches of the Social Democratic Federation and of William Morris's Socialist League would merge themselves in the new body. Some Socialist League branches and local Fabian Societies were in fact taken over; but the bulk of the SDF, under Hyndman's leadership, remained aloof, and the ILP was based mainly on the local Leagues and Labour Parties which had been formed since 1889, on a basis of independence of the older parties, but without any very definite doctrinal allegiance to Socialism.

The Bradford Conference, however, adopted a plainly Socialist basis, by defining its objects as "the collective ownership and control of the means of production, distribution, and exchange". The ILP went on to define its "Methods", declaring that it stood for "representation of the people in the House of Commons by men in favour of the object of the Party, and rigidly pledged to its policy", and for "the federation of all organisations in Great Britain and Ireland seeking to realise the object of the Party by the Independent representation of Labour on all legislative, governing and administrative bodies".

Hardie was Chairman of the Independent Labour Party from its foundation until 1900, when a system of changing the chairman every three years was introduced. For the rest of his life, even after the Independents had succeeded in bringing the Labour Party into existence, it was with the ILP that his name was most closely associated; and the ILP was always nearest to his heart. From 1893 he was Member for the ILP as well as for the unemployed; and his strenuous work in the House of Commons did not prevent him from bearing the brunt of propagandist activity on its behalf.

Hardie promptly followed up his first sensational appearance at the House of Commons by further demonstrations. He moved an amendment to the Address demanding legislation on behalf of the unemployed—the first appearance of the "Right to Work" propaganda with which his name was thereafter closely associated—and on occasion after occasion he tried to force the Government to take action both on this question and for the legal eight hours day. But these matters did not give rise to the most sensational incident of his early parliamentary career. This occurred in 1894, when within the span of a few days the French

149

President was assassinated, the Duchess of York had a baby, and 260 miners lost their lives in a colliery disaster at Cilfynydd, in South Wales. The Government promptly moved votes of condolence with the French people, and of congratulation to the Queen. When the former vote was moved, Hardie asked whether the Government proposed to bring forward a similar vote of condolence with the relatives of the dead miners, and was met by Sir William Harcourt with the offhand reply that he could easily dispose of that matter by saying at once "that the House does sympathise with these poor people". The tone of the answer moved Hardie to fury, and he proceeded to move an amendment to the congratulatory address to the Crown, asking the Queen to express her sympathy with the victims of the mining disaster, and the House to assert its abhorrence of a system which made unavoidable the periodic sacrifice of miners' lives.

Hardie was howled down, in a famous House of Commons scene; and he was also roundly denounced in the press as a wild firebrand, a mannerless agitator, and a person ready to go to all lengths in search of notoriety. On this last point at least, those who denounced him were mistaken. Hardie's indignation was perfectly genuine. He knew from his own experience the human meaning of a great colliery disaster : it made him mad to see how little the well-fed rows of MP's cared for the sufferings of the common people.

Before this incident, Hardie had been very much to the fore in championing the cause of the Hull dockers during their great strike of 1893, and also in standing up in the House for the Miners' Federation, which organised that year its first great strike for the minimum wage. In 1894 he added to his responsibilities by turning *The Labour Leader* into a weekly, and making it the semi-official organ of the ILP, which had grown big enough to feel the need of a weekly paper of its own, especially as Joseph Burgess had, that year, to give up *The Workman's Times.* For ten years Hardie added to his other tasks the editing of a weekly paper : only at the end of 1903 did he find it too much for him, and hand over *The Labour Leader* to other control as the fully official organ of the ILP.

In 1895 came a General Election, and Hardie lost his seat at South West Ham, where he was beaten in a straight fight by a Tory by 4,750 votes to 3,975. It was a disastrous election. The

150

ILP put twenty-nine candidates in the field, and not one of them was returned. Burns and Havelock Wilson held their seats; but they both reckoned now as "Lib-Labs". A long period of Conservative rule set in.

PROPAGANDIST

Hardie used this opportunity to make his first visit to America, whither Frank Smith, his devoted friend, ex-Salvationist and fighter for Labour of many forlorn hopes, went with him. He was back before the end of the year, and was soon in the thick of the struggle for the right of open-air meeting which reached its height in 1896.

Late this year, the Conservative Member for East Bradford died, and the ILP decided to put Hardie forward for the vacancy. Bradford was one of the main strongholds of Socialism, and in West Bradford Ben Tillett had put up good fights in 1892 and 1895. Blatchford had been at one time candidate for East Bradford, which returned a Tory and a Liberal alternately; but Blatchford had retired, finding the job of standing for Parliament by no means to his taste. Hardie had a three-cornered fight, and came in last, with 1,953 votes, the Conservative holding the seat with 4,921 against the Liberal's 4,526. The result was disappointing, though Hardie had not expected to win. He made no further attempt to re-enter Parliament until the General Election of 1900. For the next few years he toured the country speaking, edited *The Labour Leader,* and continued to preside over the affairs of the ILP.

Financially, Hardie was often hard put to it. For his speaking, he charged a total sum of £3 for each meeting which involved travelling, and nothing for meetings which did not. He reckoned that this sum barely covered his travelling incidental expenses. By 1896 *The Labour Leader* was just covering its costs; but it was burdened with old debts, and Hardie's income from it was small. He could have received enough to live on comfortably as a gift from more than one well-to-do Socialist; but he rejected these offers, and managed as best he could, sending a pound or 25/- a week back to his home in Cumnock when he was away, and living sparsely, with no extravagance except tobacco. He was constantly accused by Liberals of accepting Tory gold, and by both Tories and Liberals of feathering his nest at the workers' expense; but no charges were ever less justified. Calumny, in fact, followed him everywhere in those days; during the Bradford election a rumour was put about that he had been twice divorced—he, most faithful and affectionate of husbands and fathers. He minded these charges, and they sometimes made him bitter; but for the most part he ignored them.

The close of the century was shadowed by the approach of the South African War. Hardie, needless to say, was what was called a "pro-Boer". The ILP, both before and after the outbreak, protested against the war as a war of imperialist aggression. Hardie took an active part in the Stop the War Movement, and wrote and spoke incessantly on the unpopular side. "This war," he wrote,

> is a capitalist war. The British merchant hopes to secure markets for his goods, the investor an outlet for his capital, the speculator more fools out of whom to make money, and the mining companies cheaper labour and increased dividends. We are told it is to spread freedom and extend the rights and liberties of the common people. When we find a Conservative Government expending the blood and treasure of the nation to extend the rights and liberties of the common people, we may well pause and begin to think.

THE LRC AND THE LABOUR PARTY

In the midst of the war excitement Hardie's plan of the "Labour Alliance" came at last to birth. The Trades Union Congress of 1899 approved, by 546 votes to 434, the proposal that the Parliamentary Committee should convene a special conference to form a federal body of Trade Unions, Socialist Societies, and other working class organisations in order to promote Independent Labour representation. A move on similar lines was made at the Scottish Trades Union Congress; and early in 1900 first the Scots formed a Scottish Workers' Representation Committee and then in London the Trade Unions and the Socialists formed the Labour Representation Committee, which six years later became the Labour Party.

The Trades Union Congress resolution had been ambiguously worded; and the delegates who met to form the LRC held divergent views about its character and purpose. There were Trade Unionists, of a type strongly represented on the Parliamentary Committee, who hoped that it would merely revive the "Lib-

Lab" traditions of the Labour Electoral Association, which had petered out a few years before. On the other hand, the delegates of the Social Democratic Federation wanted the conference to pledge itself to a full-blooded Socialist programme, based on the doctrine of the class war—a proposal which, if it had been adopted, would simply have meant that the Trade Unions would have repudiated the movement and rendered the entire plan abortive. Keir Hardie's policy was to steer between these two extremes—to push the Trade Unions towards Socialism just as far as they could be induced to go, but to refrain from trying to push them any further. This middle course was implicit in the policy of the "Labour Alliance", which Hardie had been pressing for more than a dozen years; and in the end it was his proposal that prevailed. He moved:

> That this Conference is in favour of establishing a distinct Labour Group in Parliament who shall have their own Whips and agree upon their policy, which must embrace a readiness to cooperate with any party which, for the time being, may be engaged in promoting legislation in the direct interest of Labour, and be equally ready to associate themselves with any party in opposing measures having an opposite tendency; and, further, members of the Labour Group shall not oppose any candidate whose nomination is being promoted in terms of Resolution I.

This resolution was, of course, a compromise. Keir Hardie would have much preferred, if it had been practicable, to persuade the Trade Unions to create an independent party, fully committed to Socialism, and entirely free of entanglements with the Liberals. But he realised that no proposal of that sort would have stood any chance of bringing in the Trade Unions. It is possible to argue that the foundation of the Labour Party on the basis of an alliance between the Socialists and the Trade Unions was a mistake, and that the Socialists would have done better to go on their way without compromising in order to win Trade Union support. But it is clear that, if the Trade Unions were to be brought in, nothing more socialistic than Hardie's resolution was practicable at the time.

The foundation of the Labour Representation Committee and of its companion body in Scotland was followed immediately by the "Khaki Election" of 1900. At this election Hardie was put forward for two seats—the Tory stronghold of Preston and the Liberal stronghold of Merthyr Tydfil. Both were double constituencies, and in both there were only three candidates, Keir Hardie and the two sitting MP's. At Preston, where the poll was held the earlier, Hardie was soundly beaten, polling 4,834 against 8,944 and 8,067 for the two Tories. At Merthyr, on the other hand, he was elected in company with D. A. Thomas, the Liberal anti-war coalowner, by a handsome majority over the second Liberal. Thomas polled 8,598, Hardie 5,745, and Morgan, the other Liberal, 4,004.

Thus Hardie returned to the House of Commons under the auspices of the LRC. But he had only a single colleague—Richard Bell, Secretary of the Railway Servants; and before long Bell quarrelled with the LRC and returned to the Liberal fold. Hardie was in effect as isolated in the Parliament of 1900 as he had been in that of 1892. But he had now a safe seat. The Welsh miners had not forgotten his famous protest in the House of Commons on the occasion of the colliery disaster of 1894.

He found opportunity for further protest in 1901, when Edward VII succeeded to the throne. He then opposed the new Civil List, not only on the score of its amount, but also on the ground of his objection to the Monarchy as an institution. On this occasion John Burns acted with him; but only two other British MP's, reinforced by 54 Irish, voted for his motion. In April he moved in the House a resolution, which was talked out, in favour of the Socialist Commonwealth; and he continued his efforts on behalf of the unemployed and the eight hours' day. But in Parliament he was helpless. The effect of his single-handed protests had worn off. Moreover, the strain of overwork was beginning to tell upon him. This year he had the first serious touch of illness in his life.

The following year he was ill again, and both his parents died. In 1903 he presided over a big national conference on unemployment at the Guildhall, but was taken ill again, and had to undergo an operation for appendicitis. He was sent abroad to recover, and went on a continental tour, in the course of which he strengthened his friendships with many foreign Socialist leaders. It was this illness that compelled him to give up *The Labour Leader,* and hand the paper over to the ILP. He recovered, to renew his agitation on behalf of the unemployed and to take part in the Amsterdam International Socialist Congress of 1904; but a good deal of his vigour was gone.

Meanwhile the LRC contingent in the House of Commons was being gradually reinforced. David Shackleton, of the Textile Workers, was elected for Clitheroe in 1902; and in the following year Arthur Henderson won Barnard Castle, and Will Crooks Woolwich. There were the beginnings of a real Labour Group. Henderson and Crooks were Fabians, as well as Trade Unionists; and Shackleton, though no Socialist, was sound on Labour questions. In the country, the challenge to Trade Unionism embodied in the Taff Vale Judgment, which threatened to abolish the right to strike, was bringing the Unions into the LRC, and the ILP was consolidating its position in the northern industrial areas. When, towards the end of 1905, the Tory Government resigned and the Liberals took office, the LRC was ready to make a much more formidable electoral challenge than had been possible six years before.

In the ensuing general election Hardie retained his seat at Merthyr without difficulty. D. A. Thomas again headed the poll with 13,971 votes; Hardie was second, with 10,178; and the second Liberal polled 7,776.

STATESMAN

Elsewhere, the Labour candidates were returned on the crest of the Liberal wave, mostly in straight fights with Conservatives or in conjunction with a Liberal for seats returning two MP's. The Labour Party, as it now decided to call itself, came back to Parliament 30 strong, in a House in which the Liberals had a large absolute majority over Conservatives, Irish and Labour combined. Hardie was chosen, practically as of right, to be Leader of the Party in the new House of Commons.

In 1906, when the Party's main task was to push through the Trade Disputes Bill and thus undo the effects of the Taff Vale Judgment, Hardie was relatively in his element. But he was not cut out for the job of leading a party which found itself rather working in with the Liberals than opposing them, and bargaining for concessions rather than seeking opportunities for dramatic protest. Moreover, his health was bad; in 1907 he suffered a renewed breakdown and was ordered away on a voyage round the world in the hope that his vigour might be restored. It was on this journey that he made the visit to India of which he after-wards recorded his impressions in a book—*India: Impressions and Suggestions,* published in 1909. But the journey was far from restful; for he was vengefully pursued throughout India by reporters who denounced him as a sedition-monger. His offence was that he had shown his full sympathy with Indian Nationalist aspirations, and had denounced the exploitation of the peasants and the destruction of native rights and customs in the interests of British capitalism.

From India Hardie went on to Australia and New Zealand and then to South Africa, where he again got into trouble on account of his advocacy of native rights. He returned to England in the spring of 1908, much better in health, and was welcomed home at a great reception in the Albert Hall.

During Hardie's absence, the Labour Party had been led by Shackleton, and he did not resume leadership on his return. Instead, Arthur Henderson became leader; and Hardie was much happier as a back bench member—the more so because there were troubles brewing over which he felt compelled to take up an attitude of his own. The militant suffrage movement had been sharply dividing the Labour organisations before his illness; and Hardie was much more disposed to sympathise with the militant tactics than most of his colleagues, even when Mrs Pank-hurst had declared that the Women's Social and Political Union would draw no distinction between Tories and Socialists until its demands had been met. In addition there was trouble inside the ILP, of which a section was denouncing the Labour Party's sub-servience to the Liberals and demanding a more forthright Socialist policy in the House of Commons. This trouble centred largely round Victor Grayson, a young ILP member who in 1907 had been elected as Socialist MP for Colne Valley without the endorsement either of the Labour Party or of the national head-quarters of the ILP. Grayson, unwilling to accept the Labour Party's discipline, was refused its whip. The ILP accepted him after his election; but he was continually at loggerheads with Snowden and MacDonald, who had been leading it in Hardie's absence, as well as with the Labour Party in the House of Com-mons. Grayson's line was to emulate Hardie's earlier achieve-ments by making "scenes" on behalf of the unemployed; but whereas it had been possible for Hardie to play a lone hand when he had no colleagues, it was a very different matter when Grayson moved motions and made protests without any prior consultation with the Labour Members, and then denounced them as traitors to their class if they failed to back him up. Hardie, it is clear, half sympathised with Grayson; but as a leader of the ILP and the Labour Party, and one who had been most intent on imposing party discipline on reluctant semi-Liberal Trade Unionists, he could not possibly take Grayson's side without danger of breaking up the Party. Consequently, he sided reluctantly with Ramsay MacDonald and Philip Snowden, who had no sympathy at all with Grayson; and when, in 1909, Grayson won a victory over the National Council at the ILP Conference, Hardie, MacDonald, Snowden, and Bruce Glasier all resigned their seats on the Council, of which Hardie alone had been a member since its inception in 1893.

From 1909 until 1913, when he was persuaded again to become Chairman in order to preside over the "Coming-of-Age" Conference in 1914, Hardie was off the governing body of the ILP; nor did he return to the leadership of the Labour Party, which passed from Henderson to G. N. Barnes, and then to Ramsay MacDonald. He was undoubtedly unhappy through these latter years. He hated bickerings inside the Socialist movement; and he was continually torn between his feeling that he must remain loyal to the party which he had brought into being and his sense that it was coming to be more and more subservient to the Liberal Government, and more and more like those very "Lib-Labs" whom he had denounced so fervently in his efforts to create it. His uneasiness increased after the two elections of 1910, when the Liberals, having lost their independent majority, came to depend on Labour and Irish votes, and the Labour men did not dare to vote against them for fear of bringing the Government down, and thus wrecking the chances both of Irish Home Rule and of the restoration of Trade Union rights, which had been further menaced by the Osborne Judgment—denying the legal right to take any part in political action. In addition, the "Lib-Lab" tendencies in the Party had been strengthened by the accession of the Miners' Federation, which had come over to it in 1909; and Lloyd George's Insurance Bill of 1911 drove a wedge between the Socialists, most of whom denounced it as a step towards the "Servile State", and the Trade Unionists, most

157

of whom supported it as likely to relieve their funds of serious drains and to bring them in new recruits through their power to administer the new insurance schemes as agents of the State.

Keir Hardie was unhappy, because his instincts were with the rebels, whereas his sense of loyalty to the Party bound him fast to a policy of cooperation with the Liberals. He was unhappy too because he saw war coming, and no sentiment was stronger in him than his belief in international working-class brotherhood. Illness had kept him away from the Stuttgart International Socialist Congress of 1907; but at the Copenhagen Conference of 1910 he moved, on behalf of the ILP, an amendment to the official resolution on the war question, with the object of pledging the international working-class movement to resort to a General Strike as a weapon against war. No vote was taken on his amendment, which was referred by agreement to the Bureau for further consideration and there buried. But Hardie's speech indicated very plainly his growing sense of the imminence of a fratricidal war which he felt would wreck all his hopes.

At the two General Elections of 1910 he held his seat without difficulty. In that year he also presided over the Labour Party Conference at Newport; and in the following year he was very active both in the House of Commons and elsewhere on behalf of the railwaymen in their great strike. In 1912 he went on a rapid lecture tour in Canada and the United States, and also attended the Special International Socialist Conference which was held at Basle to deal with the situation arising out of the war in the Balkans. In 1913 he resumed, as we have seen, the chairmanship of the ILP, and was abroad several times at various conferences, as well as in Dublin in connection with the famous strike led by James Larkin of the Irish Transport Workers' Union. But he found time to struggle hard in Parliament against the "Cat and Mouse" Bill, by means of which the Government was seeking to checkmate the militant suffragettes.

In 1914 Hardie presided over the ILP's "Coming of Age" Conference at Bradford, and gave to the delegates his personal interpretation of what he had done.

> I think I have shown that I can be a pioneer, but I am not guided so much by a consideration of policy, or by thinking out a long sequence of events, as by intuition and inspira-

158

tion. I know what I believe to be the right thing, and I go and do it. If I had, twenty-one years ago, stopped to think about what the future would bring, I would never have dared to accept the responsibility of entering the House of Commons. During those first three years my wife kept my house going, kept my children decently and respectably clothed and fed, on an income which did not often exceed twenty-five shillings a week. Comrades, you do well to honour her. Never, even in those days, did she offer one word of reproof. Many a bitter tear she shed, but one of the proud boasts of my life is to be able to say that, if she has suffered much in health and spirit, never has she reproached me for what I have done for the cause I love. . . . I said the other day that those of us who are advanced in years may easily become cumberers of the ground. I am not going to die if I can help it, but there is a dead spirit which blocks the path of the young. I am not going to stand in their way. I shall die, as I have lived, a member of the I L P, but I want the party to have freedom to grow, and I do not want young men and women to say, "We might have done this or that if it had not been for old Keir". I will accept no position that will give me standing over you. I will fight for what I think the right thing, but I will trust your judgment. While I have anything to give, it shall be given ungrudgingly to that child of my life—the I L P.

Thereafter, what energy was left to Hardie was given to the hopeless attempt to prevent the outbreak of the World War. He attended the Brussels meeting of the International Socialist Bureau at the end of July, and he as Chairman and Henderson as Secretary signed the anti-war Manifesto of the British Section of the International and spoke at the Trafalgar Square demonstration which was held on the eve of Sir Edward Grey's pronouncement in the House of Commons. He spoke also in the House, saying that if the workers had been consulted there would have been no war.

Hardie was already a sick man, and the advent of war affected him profoundly. He took his stand with the ILP and against the majority of the Labour Party, who, when war broke out, rallied to the support of the Government. He was howled down at Merthyr; but he went on speaking and writing as long as he could, sick in mind as well as in body. On 26 September 1915 he died.

The story of Keir Hardie's life has been told in this pamphlet without ornament or panegyric, as I think he would have wished it to be told. There were various estimates of his character in his lifetime. Hyndman disliked him cordially, and he could never get on with John Burns. His Socialist critics said that under an appearance of simple rugged honesty he concealed much subtlety in compassing their defeat. They were right, to the extent that Hardie was well aware of his power to sway an audience and of the value of his homeliness as a propagandist asset. But I think they were quite wrong when they suggested that he ever played for his own hand to the extent of deviating a hair's breadth from what he believed to be right. His parting words to the ILP Conference of 1914 were absolutely sincere. What annoyed many of his critics, as it annoyed George Lansbury's later on, was that he had a belief in his own inspiration—in his ability to arrive at what was right not by argument or intellect but by a deep instinct which knew the difference between good and evil. This belief was part and parcel of his religion—of the Christianity without dogmas which he had not inherited from his forbears but worked out for himself in his youth. This religious basis of Hardie's Socialism especially annoyed the Marxists, because it made him scornful of Marx's complex economic structures and of the doctrine of class war, which was sacred to all orthodox Social Democrats. In an article written in 1904 for *The Nineteenth Century* he defined as clearly as anywhere the essentially non-revolutionary type of Socialism for which he stood.

> Wherever free parliamentary institutions exist, and where Socialism has attained the status of being a recognised party, dogmatic absolutism is giving way before the advent of a more practical set of working principles. The schoolman is being displaced by the statesman. No hard and fast rule can be laid down for the application of the new methods, but generally speaking, where the Socialist propaganda has so far succeeded as to have built up a strong party in the State, and where the ties that kept the older parties together have so far been dissolved that there is no longer an effective Reform Party remaining, then the Socialists may be expected to lend their aid in erecting a new combination of such progressive forces as give an intellectual assent to Socialism, and are prepared to cooperate in waging war against reaction and in

rallying the forces of democracy. When this can be done so as in no way to impair the freedom of action of a Socialist Party, or to blur the vision of the Socialist ideal, it would appear as if the movement had really no option but to accept its share of the responsibility for guiding the State. Then, just in proportion as Socialism grows, so will the influence of its representatives in the national councils increase, and the world may wake up some morning to find that Socialism has come.

This was, no doubt, an unusually optimistic version of the evolutionary Socialist gospel; but it broadly represented Hardie's attitude, despite the reputation for violent extremism which attended him most of his life. At bottom, he was always a moderate, but one who could be easily moved to strong language and impassioned protest by the sight of injustice or oppression. These were attributes which appealed strongly to the miners and to the other workers to whom his words were chiefly addressed. Nurtured in Nonconformity, and deeply imbued with ethical ideals, these men and women responded to the new doctrines which Hardie cast in familiar phrases much more readily than to the Marxists, whose materialism shocked them and for whose class war slogans they were wholly unprepared. To say this is not to pass judgment upon Hardie's rightness, but to state a plain fact. Given the strength of British Nonconformity and its close alliance with Liberalism, there was no way in which a large working-class party could have been built up except that which Hardie was naturally equipped to pursue. He followed this path, not because it was dictated by expediency, but because that was how he, in common with most of his fellow Trade Unionists, thought and felt.

Thus there arose, chiefly under Hardie's inspiration, the British Labour Party and the peculiarly British brand of Socialism which caused much astonishment among continental Socialists. The Fabian Society is often credited with having supplied the I L P with its plans and policies; and so to a certain extent it did, by working out the implications and giving precision to the working-class demands. But the Fabians did not invent this British Socialism; it made itself, out of the stuff of contemporary society, beginning where the more progressive impulses of Liberalism left off, and taking over from its predecessor much that, in its birth-pangs, it cried out against most loudly. It was Hardie's fortune to be the pioneer of this development; and, as he said of himself, he remained a pioneer to the end. He was not a man who could bear to adapt himself to the consequences of his own propaganda success; and the leadership in both the I L P and the Labour Party passed to others who had much less of the pioneering spirit, and very much more personal ambition, than he. His last years were therefore a little pathetic, and would have been so even if his health had not failed. That it did fail was the plain consequence of putting on himself a strain too great for even his hardihood to stand. He died in his sixtieth year, quite literally worn out. There was about him a great-hearted simplicity that had grudged nothing to the cause. Because of that, he inspired great devotion; and, much as men had abused him while he was alive, there were few who failed to praise his qualities when he was no longer in their midst.

7 G. D. H. Cole
JOHN BURNS

The three men who led the London dockers to victory in 1889, and in doing so established the "New Unionism" as a powerful social force, were Ben Tillett, Tom Mann and John Burns. These three, together with Will Thorne of the Gasworkers Union, were the outstanding figures in the mass movement which brought the less skilled workers into Trade Unionism, and set a new fashion in social politics by making the "Right to Work", the "Eight Hours Day", and the "Minimum Wage" into live political and economic issues. Keir Hardie, their most memorable coadjutor in the struggle between the Old Unionism and the New, stands somewhat apart from them, because he was a miner, and the miners were old hands at Trade Unionism long before 1889. Hardie's first task was that of winning over from Liberalism to Labour a body of men who were already to a great extent organised and politically conscious, whereas Mann, Tillett, Thorne and Burns were bringing into the working-class movement a force which had till then been regarded by most of the Trade Union leaders as incapable of sustained combination or fruitful political effort. Hardie soon joined them in this task. It was a Greater London constituency that, after he had been rejected in a mining area, first sent him to Parliament, to champion the claims of the bottom dog, at the General Election in which John Burns won his seat at Battersea. But Hardie had no direct part in the great London struggles of the 'eighties out of which the New Unionism chiefly emerged. He was away in the North, fighting the miners' battles and building up the Scottish Labour Party, at the time when Burns was known all over London as "the Man with the Red Flag"— the leader of the unemployed agitation, the organiser of Radical and Socialist demonstrations, the street-corner orator who had gone to prison

163

in 1888 as the defender of the rights of free speech and public assembly.

FEATURES OF HIS CAREER

It is a far cry from the "Man with the Red Flag", defiantly proclaiming his revolutionary Socialist faith from the dock of the Old Bailey, to the Liberal President of the Local Government Board, hated intensely by every Socialist and active Poor Law reformer, and very ready to answer back in kind the taunts and recriminations of his old Socialist friends. John Burns, from the time when he took Cabinet office under Campbell-Bannerman in 1905, was regarded in Socialist circles as the very type of the renegade "lost leader", and there was nothing too bad to be said about him. He was one of the few subjects on which the protagonists of the new Labour Party and of the Social Democratic Federation, of which he had once been an outstanding member, cordially agreed. Not that the change in Burns's sentiments had been abrupt. He had cut his connection with the Social Democratic Federation as long ago as 1889, and had refused from the first to associate himself with Keir Hardie's Independent Labour Party, founded in 1893. From the very moment of his election to Parliament in 1892 he had played a lone hand, supported by his own Battersea Labour League but keeping only a loose connection with the Socialist movement as a whole. For a long while after that—indeed perhaps always—he continued to regard himself as a Socialist. But his Socialism was not as other men's Socialism, and he had a growing contempt for the doings of his erstwhile collaborators in the Socialist cause. Throughout the 'nineties, he was moving towards that very "Liberal-Labour attitude which he had been foremost in denouncing in his younger days; and his work on the newly formed London County Council, where Liberals and Labour men were actually working together in a Progressive bloc, pushed him continually in the direction of a Liberal-Labour alliance in national politics as well. Burns's position in Battersea depended on the combined support of the Liberal and Labour electors; and throughout his life Battersea was very much the centre of John Burns's world. He was born there : save for one brief interval he lived there all his life : his politics were Battersea politics and his private interests London interests radiating from Battersea Reach.

Nevertheless, Burns was not destined to die in harness as a Liberal politician. He had been an ardent "pro-Boer" in the days of the South African War, and if he had one firm conviction deep down in his mind it was a hatred of war. When Great Britain declared war on Germany in 1914, John Burns, in company with John Morley, resigned his Cabinet office, and therewith his political career. Though he remained a Member of Parliament until the General Election of 1918, when he finally retired, he did nothing politically after his resignation. He did not oppose the war: he simply faded out. Thereafter, for not far short of 30 years, he roamed about London, collected books, talked endlessly to a circle of friends and acquaintances in the National Liberal Club, but played no part at all in any public affairs. 1914 was the end of Burns's remarkable political career.

Indeed, those who knew John Burns only in the years of his retirement will be likely to think of him, first and foremost, as an inimitable *raconteur,* with the art of the anecdote, racily told, and an unlimited fund of reminiscence, in which he usually played the part of hero. His pleasure in talking about himself and in his own doings was too simple to give offence; and John Burns, when he related his experiences, was as far as it is possible to be from developing into a bore. The diary which he kept for over half a century and sometimes allowed his friends to peep into should be eminently good reading, when and if it is made available to the public.

That he had hankerings to come back to politics I myself can bear witness. He said to me one day in 1918, apropos of the reorganisation of the Labour Party which Arthur Henderson was then carrying through, that it was all on the wrong lines, and that what was needed was a "straight" Socialist Party, with no nonsense about it, and no attempt to compromise. To use his own words, "Hyndman's stuff, my boy, without the frills; and I'm the man to lead them".

That was John Burns all over. But there was never the smallest likelihood of the working-class movement after the last war accepting Burns as its leader. In 1918, when the General Election came, he had thoughts of standing for re-election at Battersea, but realised that, with a Labour candidate as well as a Conservative in the field, he would stand no sort of chance. Thereafter, as far as I am aware, he made no attempt to return

165

to politics. He had no belief in the Labour Party: the Liberal Party, as he had known it, had been smashed to pieces by the war. There was nowhere for him to go. More's *Utopia* and the history of his well-loved London became more real for him than the world in which he lived. He read endlessly: he amassed a remarkable library of books about London and about the Radical and working-class movements. He lived on so long that those who had hated him most died, and the new generation came to regard him as a historical monument rather than a man. His bodily vigour remained unimpaired almost to the last, until during the London *blitz* he was thrown violently to the ground during an air raid, and suffered a shock from which he never recovered. Not the least of Burns's assets in his days of greatness was his magnificent physical vitality. He was never tired; and his capacity for work was inexhaustible. His tremendous voice could endure a nearly incredible amount of open-air speaking: he seemed to have mastered the art of being in two places at once. How such a man can have borne being out of action for so many years, without an effort to come back, is not easy to understand. Perhaps it was made easier for him by his serene assurance that he had always been utterly right, and that everybody else was nearly always wrong. He was able to look back on his career with perfect self-approbation, quite untroubled by the hard sayings of his former friends. He was as egoistic as Cobbett, and as adept in putting his personality into everything that he said or did.

EARLY YEARS

John Burns was born in Battersea on October 20th, 1858. His father, Alexander Burns, was an engineer who had migrated to London from Ayrshire, and his brother, as he was at one period fond of reminding his audience, became a pugilist. John was himself proud, in his early days, of his prowess with his fists and would threaten to "knock off the block" of any persistent interrupter at his meetings. He was also an enthusiastic cricketer, and played regularly on Clapham Common for many years. He liked games and the open air, and owed some of his early popularity to his taste for a "rough and tumble". His father died when he was a small child, and his mother was left to bring up the family in conditions of distressing poverty. John left school at 10, and went to work first in Price's candle factory. He was next for a brief period a boy in buttons, and thereafter a rivet-boy in a local engineering works. During this time, as later, he was assiduous in attending "night-school"; and in 1872, at the age of 14, he managed to get apprenticed as a skilled engineer, serving his time in his native Battersea. He took early to politics and to temperance reform, and began his career as a public speaker on Clapham Common quite early in his apprenticeship. He took part in agitations among the apprentices, and in struggles over the right of public meeting on the Common, and thus early made his first acquaintance with the law, when he was arrested and locked up in 1876 for creating a disturbance at one of the meetings at which he was a speaker.

In the works where Burns was apprenticed was an old *Communard,* Victor Delahaye,[1] who became his close friend and

---

[1] This Victor Delahaye was an interesting person, who deserves to be better remembered than he is. An engineer by trade, he was active in the French working-class movement in Paris during the 'sixties, and was one of those who signed the *Manifeste des Soixante* in 1864. He was a member of the Paris Bureau of the International Working Men's Association and took a leading part in the Paris Commune of 1871. Escaping to London, he was elected a member of the General Council of the International, and was a delegate at its London Conference in September 1871. The following year he took part in forming in London the *Comité Révolutionnaire du Prolétariat,* a purely French body, organised by the political exiles on Marxist lines. Its statutes upheld the doctrine of proletarian revolutionary dictatorship, and membership was confined strictly to manual workers, revolutionaries of other classes being told to organise themselves apart, on the ground that "the emancipation of the workers must be the task of the workers themselves", and must be carried through under their own, and not under *bourgeois,* leadership. In 1874 this body issued in London a manifesto *A la Classe Ouvrière,* in which it called for a revolutionary proletarian party aiming at the conquest of political power and the erection of a working-class dictatorship during the period of transition to a classless society embracing the world. Delahaye was the publisher of this Manifesto, as well as one of its signatories and a member of the *Commission de Propagande.* He was then in North London, but moved later to Battersea, where Burns met him. Later, he took part in the movement for labour legislation, wrote in support of the eight hours day and other social reforms, and was a delegate at the Berlin International Conference for the Protection of Labour, in 1890.

167

exercised a powerful influence over his mind. Delahaye taught Burns his fundamental Socialist beliefs, though at a later stage he passed to a considerable extent under the influence of Engels and frequented the famous Sunday evenings at Engels's house in Regent's Park Road. He there came into close contact with Eleanor Marx, who also exercised a considerable influence on his thought. Delahaye, however, was the first inspirer of Burns's Socialism, and when the old *Communard* died, Burns paid tribute to him in an obituary notice, fully acknowledging his debt. It seems clear that Delahaye befriended him at his trade as well as in personal ways, and that he was fortunate in the conditions of his apprenticeship. No sooner was he out of his time than he got the offer of a job as engineer under the Niger Company in West Africa, where he spent a year working at his trade and incidentally found more than one occasion of showing his intrepidity in the face of danger. He cut in two with a shovel a large poisonous snake which was chasing one of his fellow engineers; and on another occasion he jumped into a shark-infested creek to dive in search of a lost propeller-blade when the steam-launch in which he and his companions were travelling had become disabled near a hostile village.

After a year in Africa John Burns came back to England, where he resumed his propagandist activities and, in 1880, married Charlotte Gale, the daughter of a Battersea shipwright. He had met her first at one of his meetings on Clapham Common, and she had witnessed his arrest on the occasion when he found himself in trouble with the police. No child was born to them until 16 years after their marriage. Burns was fond of referring to himself during those earlier years as a "practising Malthusian" by compulsion. By the time his son was born he had settled down to his work on the London County Council and in Parliament, and was no longer rushing about with the same furious speed as of old. During the earlier years of his married life there can have been very little domesticity. Burns was everywhere, and his wife did much to help him—for example in organising soup kitchens and other forms of relief during the dockers' strike.

RADICAL POLITICS

Before Burns settled down to his life's work he was able to spend a period of six months travelling on the Continent. He visited France, Germany and Austria, got to know foreign Socialists and foreign labour conditions, and came back very much better equipped for his self-imposed function of Socialist agitator. By the latter part of 1880 he was back, and ready for the fray. There was at that time practically no organised Socialist movement in Great Britain. It was the year of Charles Bradlaugh's first election as MP for Northampton, leading up to the six years' struggle which followed before he, as an "unbeliever", was allowed to take his seat. Charles Dilke, MP for Chelsea, was the leader of the main movement of the London Radicals, and was working in close alliance with Joseph Chamberlain, the Radical MP for Birmingham, who had taken the lead in 1877 in organising the advanced National Liberal Federation. 1880 was the year in which Chamberlain entered Gladstone's Cabinet as President of the Board of Trade and Dilke also joined the Government as Under-Secretary for Foreign Affairs—a post from which he migrated two years later to become President of the Local Government Board. Chamberlain and Dilke were largely responsible for the advanced Liberal legislation of the next few years, including the Reform Act of 1884 and the Redistribution Act which followed it in 1885, as well as the Municipal Corporations Act of 1882, the establishment of the Local Legislation Committee of the House of Commons (called at first the Police and Sanitary Committee) and the setting up of the Royal Commissions on Technical Education (1881) and Housing (1884). For a few years it seemed to many people that the Liberal Party was in process of converting itself, under Chamberlain's inspiration, into a Radical Party armed with an advanced social programme. Indeed, this might have come about but for the split over Home Rule. Chamberlain was as determined an imperialist as he was a social reformer; and in 1885 he resigned from the Gladstone Government over the Home Rule issue and, in doing so, brought the campaign for converting the Liberal Party as a whole to Radicalism to an untimely end.

Burns thus entered politics at a moment when party programmes and politics were exceptionally fluid and the main body of working-class opinion, represented by the Trade Unions

169

M

and the Radical Working Men's Clubs and Associations, was ranged behind the advanced section of the Liberal Party. It was in the midst of these excitements, the year after Chamberlain's entry into the Cabinet, that Henry Mayers Hyndman, having in his mind the hope of reviving an agitation on the lines of Chartism, published his first Socialist book, *England for All,* and set to work to organise the Democratic Federation, not as an explicitly Socialist body, but rather as a federation of the Radical Working Men's Clubs into a national movement based on the idea of the class-struggle, which he had imbibed from reading *Das Kapital* in a French translation. The Democratic Federation stood at the outset, not for Socialism as such, but for land nationalisation *plus* a programme of advanced Radical reform. But it failed to win the working men's clubs over from Dilke and Chamberlain, and most of those who joined it were in fact Socialists of one or another brand. Not until 1884, however, did it adopt an explicitly Socialist basis and assume the name— Social Democratic Federation—by which it became widely known.

BURNS AND HYNDMAN

This was the year in which John Burns first became connected with the Hyndmanites. From 1880 to 1884 he had been working mainly in South London, following his trade as an engineer and taking an active part in Radical propaganda. He first became at all widely known in 1883, when the police, on the initiative of the Metropolitan Board of Works, in an attempt to stem the growth of Radical agitation, tried to stop the open-air meetings which were being held regularly on Peckham Rye, Clapham Common, and other open spaces, under the auspices of the Democratic Federation, Joseph Lane's Labour Emancipation League, and a variety of Radical organisations in the Metropolis. Burns played his part in this fight for free speech—the beginning of a struggle which was to keep London in a turmoil for the rest of the decade—and the contacts thus established brought him into the SDF early in 1884. By the end of the year he was in the thick of the conflict which rent the SDF asunder —mainly on the issue of immediate political action—and in that quarrel he took the side of Hyndman against William Morris, and served as a member of the Executive of the SDF after

Morris and his supporters had broken away to form the Socialist League.

For some time before this Burns had been active in his Trade Union—the Amalgamated Society of Engineers—and in 1885 he was a delegate (incidentally the youngest there) to the ASE Conference at Nottingham, and began to make a name for himself outside London. In the same year he attended the Industrial Remuneration Conference got together by Dilke, Archdeacon Cunningham, the economic historian, and a miscellaneous collection of social reformers of many schools of thought. Burns, who was a delegate from the SDF, made a good tub-thumping Socialist speech, in the course of which he declared that he had been discharged from his employment as an engineer at Messrs. Brotherhood's for attending. He was actually out of work at this time for seven weeks, and had a taste of the conditions which he was soon to take a leading part in denouncing.

By 1885 Burns was one of the best known figures in the London Socialist movement; and he had also used his visit to Nottingham—an old Radical stronghold once represented by Feargus O'Connor—to establish connection with the Socialists and trade Unionists in that area. The consequence was that he received an invitation to contest West Nottingham as a Social Democratic and Labour candidate at the forthcoming General Election.

Quite a number of Labour candidates made their appearance at the General Election of 1885—mostly as "Lib-Labs" with the support of the local Liberal and Radical Associations, though a few were involved in three-cornered contests. Burns fought as a Socialist, against a Liberal and a Conservative, and received some support from the local Trade Unions, which were, however, divided. The Liberals did their best to induce the electorate to believe that Burns was really a nominee of the Carlton Club, brought down in the hope of splitting the Liberal vote; and there were many allegations that his election expenses were being paid with "Tory gold". Actually, this was not the case. The paymaster was a soap manufacturer, by name Barlow, a member of the Fabian Society and a friend of Henry Hyde Champion, who was at that time busy trying to organise independent Labour candidates in a number of areas, and was the

171

chief inspirer of Burns's attempt at Nottingham. The Liberals, who probably believed the "Tory gold" story (it was indeed true of certain SDF candidatures in other areas and did much to bring the SDF into discredit) furnished Burns with some excellent material for election propaganda by trying to bribe him to withdraw. Supported by a short-lived local newspaper, the *Nottingham Operative,* edited by Joseph Burgess, Burns made what was for those days a good fight for a declared Socialist. He got 598 votes, against 6,609 for the successful Liberal and 3,797 for the Conservative. Incidentally, Henry Broadhurst won the seat as a "Lib-Lab" nominee the following year.

BLACK MONDAY

From Nottingham John Burns went back to London to take up on a much larger scale his work as a propagandist and to assume a leading place in the struggle over free speech and in the growing unemployed movement. At this time trade was bad, and the "Fair Trade" agitation, the forerunner of the Tariff Reform movement, was at its height, led in London by a small group of Trade Unionists connected with seafaring and waterside trades, who were at loggerheads with the main body of organised Labour. Clashes at demonstrations were frequent between the "Fair Traders" and the Radicals and Socialists; and feeling was particularly bitter over the rival programmes of "Fair Traders" and Socialists for remedying the distress. The "Fair Traders" wanted tariffs : the Socialists traced the prevailing unemployment to the "contradictions of Capitalism", and demanded that the State should recognise the "right to work" and provide useful employment where the capitalists failed to do so.

For February 8th, 1886, the "Fair Traders" organised a mass demonstration in Trafalgar Square; and the SDF promptly decided to hold a rival demonstration at the same time and place. The rival meeting, over which Burns was to preside, was to do its best to steal the "Fair Traders'" crowd and to get a Socialist resolution adopted instead of that which the organisers had prepared. The tactics adopted by the Socialists were to occupy a large part of the Square with their own followers well before the "Fair Trade" procession was due to arrive, and to hold a preliminary meeting of their own. This they did, leaving free the pitch on the north side of the Square which had been pre-empted by the "Fair Traders". But as soon as the latter came on the scene, Burns, Hyndman, Champion, and the other Social Democratic leaders moved across to the north side, and hoisted themselves up on the railings by the National Gallery, whence they proceeded to address the crowd. There ensued a struggle, in the course of which the "Fair Trade" platforms were upset. The police, far too few to cope with the disturbance, at length agreed with Burns, who had been armed throughout the proceedings with a large red flag, that the Socialists should lead their followers in procession to Hyde Park and thence disperse them to their homes. But as the procession passed along Pall Mall, where some road repairs were in progress, trouble broke out afresh. It is said that persons standing in the windows of the Carlton Club made jeering remarks, and that there were similar incidents at other Pall Mall clubs. At all events, some of the crowd armed themselves with paving-stones and other missiles, and there was a good deal of window-smashing in Pall Mall and St. James's Street on the way to Hyde Park, while other parts of the crowd which had been in Trafalgar Square looted a number of shops in the neighbourhood of Piccadilly. It does not appear that this looting was done by the Social Democrats. The organisation of the rival demonstrations, and the news that there was likely to be trouble, had called to the scene most of the rowdy elements in the Metropolis; and some of these elements were prompt to seize their chance. While the worst looting was in progress, Burns and Hyndman were already addressing their followers in Hyde Park, and urging them to disperse—which they appear to have done without further trouble.

THE MAN WITH THE RED FLAG

The aftermath of these events, which created great alarm among the upper classes, was the arrest of Burns, Hyndman, Champion and Jack Williams, all of the Social Democratic Federation, on a charge of seditious conspiracy. Summoned on February 13th, 1885, they were released on bail after a preliminary hearing, and were not put on trial until April. William Morris stood bail for John Burns and Champion.

Burns, undeterred by the forthcoming trial, continued his open-air propaganda. He said in a speech in Hyde Park late in

February that if he was inciting to sedition in advocating a social revolution, sedition would have to be the charge against him until the grave claimed him. Disclaiming incitement to riot, he said that hunger and poverty knew no law, and denounced Parliament and Government for bolstering up the privileges of the rich. When at last his trial came on, he defended himself in a speech which became famous under the title *The Man with the Red Flag*. In relation to the proceedings during and after the Trafalgar Square meeting, he represented himself as having done his best to prevent violence and threw the blame for the rioting on the "Fair Traders" and the roughs who had joined the demonstrations. Not too ingenuously, he tried to dispel the impression that the Social Democrats had deliberately organised the breaking-up of the "Fair Trade" meeting; but he was on better ground in showing that he had done what he could to stop the rioting after the crowd had left the Square and during the march to Hyde Park. His fellow-defendants followed, with rather less boldness in proclaiming their revolutionary faith, a broadly similar line; and the surprising result of the trial was an acquittal. The jury did indeed add a rider to the effect that they considered the language of Burns and Champion to have been highly inflammatory, and greatly to be condemned; but on the facts laid before them they acquitted these two defendants, as well as Hyndman and Williams, of any seditious intent.

Burns and his fellow-Social Democrats thus scored a very considerable triumph, which helped greatly to consolidate Burns's position as the recognised leader of the London unemployed and of the Metropolitan Radical Federation in its struggle with the police over the right of open-air meeting. But the events of "Black Monday", as the day of the riots came to be called, had another sequel in the resignation of the London police chief and his replacement by Sir Charles Warren, who was supposed to be a stronger man and was during the next few years to wage a ceaseless conflict with the Radicals and Socialists of London.

UNEMPLOYMENT AGITATION

1886 was a bad year. Trade Union unemployment, which had stood at between 2% and 3% in 1882 and 1883, rose above 8% in 1884, above 9% in 1885, and above 10% in 1886; and as these figures reflect mainly the position in the skilled trades, it can be taken as certain that the rate in all occupations was a good deal higher. Not until well on in 1887 did the position substantially improve, as the forces which led up to the boom of 1889-90 began to show their effect. All through the latter months of 1886 Burns was busy addressing unemployed demonstrations, preaching an undiluted gospel of revolutionary Socialism, and at the same time joining forces with other sections of London Radicalism in the struggle with Sir Charles Warren. Neither he nor the other Social Democrats made any attempt to stand for Parliament at the election of that year. The tiny polls of the SDF candidates who had been aided by "Tory gold" had discredited the parliamentary ambitions of the Socialists; and the break-up of the Chamberlain-Dilke Radical group and the struggle over Home Rule made the situation difficult for third-party candidates. Even Dilke lost his Chelsea seat, and the Radical movement of which Chamberlain had been the leader came definitely to an end. The majority of the sitting "Lib-Lab" MPs held their seats as supporters of Gladstone; but several were beaten, and there were only two victories to fill the gaps.

Throughout the rest of 1886 the Socialists continued their agitation on behalf of the unemployed. They were, indeed, under Champion's clever inspiration, continually fertile in fresh devices for drawing attention to their cause. In the autumn, as the time for the Lord Mayor's Show drew near, they decided to organise an unemployed march to accompany it through the streets. They issued a handbill, calling on the workers "Leave your slums, and follow the pageant along the thoroughfares in silent and solemn order".

Sir Charles Warren promptly met this threat by prohibiting the proposed processions; and the Socialists decided not to challenge his order directly. Instead, they summoned their followers to meet in Trafalgar Square after the Lord Mayor's Show was over. This too was forbidden; but this time the Socialists decided to defy the prohibition. Immediately the procession had passed, a number of Socialist speakers, including Tom Mann and John Ward, seized points of vantage and began to address the assembled crowds. Ward was at once arrested—only to be let off with a token fine—but Mann contrived to make his speech and declare his Socialist resolution carried before the police were able to disperse his part of the assembly.

175

The newspapers were full of stories of the struggle between the SDF and the police, and an immense amount of publicity was secured. A week or so later, the Socialists organised yet another demonstration in Trafalgar Square. The police made plans to deal with the situation, including the stationing of artillery in the Square. The Socialists got wind of this, and wrote to Sir Charles Warren offering to provide a force of Special Constables to keep the peace, and promising to provide competent artillery-men (Champion was an ex-officer of artillery) to take charge of the guns. The ridicule was effective, and they were allowed to hold their demonstration in peace.

At the beginning of 1887 the leaders of the unemployed move-ment hit on yet another device. Burns and other Socialist leaders began to lead demonstrations of the unemployed on Sundays to the principal London churches, inviting the incumbents to preach suitable sermons about the distress, and holding meetings of their own outside the churches for the statement of their grievances. Burns organised one of these "Church Parades" to Battersea Old Church in January 1887, and followed this up in February with a monster procession to St Paul's Cathedral. One of the banners carried by the six processions which converged on St Paul's bore the inscription "My house is a house of prayer, but ye have made it a den of thieves". There were disturbances dur-ing the sermon, when the preacher, Dr Gifford, declared that there must always be the rich and the poor; and at the conclu-sion of the service Burns made a sensation by singing a new version of "Dare to be a Daniel" with the theme "Dare to be a Freeman". Thereafter three large meetings were held without disturbance on the Thames Embankment.

BLOODY SUNDAY

This was nearly the end of the great unemployed movement of the 'eighties; for as trade improved the basis of the agitation disappeared, and the Socialists had to turn their attention to other means of rousing the people. But they carried on with the demonstrations, in face of improving trade, until the end of the year; and the final stages were marked by another dramatic con-flict with the police. In the autumn of 1887 the battle of Trafalgar Square was resumed with all its old intensity. On October 18th the police dispersed a Social Democratic demonstration in the Square, making twenty arrests; and, when the Socialists reassembled on the same day in Hyde Park, the police again broke up the meeting. This did not daunt the Socialists, and during the next few days they held a whole series of demonstrations, culminating on the Sunday in a mass meeting in Trafalgar Square and a procession to attend divine service in Westminster Abbey.

These proceedings were unmolested, and the next serious clash arose out of a Trafalgar Square demonstration convened not by the Socialists but by the Metropolitan Radical Federation, in which also Burns was active, for the purpose of protesting against the imprisonment of William O'Brien, the Irish Nationalist. The Government prohibited the proposed assembly; and Radicals and Socialists joined forces to defy the ban. On the appointed day, November 13th, 1887, known thereafter as "Bloody Sunday", the Government garrisoned the Thames bridges and successfully beat back the South London contingents which attempted to cross—not without a good many injuries to both demonstrators and police. Sir Charles Warren also posted a cordon of police all round Trafalgar Square, and had the Life Guards stationed ready within call.

The display of force was great; but the demonstrators, headed by Burns and Cunninghame Graham, attempted to reach the Square. They were beaten back, but not until there had been a fierce struggle in the Square itself. Graham and Burns were among those arrested.

This affair created a huge sensation. Many thousands of special constables were sworn in, and for the next fortnight Trafalgar Square was in an intermittent state of siege. A huge police garrison held the Square on the following Sunday, and on the Sunday after that; and on Monday, November 28th, in the course of a further conflict, a man, Alfred Linnell, was so badly injured that he subsequently died. This led in December to a tremendous funeral procession through the streets, culminating in a service in Bow Cemetery, where Stewart Headlam preached the funeral sermon and William Morris's *Death Chant,* composed for the occasion, was sung.

Meanwhile, Burns and Cunninghame Graham had been released on bail, Headlam standing bail for Burns and R. B. Haldane for Graham. Their trial came on in January 1888, when Graham was defended by Asquith. Burns defended himself. The result was a sentence of six weeks' imprisonment without hard labour, the jury declaring the prisoners not guilty of "riot", but guilty of "unlawful assault".

These events, including the six weeks in prison, were of considerable importance in determining Burns's future career. He was still earning his living as an engineer; but for some years past he had found it difficult to get employment with any ordinary firm, owing to his political activities—and, no doubt, his demands for time off to attend to them. By 1887 this problem had been conveniently solved. Lorraine, the inventor, who was an active member of the Democratic Club, then the principal haunt of the London left-wing intellectuals and Social Democratic leaders, took him on as assistant, and was generous in allowing him time away for his numerous political engagements. Some time in 1888 this employment ceased, and he found work for a time as engineer in Hoe's Printing Works. But his political activities were really inconsistent with his position as a wage-worker; and there can be no doubt that he was intent on escaping from the factory and giving himself over entirely to politics.

BURNS AND THE LCC

His chance came largely through his close association with the Metropolitan Radical Federation, which had its headquarters in Battersea, but grouped together most of the active working-class bodies all over London. This association of Burns with the wider Radical movement grew mainly out of the troubles of 1887. We find him, in 1888, soon after his release from prison, urging at the International Trade Union Congress held in London that the battle of the workers should be transferred "from the bench and the workshop to the legislative platform". The immediate objective on which he had his eye was a seat on the new London County Council, which Parliament was then in process of setting up. For this he was bound to need, in his native Battersea, support much wider than could be given him by the local branch of the SDF, and, without breaking with that body, he began to woo the other groups of Radical Reformers who were associated with the Metropolitan Radical Federation.

In March 1889 he got what he wanted, and was elected as

one of Battersea's first representatives on the London County Council. At the same time his supporters founded the John Burns Fund, with the object of assuring him an income of two guineas a week (raised to £5 in 1892) in order to enable him to devote his whole time to the LCC and to his other political activities. The SDF leaders did not at all like any of these developments. They regarded the terms on which Burns got elected to the LCC as a denial of revolutionary Socialism; and from that time on he had little to do with Hyndman and his followers, though the final break was not to come just yet.

Almost at once, however, there was a dispute. Burns was acting at this time most closely in association with Henry Hyde Champion, who had founded the *Labour Elector* in June 1888, almost immediately after Keir Hardie's by-election contest in Mid-Lanark. Champion was aiming at this time at the promotion, wherever possible, of independent Labour candidates, and elsewhere at swinging the local Labour vote to the side of the candidate who promised the more forward labour policy. In March 1889 Burns joined the Board of Champion's *Labour Elector;* and in March he and Champion, much to the annoyance of the local SDF, supported the Liberal candidate in an election at Kennington, next door to Burns's own LCC constituency. This led to a breach with the Battersea SDF; and Burns founded the Battersea Labour League as an offshoot of the John Burns Fund and began to build it up as a political association under his personal leadership. Later in the year, however, when the Battersea Liberals invited him to stand for Parliament at the next election as a Liberal and Radical candidate, he gave an unqualified refusal. He regarded himself as a Socialist and an Independent Labour man. He was willing enough to court Radical voters; but he would still have nothing to say to the Liberal Party.

THE LONDON DOCK STRIKE

In August of the year in which Burns became an elected member of the LCC the famous Dock Strike broke out. Burns had nothing to do with its beginning; but no sooner had it begun than he and Tom Mann and other leaders of the London "Left" hastened to the aid of the mostly unorganised strikers. Throughout the following weeks Burns was very much in his element. In

179

effect, he constituted himself the leader of the strike, with Mann and Tillett as his principal lieutenants. His untiring energy, his stentorian voice, and his genius for publicity all served the strikers well. His very egotism helped; for it went to the making of him as a racy speaker who knew how to identify his audience with him by identifying himself with it, and stating everything in a sharply personal way that made him an idol to his hearers. The London dockers were a miserably paid, casually employed body of men, gathered together from all manner of places and upbringings, and for the most part quite incapable of following any complicated argument. Burns knew exactly how to talk to them, and above all how to cheer them up during the bad times when the strike seemed again and again to be on the point of collapse for want of money to keep the men from sheer starvation. And while John Burns orated and got on the right side of the journalists, his wife looked after the soup-kitchens and made friends with the strikers' wives.

This is not the place to tell the oft-told story of the Great Dock Strike of 1889. It is well-known how the contributions sent across the world by the Australian Labour movement saved the situation, and how, aided by the mediation of Cardinal Manning and others, Burns and his Committee successfully wrung from the port employers the concessions of "no victimisation" and "the docker's tanner"—that is, a minimum rate of sixpence an hour. What concerns us here is that Burns's work in the Dock Strike raised him to a position of easy pre-eminence among the leaders of London Labour, and made him famous all over the country.

In *The Story of the Docker's Strike,* written immediately after its conclusion by Llewellyn Smith and Vaughan Nash, later highly placed Civil Servants but at that time two young men from Toynbee Hall who were doing their best to help, John Burns appears as the unrivalled hero. The impression of his inspired leadership of the strikers, especially at those moments when the movement appeared to be on the point of collapse, is very vivid; and the authors give one clearly to understand that without Burns the dockers would never have won their victory. His position, from his arrival on the scene almost at the beginning, was that of Secretary of the Finance Committee; so that

180

he shared with Tom Mann, the Treasurer, the onerous responsibility of gathering in and dispensing the money and the supplies which were available for meeting the strikers' needs. The two authors pay tribute to the effective rough justice with which he carried out his onerous task. That, however, was very far from being the whole of the responsibility which he took upon himself, though, as an engineer, he had no direct part in the dispute. He was, in addition, both the principal orator and the principal negotiator at every stage. When he was absent ill for a single day, everything began to go wrong. It was Burns who cheered the men up when they were downhearted, Burns who told them to beware of over-confidence when they thought they were winning, Burns who dashed about everywhere, conspicuous in his white straw hat, successfully making the men keep order when trouble threatened over blacklegs or over the distribution of the all too scanty relief. Again, it was Burns who interviewed the journalists, and saw to it that the strikers got their case stated sympathetically in the press—as to a very remarkable extent they did. And it was Burns who went to talk to the Lord Mayor, to countless would-be mediators, to Cardinal Manning, whose influence finally prevailed in getting the dock directors to accept the substance of the men's demands, and to the dock directors and managers themselves, when at length they consented to talk instead of issuing written ultimata to their disobedient servants. How Burns accomplished all that he did accomplish, goodness only knows. No physique short of the magnificent could have endured the strain; and no personality short of the magnetic could have pulled off the feats to which even Burns's enemies paid tribute. He managed, moreover, to keep on excellent terms with the police, who recognised that he could keep order where they were powerless without his aid. Apparently the white straw hat, which became famous, was a police suggestion for making Burns conspicuous in order to make it easier for him to get the ear of the crowd. That historic hat, by the way, is said after the strike to have become the property Madame Tussaud's, where it served as crown to a waxen effigy of the notable strike-leader. For the strike brought Burns, greatly, I am sure, to his satisfaction, the fashionable tribute of a place among Madame Tussaud's waxworks.

TROUBLES WITH THE TUC

But though Burns was famous, there were others besides the
SDF leaders who disliked his meteoric rise. The 1889 Trades
Union Congress was held at Dundee, during the closing week of
the dockers' strike. Burns, busy in London, was not present; but
he had been nominated as a delegate by the West London
Engineers. Before the Standing Orders Committee, Robert
Austin, as General Secretary of the Amalgamated Society of
Engineers, objected to Burns's credentials, on the ground that he
had not been chosen by the Society as a whole. Congress decided
to accept his delegation; but owing to his work in London he
was unable to take his seat. However, many of his friends were
at Dundee; and at the very time of Congress a by-election was
pending, owing to the death of the sitting Member. A mixed
collection of Socialists and Trade Unionists, urged on by
Cunninghame Graham, invited Burns to stand; but after dally-
ing with the idea he withdrew, and announced that he proposed
to contest the Battersea parliamentary division. It has been often
said that the Liberals bargained for his withdrawal at Dundee
by promising not to oppose him at Battersea when the next
General Election arrived.

During 1890 Burns was busy for the most part with his work
on the London County Council, where he constituted himself
the principal champion of direct employment in place of the
use of contractors for Council work, and was also active in
urging the acceptance of the eight hours day for Council
employees, of a forward housing policy, and of the adoption of a
Fair Wages Clause in all Council contracts. In September he
made his first appearance at the Trades Union Congress, and
took an exceedingly active part in the debates. He supported
James Macdonald, of the London Trades Council, in a Socialist
amendment to the hardy annual resolution advocating Labour
representation, moved a resolution demanding help for the
Amsterdam dockers, then on strike, and pressed strongly for the
eight hours day and the Fair Wages clause in Government contracts. Just before the Congress, speaking in Battersea, he had
delivered a violent attack on the reactionary Trade Union
officials who dominated its proceedings, and at Congress itself he
coupled this with a quite different onslaught upon "journalistic
blacklegs, dead-stumped parsons, and self-seeking lawyers" who,

he said, were trying to get the movement for Labour representation into their own hands. He accused the Congress of leaving the road open to such adventurers by failing itself to organise the movement along the proper lines, and had an acrimonious dispute with John Wilson, the leader of the Durham Miners and a protagonist of the Old Unionism against both the New Unionism of the Dockers and the movement for independent representation of Labour.

The attitude of Burns at the Trades Union Congress of 1890 illustrates very clearly the line which he was to take during the next few years. He was no less hostile to the Old Unionism than Keir Hardie and the rest of the Socialists; but he was also increasingly hostile to many of the Socialists who had been his allies in this particular struggle. What he appears to have wanted at this stage was a Socialist movement in politics based directly on the Trade Unions and excluding most of the intellectuals who were active in the spreading movement for Labour representation. He wanted the Trade Unions to throw off *laissez faire* and to take up the advocacy of the Right to Work, the Fair Wages Clause, the Eight Hours Day, and the development of "gas and water" Socialism; and he believed in the practicability of a Trade Union Socialist Party working along these lines. That was where he fell out, acrimoniously as his wont was, with the group round Keir Hardie, Cunninghame Grahame and Champion that was busy creating the local movements which were to lead early in 1893 to the formation of the Independent Labour Party. The consequence was that Burns, despite his popularity, found himself more or less isolated. He was against both the organised groups which were contending for mastery of the Trade Unions; and he sided now with the one and now with the other in a way that laid him open to continual charges of personal bad faith and desire for self-aggrandisement. That the desire to become a recognised great man was strong in him is undoubtedly true; but I think his attitude was quite consistent through these years, and looked inconsistent only because there were so few others who adopted it.

OLD AND NEW UNIONISM

Burns's attitude to the Old Unionism is excellently summed up in an article which he contributed to *Justice,* the organ of the

SDF, in 1887. "Constituted as it is," he wrote, "Unionism carries within itself the source of its own dissolution . . . Their [the Unions'] reckless assumption of the duties and responsibilities that only the State or the whole community can discharge, in the nature of sick and superannuation benefits, at the instance of the middle class, is crushing out the larger Unions by taxing their members to an unbearable extent. This so cripples them that the fear of being unable to discharge their friendly society liabilities often makes them submit to encroachments by the masters without protest. The result of this is that all of them have ceased to be Unions for maintaining the rights of labour, and have degenerated into mere middle and upper class rate-reducing institutions." In effect, Burns, in common with the other leaders of the New Unionism, was opposed to the friendly benefit type of Society, and held that the Unions, instead of trying to meet the needs of their members by levies on their wages, should give their main energy to demanding that the State should assume the burden of maintaining the unemployed, the sick, and the aged. He was an emphatic State Socialist, and was in this matter entirely at one with Keir Hardie and the rest of the New Unionists, and opposed, as soon as the issue had to be clearly faced, to the Hyndmanites, who regarded demands for social reform made upon the capitalist State as having at most a propaganda value, and did not at all expect the State, in its existing form, to turn into an instrument of social welfare. But Burns was also opposed to the New Unionists because he disbelieved entirely in their attempt to create a new party by bringing together a heterogeneous assembly of advanced social reformers. He had come to believe that the right way was to win over the Trade Unions to a policy of political action for social reform, and to rely on a political movement based directly on the Unions rather than on a partnership between the Unions and an independent Socialist organisation.

At this 1890 Congress Burns had a remarkable stroke of luck. Although it was the first Congress he had attended, he stood for election to the Parliamentary Committee, then the governing body between the annual gatherings. He was defeated, coming second among the unsuccessful candidates; but one of those elected resigned, disapproving of the socialistic tone of the proceedings, and the next man on the list refused to serve. Burns thus found himself, doubtless to his own as well as to others' surprise, a member of the governing body of the Trade Union movement.

IN PARLIAMENT

He was still regarded at this time as a "left-winger" and a leader of the new, agressive Unionism; and, when the Scottish railwaymen struck in December, he promptly hurried north to help them. Their strike collapsed; but in 1891 he had better fortune, when he took a leading part on behalf of the London omnibus workers, who scored a remarkable victory with his help. For the rest, during this year and the next he gave most of his attention to the L C C and to nursing Battersea in preparation for the coming election. He did nothing at the Trades Union Congress in either year, and did not seek re-election to the Parliamentary Committee. It seemed as though he were dropping out of the Trade Union movement now that he had ceased to be a working engineer, and were meaning to give all his time to politics. In the L C C he scored a big success by securing in 1892 the adoption of a Fair Wages Clause which became in subsequent years a model for similar clauses in many other towns.

This was the year of the General Election in which the first "Independent" Labour candidates were returned to Parliament. Of the three, Burns at Battersea, Keir Hardie at South-West Ham, and Havelock Wilson, the Seamen's leader, at Middlesbrough, Burns and Hardie had no Liberal opponents. Burns won Battersea in a straight fight with a Conservative, by 5,616 votes to 4,057; and Hardie won his seat by 5,268 to 4,036, after the "Lib-Lab", Joseph Leicester, had withdrawn. Wilson alone was elected in a three-cornered contest. At once the question arose whether the three were to act together as an "Independent Labour" group. But Wilson, who, though the local Liberals had opposed him, was really more Liberal than Labour, stood aloof; and Hardie's offer to act under Burns's leadership led to nothing. Indeed the two were very soon at loggerheads over tactics. Hardie, who described himself as "the Member for the Unemployed", was determined to force the question of unemployment to the front in defiance of parliamentary procedure and decorum,

185

whereas Burns, schooled by his experience on the L C C, was equally determined to observe the rules, and was in addition jealous of Hardie's rising popularity and of the position of natural leadership in the Socialist movement which became definitely his with the foundation of the Independent Labour Party under his chairmanship in January 1893. Burns gave no support to Hardie's motions on behalf of the unemployed, or to the "scenes" with which he upset the House. Burns's maiden speech was not made until February 1893, on the Registration Bill : for the time being his line was to wait and to watch until he felt he had mastered the Commons atmosphere. He had, however, a good *alibi* on the occasion on which he was most accused of letting Hardie down; for he was away speaking for John Lister, the Independent Labour candidate at the Halifax by-election.

RUPTURE WITH THE S D F

In 1893 Burns's quarrel with his old colleagues of the S D F proceeded to a final rupture. He had left the S D F in 1889, but had proceeded on friendly terms with many of its members. But now a quarrel arose over the second Battersea seat on the L C C, which fell vacant. The local S D F and some of the Trade Unions wished to put forward a Labour candidate; but Burns gave his support to the nominee of the local Liberal and Radical Association. The Socialists accused him of being actuated by self-interest, because he depended for his position both in Parliament and on the L C C on Liberal as well as Labour votes; and a violent quarrel ensued, in the course of which Burns was roundly denounced and repudiated by the National Executive of the S D F. He was none the better loved when the Liberal beat the Labour nominee, and won the seat.

This did not prevent Burns from reappearing at the Trades Union Congress of 1893 as an advocate of Socialism. On this occasion the mover of the Socialist amendment to the resolution on Labour representation in Parliament (moved by Ben Tillett) was again James Macdonald. Burns supported him, but in the year of the formation of the I L P went out of his way to denounce "bogus independent Labour parties" and to attack "arrant frauds who are going about the country in the name of independent Labour and Socialism, doing everything to disintegrate Labour and Trade Unionism". He said he wanted Trade Unionism and Socialism to be blended together, and that if they were so blended they would be invincible.

The sequel to this attack was that Burns was not only elected again to the Parliamentary Committee, but also made Chairman of it—so much did his hostility to the I L P endear him to many of the Old Unionists whom he had so often opposed. The following year, 1894, it fell to him as Chairman of the Committee to open the proceedings, and he dwelt with satisfaction upon the large number of Town Councillors and other local government representatives who were among the delegates. At a later session he made a strongly Socialist speech in support of a resolution advocating the nationalisation of land and minerals; and at the end of the year, sent to America as a Congress delegate to the Convention of the American Federation of Labour, he again spoke very definitely for Socialism.

During this same year Burns is said to have been offered the post of Under-Secretary to the Home Office in Lord Rosebery's Government, with the idea that he should take in hand the revision of the Factory Acts and the preparation of a Bill dealing with the vital question of Workmen's Compensation. This must have been in some respects a tempting offer; for the matters with which he was asked to deal were near his heart. But he was not yet ready to throw in his lot with the Liberals, or to be ranked with the "Lib-Lab" Trade Union leaders whom he had so fiercely denounced. He refused the offer, and retained his status as an independent Labour representative, though he remained aloof from Keir Hardie and the I L P. At the General Election of 1895 he was re-elected for Battersea by the fairly narrow majority of 5,010 votes to the Conservative's 4,766. The defeat of Hardie in South-West Ham and the fact that Havelock Wilson, who was re-elected at Middlesbrough, counted by this time among the "Lib-Labs", left Burns as the only Labour Independent in the House of Commons, now with a Conservative majority which was to endure for 10 years. During this year Burns acted as Vice-Chairman of the Trades Union Congress Parliamentary Committee; and at the Congress in September he appeared as sponsor of a scheme which at once brought down upon him the further wrath of the Socialists and ended his own active connection with the Trade Union movement.

This was altogether an extraordinary affair. The Congress of 1894 had instructed the Parliamentary Committee to bring up to the next Congress a scheme for the revision of the Standing Orders. The Committee, mainly at the instigation of the Tory Secretary of the Cotton Spinners' Union, James Mawdsley, not merely prepared a revised draft, but decreed that the new Standing Orders should govern the proceedings of the 1895 Congress, at which they were due to be ratified or rejected. It was proposed under the new Orders to exclude from the Trades Union Congress the local Trades Councils, which had been in effect its founders, on the plea that the presence of their delegates, side by side with those of the national Trade Unions, involved "dual representation". It was further proposed to exclude from sitting as a delegate at Congress any person who was not either a full-time Trade Union official or a workman actually working at his trade. This latter proposal, aimed principally at the I L P, meant excluding Henry Broadhurst, the former secretary and the leading figure among the Lib-Labs, and also Burns himself. Nevertheless, Burns not merely supported the proposals and the high-handed action of the Parliamentary Committee in disqualifying in advance most of those who could have been relied on to vote against them, but actually took the leading part in pushing the new Standing Orders through Congress in opposition to the Socialists who had survived the purge. He himself was able to do this because he was entitled to act as Vice-Chairman of the Parliamentary Committee until the Congress ended, though he was disqualified from standing for election again.

Burns's motive in taking this line was undoubtedly his strong hostility to the Independent Labour Party and all its works. He was prepared in order to defeat the followers of Keir Hardie, to ally himself with the most reactionary elements in the Trades Union Congress. Perhaps he hoped, in doing this, to help on the cause of the Trade Union–Socialist Party which he still apparently desired. But, if this was in his mind, he went a strange way about it in consenting to his own exclusion; for he was the only possible leader for such a party, if it had stood any chance of coming into existence. His enemies said that he had gone over entirely to the "Lib-Labs" and abandoned his Socialism; but I think this is too simple a way of stating the case. It seems more likely that he had given up hope of getting what he wanted through the Trades Union Congress, and was already hunting about for alternative methods of rallying Radical opinion to a form of "gas and water" Socialism reminiscent of Joseph Chamberlain's projects of the '70s and early '80s.

At all events, in 1895 Burns dropped out of the Trade Union movement, and for the next few years pursued a busy but uneventful career in parliamentary and municipal affairs. His one child—a son, who died, much to his grief, in 1922—was born to him, I think, in 1896, and his domestic life had some chance now that he was no longer ceaselessly about on propagandist work. He laboured hard, however, in London politics as well as in Parliament. Keeping on friendly terms with the Trades Union Congress, he introduced an Eight Hours Bill on its behalf in the House of Commons in 1897; and two years later, when London government was further reformed by the institution of the Metropolitan Borough Councils, he strongly advocated that the powers of the Boards of Guardians should be transferred to them as an instalment of Poor Law reform.

In common with many Radicals, Burns opposed the South African War; and in the "Khaki Election" of 1900 he came near to losing his seat at Battersea, winning by 5,860 votes to 5,603. This was the year in which, in accordance with a resolution carried at the 1899 Trades Union Congress, the Trade Unions and Socialist Societies joined hands to form the Labour Representation Committee, direct forerunner of the Labour Party. Burns attended the inaugural Conference of the L R C and there, contrary to what might have been expected of him, supported the I L P representatives in opposing the proposal that L R C candidatures should be confined to manual workers. He thus opposed the group which desired to create a purely Trade Union party; but, though the proposal was defeated, he did not stand at Battersea as a nominee of the L R C. Instead, we find him, later in the year, joining forces with Tom Mann, W. M. Thompson and others to summon a Democratic Convention, out of which emerged a National Democratic League with a purely Radical programme of parliamentary and electoral reform. This

189

League, sponsored mainly by *Reynolds' Newspaper,* of which Thompson was editor, and based largely on the Radical opposition to the South African War, appeared at the time to be a possible rival to the L R C, which made at the outset only very slow progress. It included a good many active Socialists, such as Mann and Robert Smillie, together with old anti-war "Lib-Labs" and the more advanced elements in the Liberal Party. Lloyd George was at one time Vice-President, and Charles Duncan, of the then militant Workers' Union, and John Ward, of the Navvies, were among its active members.

IN OFFICE

With this new grouping Burns allied himself loosely; but his main propaganda during the next few years was on the theme of Municipal Socialism. On this subject he wrote, in 1902, the longest letter ever published in the correspondence columns of the *Times.* This was reprinted as a pamphlet; and several speeches of his on the same subject and on such matters as rating reform also enjoyed a wide circulation. In 1903, when Chamberlain launched his tariff campaign, Burns's mind harked back at once to the old days of the "Fair Traders"; and he engaged in vehement controversy with the Tariff Reformers. He stumped the country in the Free Trade cause; and the effect was to bring him very much closer to official Liberalism—the more so as men such as Lloyd George and John Morley, who was his closest friend and associate among the Liberals and was to be his companion in exile when war came in 1914, were gaining influence rapidly in the Liberal Party. It came as no great surprise to the public when Campbell-Bannerman, on forming his Liberal Government towards the end of 1905, offered Burns the position of President of the Local Government Board. Nor was anyone surprised when Burns accepted the offer.

The tradition of his manner of accepting it deserves to be true. He is said, on receiving the offer, to have slapped the Prime Minister on the back, and to have exclaimed, "Bravo, Sir Henry! Bravo! This is the most popular thing you have done yet."

For the next eight years John Burns was at the head of the department of which, in opposition, he had been the keenest and

190

most persistent critic. The question was—what would he do to reform it, and to change the Poor Law system which it administered through its strong control over the local Boards of Guardians. On the main question of Poor Law reform, the new President had for the time being in effect no power to change the system; for his predecessor in office had recently appointed a Royal Commission on the Poor Laws, and the natural course was to wait for its Report before proposing any major measure to Parliament. Burns, on taking office, freely expressed his confidence that much more than most people supposed could be done by administrative action under the existing law—that is, by rescinding the more oppressive of the Orders then in force and replacing them by new ones which would encourage the Guardians to an attitude of greater clemency. He did actually pursue this policy with some success in promoting the better treatment of pauper children. But in relation to most matters, he appears to have found the opposition to change among the officials of his department too powerful to be overcome—and even to have been talked by these same officials into an attitude of acquiescence in many of the evils which he had formerly denounced. It soon became a widespread opinion that Burns, for all his bluster, was a man easily managed by the accomplished Civil Servant who was ready to flatter him to the top of his bent.

The most significant form this flattery assumed was that of telling Burns that, as a "strong" man, he could dare to do things which previous Presidents of the Local Government Board had left undone out of cowardice. The officials, in fact, very successfully, diverted his attention from the reforms they disliked to reforms of a very different kind, which they had long been itching to make. It is an unquestionable fact that there existed in the administration of the Poor Law under the Boards of Guardians a good deal of petty corruption—some on the part of actual Guardians, but much more on that of workhouse masters and other local officials, who were so placed as to be able to score a good rake-off on contracts for food and clothing and other necessaries supplied to the inmates. This corruption was, of course, confined to a limited number of places and was part of an old, bad tradition, and not a new growth. But there it was; and the Board's officers were particularly eager to pounce upon it in areas where it happened to coexist with a local Poor Law policy of which they disapproved.

They found their chance in Poplar, an area which was a major battle-ground in the conflict over Poor Law policy. For a very long time, the Poplar Board of Guardians had been among the most determined exponents of the classical principles of "deterrence" and "less eligibility", ruthless in the refusal of outdoor relief and niggardly when they were forced to grant it, set on reducing the poor rates by every possible expedient and above all by compelling applicants and their families to enter "the house", and at perpetual war not only with the Socialists, but also with all the more humane reformers who were trying to make the Poor Law system less cruel and degrading. This policy had provoked, some years before Burns went to the Local Government Board, a powerful reaction; and Will Crooks, George Lansbury, and a handful of keen Socialists had been elected as Guardians in Poplar, and had set to work with energy to bring the Poplar Board round to a different point of view. They had gradually succeeded; and the Poplar Guardians, from being the "strictest", had become the most generous Board in the whole country, insisting especially on paying what were in effect regular pensions to the old out of the rates and on improving enormously the treatment of the able-bodied paupers and their dependants. The Local Government Board officials, before Burns's advent, had waged fierce warfare against the new Poplar policy, and had explored every possibility of disallowing it. But the Poplar Guardians showed themselves clever at keeping just within what the law allowed them to do; and the central officials had been unable to catch them out—until Burns came on the scene.

Actually, the storm which, at the beginning of 1906, burst about the heads of the Poplar Guardians had been brewing before Burns took office. The LGB officials had good evidence of the prevalence of corrupt practices in the area in connection with the purchase of workhouse stores and other supplies; and this evidence incriminated not only some of the local officials, but also some of the elected Guardians, including a few members of the Labour group. It did not, of course, touch Crooks, who was Chairman of the Board, or George Lansbury, personally; and it was not a new thing, but a survival from days before Labour had won its place on the Board and introduced the new policies of which the LGB disapproved. But it could be made to serve very conveniently as cover for an attack on the new policy of the Poplar Guardians, and it could be plausibly argued that they had shown much more zeal in giving away the ratepayers' money than in reforming the abuses of the administration. Actually the Poplar Board had for some time been urging on the LGB a centralised system of purchasing supplies on behalf of the various London Boards; and this proposal, if it had been acted upon, would have been an effective way of checking many of the abuses. But centralised purchase savoured too much of Socialism to be acceptable to the central authorities; and the Poplar plan had been rejected.

The situation when Burns took office was that the LGB officials had everything ready for launching a thunderbolt at the Poplar Guardians in the form of a public inquiry, to be held by an LGB inspector, in which charges of corruption and of "lax" Poor Law administration were to be mixed inextricably together. There were deep official fears, on Burns's advent, that the whole affair would be quashed; and the first task before the permanent officials was to persuade Burns that, as a strong man, he ought to go on with it, and that nothing could better display his impartiality and his fitness for office than to begin operations with an exposure of abuses on "his own side"—for so the public would interpret what he was being asked to do.

These tactics succeeded. Burns was persuaded to regard himself as the strong man, the sea-green incorruptible; and the official who conducted the inquiry was allowed to treat the corruption and the humane policy of the Poplar Guardians in effect as a single charge, so as to bring on the Socialists the odium of the corruption, and to induce public opinion to believe that "laxity" of administration and petty corruption walked naturally hand in hand. Seldom has an "impartial" inquiry been less impartially conducted, or more rapturously taken up by newspapers and politicians who saw in it the means of bringing the then brand-new Labour Party into disrepute. It is no wonder that this one episode earned Burns the unforgiving hatred of his former collaborators in the Labour and Socialist movements, or that many of them believed that he had done what he did out of personal spite and for the deliberate purpose of discrediting the Labour Party and bringing Socialism into obloquy.

That these were Burns's motives I do not believe. I think he was flattered into acting as he did—though if he had been a man of stronger loyalties he would not have been persuaded as he was. At all events, the Poplar Inquiry and its entirely indefensible conduct made Burns, within a few months of his assumption of office, easily the most hated man in Socialist and Labour circles all over the country.

LIBERAL REFORMS

The affair of the Poplar Board of Guardians was by no means the only matter over which John Burns was at loggerheads with his former fellow agitators. The Local Government Board of those days was in effect still little more than the old Poor Law Board under a changed name; and in its administrative policy the "principles of 1834" still to a great extent held sway. But by this time Labour and other progressive Guardians inspired by quite different ideas had been elected in considerable numbers and with many of them it was a tenet of faith that the State had an obligation to provide decent maintenance for the aged, good conditions and a sound upbringing for the children, and either work or a tolerable living income for the ablebodied unemployed. In relation to the old people the pressure was somewhat relieved when Old Age Pensions, subject to a Means Test, were started under the Act of 1908; but the sum allowed was manifestly too little to live upon, and accordingly the need for supplementary relief remained. The question of Old Age Pensions had been under discussion for many years, and there had been active controversies between the advocates of contributory and non-contributory schemes. The Liberals decided on a non-contributory plan, which was the easier to work; but this led to their putting the scale of benefit very low—so that the social reformers were far from satisfied, and many old people continued to be driven into the workhouses or to depend on supplementary outdoor relief. Burns did a very little to improve the position of these classes, but much less than had been hoped for. In improving the treatment of the workhouse children he was rather more successful; but the crux of the matter, as ever in disputes over Poor Law policy, was still the question of the able-bodied unemployed. Over this issue, the incompatibility between the conflicting policies was greatest; for in face of the prevailing levels of wages for the less skilled or less organised occupations, there was no way at all of reconciling the principle of "less eligibility" with that of maintaining the unemployed at a tolerable standard of living. There was also the vexed question of the "labour test". It was widely regarded as wrong in principle to pay relief without setting men to work where work could be found. But, whereas the Socialists contended that the work must be either useful work or training for useful work, and must be paid for at wages sufficient for decent living, the old school of Poor Law administrators believed in a "Labour test" imposed rather as a test of the applicant's endurance than on account of any value in the work done, in respect either of what was produced or of its educational quality. Stone-breaking was still widely used as the test, not only for the casual tramp, but for the unemployed who were thrown out of work by economic depression. When, therefore, some of the more progressive Boards of Guardians—with Poplar again in the forefront—began to organise Farm Colonies and similar experiments, with the object of training unemployed townsmen for usual work on the land, there were bitter disputes with the Local Government Board, which either disallowed the experiments or insisted on treating the Farm Colonies as "branch workhouses" and subjecting those sent to them, despite the hard work which they had to do, to the standard pauper dietaries intended for sedentary workhouse inmates.

DISAGREEMENTS WITH REFORMERS

It would take too much space to go into these controversies, which are fully explained in Sidney and Beatrice Webb's great *History of the Poor Law,* and illustrated in the autobiography of George Lansbury, and in such works as Haw's *Life of Will Crooks.* It is enough to say that Burns's boast that he could largely reform the Poor Law by administrative changes without need for fresh legislation was not borne out in practice, and that the officials of the Local Government Board so contrived matters that for every administrative change for the better there was a balancing instance in which Burns was persuaded to turn his authority against the more progressive Boards of Guardians.

When, in 1909, the Royal Commission on the Poor Laws at length issued its Majority and Minority Reports, and the question of legislation was forced to the front, the quarrel between Burns and the reformers came to a head. Both Majority and Minority among the Commissioners wanted sweeping changes in the law; and the Minority Report, signed by Beatrice Webb, George Lansbury and others, proposed the complete break-up of the Poor Law and its supersession by organised public provision, free from all pauper taint, covering the essential health and unemployment services under the auspices of the elected Councils of town and country areas. The National Committee to Promote the Break-up of the Poor Law (later re-named the National Committee for the Prevention of Destitution) was set up to organise a nation-wide campaign in support of the proposals of the Minority Report; and a very large body of public opinion was speedily mobilised behind it.

Burns, however, was against this sort of Poor Law reform and continued to boast of his own success in achieving what was needed by administrative methods. The whole Government, moreover, decided to proceed on quite different lines from those advocated by either Majority or Minority of the Commission. The health problem they decided to tackle by means of a system of contributory sickness insurance, on the model of Bismarck's German legislation; and the problem of unemployment was to be dealt with partly by an experimental system of contributory unemployment insurance, applied compulsorily in the first instance to a few selected trades, and partly by the development of the Labour Exchanges instituted under an Act of 1909 to cover the whole range of areas and employments.

Burns is said to have remarked, soon after the publication of the Government's insurance scheme, that it had effectively "dished the Webbs"; and it did in fact make impracticable a large part of the plan set forth in the Minority Report of the Poor Law Commission. Indeed, it did more than that; for by covering a part of the field in an alternative way, it made much less likely the finding of parliamentary time for the reform of the Poor Law itself, and thus left Burns free to carry on with his policy of piecemeal administrative change. The Poor Law was not in the event reformed by legislation until 1929; and the reformers laid on Burns a large part of the blame for the miscarriage of their projects.

In the meantime the Local Government Board had been called upon to take action in a quite different field. The one major piece of legislation that stands to Burns's credit over the eight years during which he held office is the Housing and Town-planning Act of 1909, notable both as a development of public housing policy and as the beginning of town-planning legislation. Looked at from the standpoint of today, the Act seems a very timorous and tentative measure; but at the time it was regarded as a big advance. Until 1909 the main part of the housing powers open to Local Authorities was "adoptive"—that is to say, it came into force only where a particular local Council chose to "adopt" it. The Act of 1909 conferred house-building powers on all Local Authorities and also strengthened considerably the powers under the "Cross" and "Torrens" Acts to clear slum areas and demolish or secure the renovation of insanitary dwellings. On the town-planning side the steps taken in 1909 were very modest. In general, the initiative in making town-planning schemes was left with Local Authorities and private landowners; and, though the Local Government Board was empowered to make a scheme where the appropriate authority failed to do so, it was clearly contemplated that resort would be had to this power only in very extreme cases. Still, a beginning was made; and under more favourable conditions and with a more advanced central department a good deal might have been accomplished. Unfortunately, the Act was passed at a time when private building activity was at a very low ebb, and was ebbing yet further under the influence of the controversy over Mr. Lloyd George's land duties. Moreover, the Act merely empowered the Local Authorities to act; and there was still no question of financial aid from the central Exchequer. Under these circumstances, little had in fact been done before the outbreak of war in 1914 brought nearly all house-building to a standstill.

LAST YEARS OF OFFICE

In 1910 John Burns had twice to face his Battersea constituents in the General Elections resulting from the conflict with the

House of Lords over the Budget of 1909. He had won easily in 1906, against a Conservative, by 7,387 votes to 5,787. In January 1910 he was elected by 8,540 to 7,985, and in December of the same year by 7,838 to 6,544. Shortly after this, there began the wave of strikes which marked the growing disillusionment of the working classes with the fruits of Liberal government. Burns played an active part, with Winston Churchill and Lloyd George, in the negotiations in connection with the London transport strike of 1911; and when the second strike broke out at the London docks in the following year, he again attempted to mediate—this time without success. Apart from these interventions on the scene of his earlier triumphs he did nothing very notable during his later years at the Local Government Board— unless indeed his continued opposition to the Minority Report is to be so regarded. Early in 1914 he was transferred from the LGB to the Board of Trade; and he was President of the Board of Trade during the Ulster crisis which immediately preceded the European War. Over Ulster Burns took in conversation a strong line—openly blaming his Cabinet colleagues for their pusillanimity in handling Sir Edward Carson and the recalcitrant army officers of the "Curragh Incident". But before this trouble could come to a head, German action precipitated the European War; and, as we have seen, immediately upon the decision of the Cabinet to declare war on Germany, Burns and John Morley resigned from it and retired into private life.

There has been much argument about the motives which underlay John Burns's resignation from the Cabinet in 1914. It has been asserted, on the one hand, that his sympathies were pro-German, and, on the other, that his resignation was prompted mainly by a feeling that nothing should induce him to remain a member of a Government responsible for conducting even a righteous war. That he had been critical of Sir Edward Grey's foreign policy is certain, and he almost certainly believed that the war could have been averted if British foreign policy had taken a different shape during the years of Liberal government after 1905. That he was "anti-war" after the war had actually begun there is no evidence; and, as he never publicly explained what his motives had been, the world must be left to guess— unless indeed he has left behind him papers which will provide the explanation. I think his main motive was an intense dislike of war and of responsibility for it, accentuated by his mistrust of the foreign policy of the "Liberal Imperialists" who had dominated foreign policy within the Asquith Government. But Burns's attitude was certainly not one of absolute pacifism. His line over Ulster by itself disproves any such assumption.

After 1914 John Burns, though he lived on for nearly 30 years, in full physical vigour almost to the end, had no public life. In Parliament, from the outbreak of war to his retirement at the General Election of 1918, he said nothing; and when the war was over he found no road leading back into politics. As we have seen earlier, he vanished entirely from the view of the public; and gradually the old, bitter memories died away, and those who had cherished them most angrily, such as Hyndman, disappeared from the scene. Burns had always about him something of the air of a sea-captain—even if this was mainly due to his reefer-jacket. In his latter days he was even more like a sea-captain, pottering busily about and remembering ancient voyages.

CONCLUSION

What manner of man was Burns, underneath his boastful self-confidence? Honest, undoubtedly, in the sense of being personally incorruptible; but apt to do things that looked dishonest under the impetus of his vast egoism and his readiness to push other men out of the road. Frugal, and with a thrifty belief in temperance and strenuous living. Unsparing of himself, whenever there was something he wanted to do, but always with a minute to spare when he saw any limelight he could bask in. A magnificent mob-orator in his great days, and, like most mob-orators, one whose speeches did not stand too well the test of being written down. As for his social philosophy, it can be almost summed up in the phrase that he believed in the State doing things—provided we include in our conception of the State the organs of local as well as central government. Burns was a "gas and water" Socialist much more completely than the Fabians to whom the name is often applied. He was also a believer in State-action in other fields—in legislative regulation of hours and wages, in State provision for what we call nowadays "Social Security", and in orderly administration even to the length of bureaucracy—provided of course that the bureaucrats were, or at any rate seemed to be, on his side. Although he was in his time an active Trade Unionist, he was always a little scornful of Trade Unionism as a voluntary movement, and believed that its functions in protecting its members ought to be taken over largely by the State. He believed for some time in the notion of a Labour Party based directly and exclusively on the Trade Unions, and professing a collectivist gospel; but, strike-leader though he was, he had no great belief in the power of the Trade Unions to achieve lasting results by industrial action. He ended his political career in the Liberal Party, not because he was ever really a Liberal, but partly because he was a strong believer in Free Trade, and partly because he could not get his own way in the Labour movement, or bring himself to work with Keir Hardie and the Independent Labour Party, even when he was broadly in agreement with what they wanted. In a sense, he must be pronounced a failure, because he got himself into a false position from which he found no retreat— or at least none that his egoism would allow him to take.

With all his faults, however, Burns did big things in his day. The great Dock Strike of 1889 would almost certainly have been lost had he not been there to lead it; and no man had so much to do as he with bringing the less skilled workers into the Labour movement and creating in London the forces that went to the making of the Labour Party. On the London County Council he did excellent work: and his failure at the Local Government Board was partly redeemed by his part in the Housing and Town Planning Act of 1909. He owed his position at the first working-class man to reach Cabinet rank to his own qualities, good and evil, and not to his place at the head of any great organisation; and, finally, there was something highly characteristic about his manner of leaving public life abruptly and without a single word of explanation, and thereafter making for himself a very full and seemingly happy private life of his own. That he was an original thinker no one will claim. He picked up his doctrines and policies from others, and added nothing to them : that was what made it possible for Hyndman to declare that he and a few of his fellow-members of the SDF had taught Burns everything he ever knew. This was not quite true; for he had learnt a good deal from Victor Delahaye before he ever met Hyndman and his friends, and he learnt a good deal more from Engels later on. But it was true that while Burns was the orator of the SDF he said in the main what Hyndman and Champion told him to say, rather than anything that he had thought out clearly for himself. That was why Hyndman was so angry when Burns broke away from him, and also why Burns was able to break away so easily. His revolutionism, fiery as it seemed for a time, was not deep-seated : his belief in himself went much deeper, and so did his single clear idea that the State ought to be doing for the people a great many things which its rulers were showing no inclination to allow it to do.

8 Margaret Cole
BEATRICE AND SIDNEY WEBB

INTRODUCTION*

If this booklet were an old-fashioned fairy tale, its plot might be summarised somewhat as follows :

"Once upon a time there were a boy and a girl who were very nearly the same age. They did not meet when they were young. They were born and brought up in quite different classes in society and learned to live in quite different ways. But as they grew older they both became deeply interested in the way in which their country was run and in the welfare of ordinary people, and this common interest at last brought them together. They met; they were married and lived happily ever after, and when they died they were buried in Westminster Abbey. And though, while they were apart, they were One and One, when they came together they made not Two but Eleven."

The last sentence is drawn from an inspired plea made by Sidney Webb in the course of his courtship; and it is almost a literal statement of fact. For great as were the individual gifts of each partner—gifts which, although Beatrice modestly described them as "second-rate", made it certain that they would both have played a part in English social history even if they had never met—their combination was as effective as a chemical rather than a mechanical process. It resulted in the terrific output of writing, organisation, and agitation which this study can do no more than briefly sketch, but which has deeply affected both the social thought and the social organisation of Britain. So far as I know, there has never in this country been a Partnership like the Partnership of Sidney and Beatrice Webb; I think it improbable that there will ever be another.

It was not merely a Partnership; it was also a lifelong

* A brief preface by C. R. Attlee has been omitted.

romance. Since the publication of *Our Partnership*[1], with its simple-phrased references to their emotional relationship, everyone can see that the one-time description of the Webb ménage as "two typewriters clicking as one" was superficial nonsense. They were, it was true, complementary to a remarkable degree. Sidney brought to the common fund an exceptional gift for quick and rapid drafting, in "a faultless handwriting" (compare Beatrice's scrawl, sometimes unreadable even by herself!), for tearing the heart out of books and documents which made her head ache to read, and for remembering almost any fact with which he had ever had nodding acquaintance, which, to put it at the lowest, made their joint literary output many times greater than Beatrice could ever have achieved alone : she, for her part, excelled in the spoken interview, in the extraction of information —and sometimes of money—from individuals, and she had, when she was in a position to use it, a vivid descriptive style to which he could lay no claim. It would seem, also, that she, rather than he, had intuitive flashes in which she suddenly "saw" the shape of a book or the answer to a social problem[2]; whereas he adhered more steadfastly to a line once adopted, and when she showed signs of weakening, whether in the matter of attending Society dinners or of disliking the Soviet-German Pact of 1939, he gently but firmly drew her back to the proper path.

This perfect mutual "dovetailing" made them a unique combination; it accounted for a great deal of their strength and steadiness, though it could at times prove a weakness, since when their combined judgment was wrong—and nobody can always be right—they were so thoroughly and *unassailably* wrong. But it was not nearly the whole of the "truth about the Webbs", as everyone realised who ever had personal relations with them. They were deeply, almost youthfully in love till death did them part, and both found in their marriage an unshakeable happiness, an emotional as well as an intellectual satisfaction so profound that Sidney, at least, seemed scarcely to need the companionship of any other person in the world. This

[1] *Our Partnership,* by Beatrice Webb, edited by Barbara Drake and Margaret Cole. Longmans Green & Co. 1948.

[2] Their plan for the reform of the English political system and the idea that poverty should be regarded and treated as a social nuisance both came to her, as she has recorded, "in a flash".

gave the basic security upon which all their 50 years' life-work was built; it is all the more astonishing to contemplate when one realises that they might very easily not have married at all. They were both over 30 when they first met; neither was the other's first love; their social provenance was so different that the engagement had to be kept a secret until Beatrice's father died, and several of her former friends were estranged from her by her marriage. It was a step in the dark, albeit a well-considered step; but no one at the time could have prophesied that it would have so triumphant a result.

BEATRICE

Beatrice Webb came from the executive classes. Not from the aristocracy; her great-grandfather, John Potter, had a small draper's shop at Tadcaster and a small farm nearby, and her grandfather Richard started life as a shop assistant and rose, in the palmy days of the industrial revolution, to ownership of a cotton warehouse in Manchester and thence to the position of one of the leading Radical business-men of Lancashire, amassing a reasonable fortune on the way. His son, another Richard, was brought up, it is true, to be a Victorian "gentleman"; he was sent to a public school and to London University, was called to the Bar—without intending to practise—married the brilliant daughter of a well-off merchant in Liverpool, and would in all probability have settled down on an estate in the country with an eye to a Parliamentary career had not the financial crash of 1847-8 removed most of his inherited wealth and forced him to go back to business to make a living. He was not, certainly, reduced to any distress; he became immediately a director of the Great Western Railway and a partner in a timberworks at Gloucester—out of which he made handsome profits during the Crimean War; he played a part in a great many enterprises of various kinds, and kept up very comfortable establishments for his wife and his nine daughters. But he had ceased to be a *rentier;* he was a business man, and Beatrice in her girlhood very soon observed that he and her mother and all the friends and acquaintances who came in and out of their various houses belonged to the class who did nothing manual for themselves, but "habitually *gave orders*". Almost from the time that she could think in general terms at all, it was borne in upon her that

British nineteenth-century society comprised a top stratum which *gave orders* and a vast foundation, called impersonally "labour", which carried them out.

Beatrice was the eighth of nine daughters, all of whom made excellent marriages in the conventional sense; her only brother died when a very little boy. She was a delicate, rather lonely, and sometimes unhappy child; ill-health prevented her from the companionship of school life; she was seven years older than her younger sister, and her mother seems to have had little sympathy for her in her early youth. "Beatrice", she wrote in her diary, "is the only one of my children who is below the general level of intelligence"—a really staggering misapprehension. Further, the child herself suffered from the introspectiveness which so often goes with ill-health, and like many another Victorian child, often wondered anxiously—sometimes in the diaries which she began to write when she was very young—whether she was being good enough, or hard-working enough, and whether she was not, perhaps, becoming "a frivolous, silly, unbelieving woman". (In after years, she occasionally meditated on Sidney's good fortune in possessing "a robust conscience").

She was not, therefore, a happy child, largely because she had not a happy temperament; but this does not mean that she was in any way a repressed or a miserable child. She intensely loved and admired her father, who was both fond and proud of all his daughters and (in contrast to many Victorian parents) gave them the same freedom of reading and action as he would have given to his sons; and at least two of the friends whom she made in her childhood proved very valuable contributors to her own development.

The first of these was her nurse, Martha Jackson, nicknamed "Dada", and herself a distant relative of the Potter family. Beatrice in her own autobiography, *My Apprenticeship*, calls Martha Jackson "the only saint I ever knew", and seems to have regarded her as something between a nurse and a mother-confessor; it was Martha Jackson who, when she was 25, took her to stay with the Co-operators of Bacup and for the first time made the abstraction "labour" take on flesh and blood; it was perhaps through Martha Jackson that Beatrice first learned, what some of her contemporary students of radical politics never learned, how to talk without embarrassment with members of working-class communities.

The other friend was that curious and crabbed philosopher Herbert Spencer, who had met the elder Potters when he was a very young man, and retained a deep admiration for Mrs. Potter in particular. Spencer's peculiar philosophy, his attempt to construct upon the researches of Darwin and other nineteenth-century scientists a "scientific" system of sociology, is remembered nowadays by hardly anyone but specialists; but he was very kind to the Potter children, especially to Beatrice. He made himself her confidant and mental guide; he was genuinely concerned about her health; he patiently read and criticised her youthful scribblings "about Greek and German philosophers"; and above all, he encouraged her intellectual efforts and set her "the example of continuous concentrated effort in carrying out, with an heroic disregard of material prosperity and physical comfort, a task which he believed would further human progress". Beatrice never swallowed Spencer's philosophy; but she greatly admired his persistent and lifelong collection of facts, and followed his methods to some extent when she came to do research work of her own. And certainly Spencer's insistence that sociology ought to be considered a science and to use scientific methods influenced her all through her life.

Meantime, she grew up into a young lady living the life of many another Victorian young lady of the comfortable classes. She "came out" in 1876; she took part in the gaieties of the London Season; she spent part of the year at various country houses owned by her father, and occasionally accompanied him on business tours abroad. After her sisters were married, and particularly after her mother's death in 1882, she undertook the management of the large Potter household and became her father's close companion and at times something approaching his confidential secretary. She entertained his friends, and as "the brilliant Miss Potter" she was a considerable success in that world of London Society which she afterwards learned to distrust and despise. She met politicians and Great Men; for a while during the early 'eighties she was very much attracted by a man much older than herself, Joseph Chamberlain, who was then at the height of his career and had not yet broken with the Liberal Party, and the possibility of her becoming his third

206

wife was discussed with her family. (This would have been an unfortunate alliance, in view of Chamberlain's later career; even at the time when she was most deeply moved by him Beatrice recognised with some uneasiness his appetite for personal power). But all the time, underneath, she was searching for a faith to live by and a life-work which should be worthwhile. It was not for some years that she found both together, and with them her life's partner.

Like other Victorian young ladies with social consciences, she devoted some time to good works, or "slumming". She worked as a visitor for the Charity Organisation Society and as house-manager and rent-collector for a block of working-class flats in Dockland; but she soon found that these well-meant attempts at relieving the depressing mass of London poverty yielded her no satisfaction, and very gladly accepted the request of her cousin Charles Booth to become one of his voluntary helpers in that great Inquiry into the Life and Labour of the People of London whose findings, issued in many large volumes over a number of years, shocked all the shockable members of the English upper classes as they realised the mass of squalor, ignorance, misery and starvation which in the Golden Age of British capitalism still filled the poorer quarters of the richest city in the world. It was in the course of this Inquiry that, in order to find out the truth about sweated labour in the tailoring trade, she got a job as a "plain trouser hand" in the East End of London, and collected evidence which she subsequently gave in public to the House of Lords committee of enquiry into sweated labour, and wrote up into her first published work. Alfred Marshall, the economist, was so much impressed with her investigations that he advised her to make herself an authority on women's labour in general; but she felt that such a study, for her, led nowhere, reached no conclusions about society, and brought her into contact only with hopeless and unhelpable groups of persons.

In 1883 she had gone—under the name of "Miss Jones, farmer's daughter from near Monmouth"—to stay with Martha Jackson's friends among the co-operators and mill-workers of Lancashire; and there, she felt, she had found real working-class people, a real social life and living institutions which the theore-tical economists of her day had never condescended to notice. Accordingly, after her work in the sweated trades was completed, she went north again—this time using her own name—to conduct by herself an enquiry into co-operation and to produce in 1890 a small book on *The Co-Operative Movement*. This book, small as it was, held the field for many years as an important study of its subject; it also brought its author into contact with a little man called Sidney Webb, recommended as one who "literally pours out information" (on the subject of working-class conditions in the eighteenth century). The Whitsun of that year saw them both attending the Co-operative Congress at Glasgow, and among the drunken crowds of the Glasgow streets, "two Socialists came to a working compact".

"You understand," said Beatrice, "you promise me to realise that the chances are that nothing comes of it but friendship."

SIDNEY AND THE FABIAN SOCIETY

By 1890 the other partner to this compact was already a considerable person in his own world, if not in Beatrice's; the long persistent legend that Beatrice picked him up out of the gutter, as it were, in the course of her social investigations and forcibly married him has not the slightest foundation in fact. But his early days were lived at a social level much lower than hers. His grandfather was an innkeeper in a small Kentish village, and all his relatives were "little folk" of one sort or another, the only one of them to attain any distinction being his cousin Fred Webb, who once rode a Derby winner. His mother kept a retail shop in Cranbourn Street, off Leicester Square; his father earned a small income as an accountant, and in his spare time was an inveterate worker in voluntary public service—he had, *inter alia,* been one of John Stuart Mill's committeemen in his Westminster election campaign. The two sons, Sidney and his brother Charles, left school when they were about 16; this was the standard of the household.

What chiefly impressed Miss Beatrice Potter, when she came to know the Webb family, was the entire absence in it of any social ambition or will-to-power. They did not seem to want to *give orders* to anyone, or to climb out of their social class, or even to make more money than they had already. The family income, she says, in *Our Partnership,* never exceeded £500 a year—a pittance in the eyes of a young woman who was to inherit double that sum for herself alone. Nor did they seem in need of society, with a large or small "s"; they did not entertain, and Sidney's recollections of his youth, as he once retailed them in the *St. Martin's Review,* are not associated with friends or sports—though Bernard Shaw says that he was a remarkably good shot with a rifle!—but almost wholly with the streets and shops of London. Towards London, indeed, he did display an emotion which most human creatures reserve for their families, their old school or their old friends; he wandered by himself all over the London of the 'sixties, with its riches and squalor; the shop-windows and their advertisements were his earliest spelling-book and *Kelly's Directory* his favourite reading. He remembered his mother lifting him up to see the Lord Mayor's Show and promising him that if he were a good boy he might himself one day be Lord Mayor of London. In his formative years he grew up a patriotic Londoner, as fervent as was Herbert Morrison a generation later; therein he had a certain advantage over his wife, who had no local habitation of her own to love.

But however modest the ambitions of the Webb household, it must soon have become clear that Sidney Webb was not destined to remain long at the economic level of a small shopkeeper and a piecework accountant. His was one of the not infrequent cases in which a family of unassuming ducks suddenly produces an unmistakable and unaccountable swan. His power of concentrated work, of memorising facts and making rapid and efficient use of them was phenomenal; immediately after leaving school he started to attend evening classes, and by this means succeeded, first in passing the Civil Service Open Examination and becoming a Second Division Clerk, and three years later (1881) in reaching the First Division with marks high enough to have entered the Foreign Office had he wished. He chose instead the Colonial Office, and was it seemed all set to become a distinguished civil servant—as a side-issue, he passed his Bar examinations four years later. But a different career was in store for him.

The first shaper of destiny for him was the man who became his only close lifelong friend—a lean, red-bearded, perverse, poverty-stricken young journalist named Bernard Shaw. They met first in 1879, at a Hampstead debating club which had christened itself the Zetetical Society; there they practised impromptu discourse upon all manner of subjects, discussed with each other the parlous state of the world and possible remedies for it, and learned to take economical holidays together. After a while, Shaw made the acquaintance of another tiny group of Socialistic debaters who called themselves The Fabian Society and met in the room of a young man of middle-class parents named Edward Pease, who had taken up cabinet-making because as a Socialist he thought he ought to have a trade. Having had some years' experience of his friend's phenomenal knowledge of facts, Shaw, the brilliant debater, decided that Sidney Webb was exactly the man needed to give weight and stiffening to the infant Society—to bottom its ideological discussions by producing *Facts for Socialists*. Accordingly, Webb was brought into the group; by 1885 he and Shaw were both members of the Society's tiny Executive Committee; in 1887 *Facts for Socialists* (which has run to 18 editions) first appeared as a Fabian Tract, to be followed a year later by another called *Facts for Londoners,* designed to provide ammunition and a policy for the Progressive Party (Liberals) in the first elections to the London County Council; by the end of 1888 Shaw and Webb were collaborating with Graham Wallas, Sydney Olivier, Annie Besant, Hubert Bland, and an eccentric named William Clarke in the series of London lectures which, reprinted as *Fabian Essays,* sold for 65 years after their first delivery and put the infant Society right on the Radical map. All this before Webb had even met his future wife.

There is no need—and no—space—to enlarge here upon the history of the Fabian Society, now well past its seventieth birthday; it is pertinent, however, to note that for a quarter of a century Webb was its chief guiding spirit both on method and on policy, which may perhaps be summed up in two phrases, "the inevitability of Socialism and the inevitability of gradualism". The second principle is clearly assumed in *Fabian Essays,* 34 years before Webb proclaimed it to the Labour Party Conference; the first implied that any reasoning person who looked at the hard facts of late Victorian society could not fail to reach the conclusion that Socialism—by which the Fabians meant State and municipal enterprise—was the only reasonable solution. But reasoning persons, if they were to be convinced, must be presented with the relevant facts set out in an intelligible manner; hence the preoccupation of the Fabians with collecting basic facts, arranging them so that their Socialist implications should be understood, and handing them out to the public by means of Fabian Tracts, series of lectures in towns and provinces, or suggestions made to individual leaders or groups. (Much of the early programmes—particularly the municipal programmes—of the I.L.P. was based on Fabian-provided material.)

The essential qualification for an active Fabian was that he should be prepared to work hard without pay, to learn to speak fluently and to deal with questioners on any relevant subject before any audience, large or small, influential or merely "seeking guidance". He was furthermore expected to be accurate in his statements, and so far as humanly possible, to verify his references and check his proposals at the bar of commonsense, and—an important point—not to make unwarranted claims for the Fabian Society, not to suggest, for example, that all Socialists ought to become *Fabian* Socialists, that the Fabian Society should dictate policy, or that it should undertake, or persist in carrying on activities which other institutions could do better.[1] It is this attitude which partly, at any rate, accounts for the long life and influence of the Society; it was an attitude very congenial to Beatrice, who joined it (and appeared at an Annual Meeting as "representative of Sowerby Bridge!"—near Bacup) a little while before her marriage in the summer of 1892;[2] it was in this spirit that the new Partnership set off to spend its honeymoon studying early Trade Union records in Dublin and Glasgow.

TRADE UNIONISM AND LOCAL GOVERNMENT

There is something highly characteristic—even if there is also something a little comic—in this opening to the lifelong work of the Webbs. They did not marry without thought or without a plan, and the plan which they made envisaged living the life they wanted to live and doing the work they wanted to do in their own way, whether or not it would have seemed attractive to others. They were never unconventional, in the ordinary sense

---

[1] See Fabian Tract 42 and Tract 70.

[2] "Sidney Webb was married on 23rd ult. to Beatrice Potter" : *Fabian News*, August, 1892.

211

of the word; they did not believe in shocking their neighbours save in so far as their political opinions were shocking; their range of enjoyment was limited, their appreciation of art, for example—though not of natural beauty—being almost non-existent, and they did not see why they should spend precious time on pleasures which they did not find pleasurable, or honeymoon among Florentine paintings when what they really wanted to look at were old rule-books and reports of branch meetings. Critics like H. G. Wells, or society acquaintances like Margot Asquith, would have appreciated them better if they had been more unconventional in their behaviour, and less comfortably confident that what they did was almost exactly what they wanted to do. Though they did not believe in overwork or in discomfort or asceticism for its own sake—their homes were always adequately staffed and comfortable if not luxurious—their most recurrent extravagance was the employment of an extra secretary!

Thanks to Beatrice's father, they enjoyed an unearned income of £1,000 a year, which in the 'nineties, with income tax at sixpence in the pound, was a considerable sum. It relieved both of them from the need to earn a living; and they proposed to devote their lives to political and research work, and to trust that such books as they might publish would in the long run pay for themselves. This hope was fulfilled; the profit-and-loss account of the great library which stands to their credit shows a favourable balance on the whole. But this result could not have been achieved if they had been dependent upon their writing for a living; it was the existence of the independent income which enabled them both to produce works of research (such as the 10-volume *corpus* on the history of local government) and also to take the risks of issuing, for the benefit of the working-class and other slender pockets, cheap editions of books like *The History of Trade Unionism* and *Soviet Communism* at highly unremunerative prices. Seldom can an "unearned income" have paid so handsome a social dividend.

Their plan of living was arranged; their house, the famous 41 Grosvenor Road on the Thames Embankment, was taken and furnished almost immediately after their marriage. Joint research and authorship was to take up most of the mornings; the afternoon, while Beatrice relaxed, Sidney was to devote to work at the London County Council, to which he had just been elected, or the Fabian Society, or whatever else he found to his hand; in the evenings they might write, or read—Sidney according to his wife, did not care for "chatter"—or upon occasion see a friend or neighbour. But public life was to be Sidney's sphere, working among his Fabian and Progressive colleagues, with the possibility of entering Parliament in due course; Beatrice resigned herself, not, one gathers, without a pang or two, to giving up the world of Society in which she had shone and became Mrs. Sidney Webb, the wife of a not-yet-very-distinguished public man and the friend of his friends—of whom she found Bernard Shaw, with all his brillance, in some ways the least easy to understand. She loyally accepted him, however, classified him to her satisfaction as a "Sprite"—a sort of Undine without human qualities—and thereafter remained firmly his friend.

Such a tidy and hundrum pattern was hardly to be carried out by two people of such qualities. Their first joint venture was in fact Beatrice's doing. During her work on Co-operation she had reached the conclusion that one of the greatest weaknesses of the massive Consumers' Co-operation Movement was its tendency to ignore or despise associations of employees; and as soon as she had finished her book on it she set herself the task of investigating Trade Unionism, then a subject practically unknown to the general public and even to economists. The task was enormous, and but for her marriage could never have been completed; but the two of them together accomplished it, and with Bernard Shaw and Graham Wallas to help in the polishing of the style they produced in 1894 their first great classic, *The History of Trade Unionism,* and in 1897 the companion volume on the philosophy of Trade Unionism and employer-worker relationships, which is called *Industrial Democracy.* The work which they did for these two books brought them closely into contact with leaders of the Trade Union movement of the '90s, both old-style craft Unionists like Henry Broadhurst of the Stonemasons and fiery young Socialists like Tom Mann of the Engineers; and their advice and counsel was frequently sought, so much so that Beatrice, whose main preoccupation this was and who, as Shaw has said, "really enjoyed hob-nobbing with Trade Union secretaries over their pipes and drinks", had, even at that early date, a vision of the Webbs becoming (in the mediaeval sense) "clerks to organised Labour". This vision came to pass, more or less, towards the end of the first world war; but not at the time of its conception. The most obvious reason for this was that John Burns, the hero of the London dock strike, the biggest figure in the Trade Union world, and due to receive Cabinet office in the 1906 Liberal Government, had no intention of being advised or tutored by the Webbs—or for that matter by anyone else; but a more important cause was their own absorption in other interests—local government research, education, and Liberal politics.

Of their local government research work, great and enduring as it was, there is space to say very little here. As soon as their Trade Union task was finished, they plunged into an even bigger and more uncharted jungle, the history and growth of English local government institutions. This was not an accident or unplanned activity; it was a fundamental Fabian belief that the associations of consumers known as Town and County Councils, etc., had a great part to play in the making of modern democracy, and to the Webbs it was obvious that reformers could not use the Councils for reforming ends unless they knew what they were like and how they had come into existence. Accordingly, they began to work upon the history of local government as they had worked upon the history of Trade Unionism; but soon found that they had taken on what would have seemed a life-sentence to most people. *After a year's work,* they discovered that they had taken the wrong starting-point; they had to scrap most of what they had done, and go back further, to 1688 or, in the case of the Poor Law, to early Stuart times, in order to make a satisfactory study. So big was the job that the first volume, on *The Manor and the Borough,* was not given to the world until 1906, and the last of the great 10, *English Poor Law History,* not until 1929. (Some half-dozen other, slighter volumes were included during the intervening years.)

The work was not, of course, continuous : subsequent pages will show the kind of strenuous other activities with which local government research had to compete in the working hours of the day. Beatrice's vivid description, in *Methods of Social Study,* of the delights of spending hour after hour "in the chancel of an old parish church, in the veiled light of an ancient muniment, in the hard little office of a solicitor, in the ugly and bare anteroom of the council chamber of a local authority, or even in a dungeon without ventilation or daylight . . . with a stack of manuscripts, or a pile of printed volumes, to get through in a given time, shows clearly enough that it was the enthusiasm of the genuine creator that was here engaged. If they should have needed any further encouragement, they might have found it in the fact that they produced some 6,000 or so pages of permanent and unquestioned value—a quarry for succeeding generations.

THE L.C.C., EDUCATION AND PERMEATION

After the ending of the Trade Union chapter in the history of the partnership, the next phase, in its public aspect at least, is mainly Sidney's, though as time went on Beatrice came to take a more and active part on the social side. It may be summarised as "The London County Council, Education, and Permeation" —and the comprehensiveness of the summary is itself indicative of the sheer amount of work which the two of them got through in the years before the last Liberal Government changed the face of party politics and Beatrice turned to reforming the Poor Law.

To begin with the first item. Sidney was elected to the L.C.C. in 1892 as a Progressive, and sat there until 1910. During that time he was a member of at least 16 important committees and represented the council on half-a-dozen other bodies; and as he was a most hard-working committeeman, an extremely skilful and ready draftsman and reconciler of opposing points of view, his influence on the day-to-day work of the Council was immense. "In the absence of any evidence to the contrary", wrote Edward Pease, "in the case of any report it must be assumed that Webb wrote it." The greatest and most permanent work that he did for the Council, however, was not, as might have been expected, in the field of direct socialisation, but in education, particularly secondary education. It is not too much to say that the present huge organisation of secondary "further" education in London County (costing over £5 million in a single year) practically owes its existence to Sidney Webb and his paid collaborator, William Garrett.

When he joined its ranks, the Council had done practically nothing for London higher education. The Government, however, had three years previously passed a Technical Instruction

215

Act which gave the newly-created County Councils power to levy a rate for education of this kind. Webb seized upon this opening, and directly after his election persuaded the L.C.C. to set up a Technical Education Committee, with himself as Chairman and three other Fabians among its membership, its first job being to conduct a full survey of the opportunities provided in London for "education above the primary level'—and to disclose its pitiable inadequacy. The words quoted have considerable point. The Committee might bear the name Technical; but Webb had no intention of letting public education for children over 12 be restricted to what are commonly regarded as "technical" subjects. What he intended to create was a real system of secondary education; and though he was working with the stream of current advanced thought and was helped by many others—such as the late Arthur Dyke Acland—it was very largely his eye for possibilities, his ready grasp of any opportunity that offered, his persuasive management of colleagues and "interests", and his unremitting attention to detail, which got the job done.

The widening of the scope, for example, was achieved by persuading the Government, with Acland's cordial assistance, to enlarge successively its interpretation of the term "technical" until, in Webb's own words, it included "the teaching of every conceivable subject other than ancient Greek and theology"— it is not certain why he left out Greek!—and by appointing really able men—men like Sir William Garnett, Sir Gilbert Frampton the sculptor, and W. R. Lethaby the architect and art critic—to be its servants and advisers. Possible opposition was largely disarmed by persuading existing institutions to take part in the scheme and setting up new ones, which might have caused rivalry and heart-burnings, only in case of proved necessity.

To keep his fellow-counsellors on their toes, Webb first fired them with a scheme for providing 500 yearly scholarships (with maintenance grants) for intelligent primary pupils, and then brought them down to earth by pointing out that the just-completed survey showed that there were practically no schools for the bright young scholars to go to, thereby forcing the Council to set about building its own secondary schools; and the interest of the parents and citizens he kept alive, not merely by writing and speaking, but by such homely devices as sending a personally-signed letter of congratulation to the parents of every successful school child. Though his attitude to primary education and the Education Act (see below) was less uniformly approved, and ended by estranging him from his fellow-Progressives, his secondary education record was so impressive that he was made Chairman of the Higher Education Committee for so long as he remained on the Council.

Meanwhile the net of his energies had spread from secondary education to take in higher education in a stricter sense. Himself self-educated after 16 by evening classes at Birkbeck College, he had long felt it astonishing and disgraceful that the commercial centre of the world did so little to tell its adolescents and adults anything about the economic and social conditions of the world they were living in. "King's College," he said of the '90s, "had a nominal professorship which was suspended. Professor Foxwell held a chair at University College, but had only a score of students, reported to be "one-half coloured." A rather elementary course of lectures was annually repeated at Birkbeck College. That was all that existed in the capital of the British Empire for a population comparable to that of the whole of Scotland (or Belgium or Holland), each of them having several universities." This state of things was naturally intolerable to a Fabian who believed firmly that study of economic and social *facts* was sufficient to turn any sensible and intelligent person into a Socialist; and in 1895 came an unexpected chance of remedying it.

A cranky old Fabian from the north, by name Henry Hutchinson, died, and when his will was read it was found that he had left his property of some £10,000 in trust to his daughter and Sidney Webb, with three other members of the Fabian Society "to the propaganda and other purposes of the said Society and its Socialism and towards advancing its objects in any way they deem advisable." To anyone less far-sighted than Webb and the colleagues whom he influenced the obvious thing to do with this windfall might have seemed to make a splash within the Fabian Society, to equip it with fine offices—as H. G. Wells wanted to do 10 years later—or to launch a raring-tearing propaganda for Socialism. 10,000 pounds, in the '90s, would have made a considerable show in either of those directions. The Webbs, however, would have none of it; neither they, nor the

217

other Fabians, wanted to make the Fabian Society showy, and they believed that the I.L.P. was doing all the propaganda required. "Reform," remarked Beatrice in her *Diary,* "will not be brought about by shouting. What is needed is *hard thinking."* Accordingly, after setting aside some provision for Hutchinson's family, the trustees divided the remainder into approximately equal parts of which one was spent on sending Fabian speakers to lecture in provincial centres, and the other went to found the London School of Economics and Political Science, an institution, in the words of Lord Beveridge, who was for so many years its Director, "where men should be free to study and teach scientifically, pursuing truth as they saw it in independence of any dogma, whether of Socialism or the reverse." "No religious, political, or economic test or qualification," said the Articles of Association of the School, "shall be made a condition for or disqualify from receiving any of the benefits of the Corporation, or holding any office therein."

The subsequent history and rapid growth of the L.S.E., "on whose buildings," it was said before the war, "the concrete never sets," is outside the scope of this book, though the Webbs long took an active part in its life and Sidney was for many years its Professor of Public Administration (unpaid). But it is important to underline the word Science in its name. It was the firm conviction of Sidney, as of Herbert Spencer's former pupil Beatrice, that the study of economics and of sociology is essentially a science and not a branch of deductive philosophy, and that effective thought on either of these subjects is prevented and bedevilled by the classical attempts to formulate them by *a priori* reasoning from "first principles", either without studying the actual facts or by relegating them to a quite lower plane of thought. They would not, of course, ever have been foolish enough to make the claim that social science could be studied exactly as though it were a physical science such as chemistry, or that ultimate values could be left out of account; they had their own stoutly-held values and expressed them quite clearly time and time again. The meaning which they attached to the word science was nearer to that of the French *science* or the Latin *scientia* ("knowledge") than the very narrow sense which it has acquired in some circles to-day. But they did very strongly hold that all hypotheses about the conduct of economic and social

218

affairs should be tested by a continuous comparison with the actual ascertainable facts—*Measurement and Publicity* was a Webbian slogan coined some twenty-five years later; they also believed that a dispassionate study of the facts would often yield conclusions quite unexpected by the student or by anyone else. For these reasons, they believed that the *method* of study in economics and sociology ought to approximate much more nearly than hitherto to the methods of the natural sciences; so Webb, with the assistance of his friend R. B. Haldane, succeeded in getting the L.S.E. degree in Economics recognised as a *science* degree in the reorganised University of London. The many thousands of ex-London students who write B.Sc.(Econ.) after their names owe it to Webb's efforts.

There is no space here to describe the reorganisation of London University, which took final shape in 1898 and turned it from a mere examining and degree-granting body into a teaching institution, with Webb as a member of its Senate. This, however, like the foundation of L.S.E. and the Technical Education Committee, was part of a process which, round about the turn of the century, was drawing the Webbs more into politics proper (and thus back into London Society). It was at this time that they followed, if they did not exactly formulate, the policy known as "permeation".

In a sense, "permeation" had been the policy of the Fabian Society for many years. Knowing themselves to be few in numbers though full of ability, and neither hoping nor desiring to become a large organisation, the Fabians had never thought of a "Fabian Government" coming into existence under that name. (Nor, indeed, of a "Labour Government"; before 1900 there was no Labour Party, and even after that it was scarcely worth the Webbs' attention before 1914). The Fabian idea was if possible to convert future Ministers and persons in key positions to Fabianism, or, as that would not be possible in most cases, to station Fabian advisers at their elbows, and to persuade parties, groups, committees, councils or what not, to endorse pieces of a Socialist programme as it were unawares. For these purposes it did not matter in theory whether the persons or groups to be "permeated" were Tories, Liberals (or Anarchists!); the Fabians were ready to try their hand on anyone, and in fact the nineteenth-century history of British social development gave some colour to the view that, for bringing about separate pieces of social change, one major Party was about as hopeful as the other. Disraeli had enfranchised the town artisans, Gladstone the miners and the agricultural workers; the Liberals had given the Trade Unions recognition, but the Tories had allowed them to picket during trade disputes.

During the latter half of the century, of course, the politically-minded working man had generally been a Liberal; early working-class candidates for Parliament stood as Liberals. But in the last decade confidence in the Liberal Party was shaken on all sides. It had split over the Irish question; its zeal for reform seemed to have waned or vanished; Chamberlain, once its greatest social crusader, had now to all appearance deserted social problems in favour of imperialist adventure, while the caucus system which he had set up within the party was unwilling to make concessions to labour or even to encourage the adoption of working-class candidates. The leadership of the party was weak and divided, and there was considerable antagonism between the supporters of Sir William Harcourt, the originator of death duties, and those of the rich racing peer Lord Rosebery. Though the Fabians and the Radicals had by clever tactics forced upon the party's 1891 conference a policy of advanced social reform (the "Newcastle Programme"), they did not believe that the existing leadership would carry it out: in contrast to their position among the Progressives of London, they had not sufficient support among the potential Ministers and influential members of Parliament. It seemed to some of the Fabians that there was much to be gained by bringing together in discussion Liberals of their way of thought and intelligent Tories who could be awakened to the inevitability of *some* social change, particularly if there could be added to the discussion civil servants and administrators already inoculated with Fabian ideas.

In this way was "permeation" born; on the Liberal side its chief participants were Haldane and Edward Grey—and to a less extent Asquith; among the Tories the chief prize was Arthur Balfour, Prime Minister from 1902 to 1905, a philosopher-politician who always had great charm for Beatrice; and a good deal of the discussion took place at dinner-parties in 41 Grosvenor Road—so convenient for the House of Commons. Beatrice was still not then a politician in her own right; she was

220

a politician's lady running a *salon*. But her personality was beginning to take on more and more importance in the political world; Grosvenor Road was beginning to be a place which counted; and her Diaries show how much she enjoyed those evenings and lunches of discussion and high-principled semi-intrigue over the future of the London County Council, the London School of Economics, the party system, the Balfour Education Bill, and so forth—enjoyed them all the more, as she candidly pointed out, because the standard of living, of dress, and of general conversation was more like "what she was brought up to" than that of Trade Unionists and their wives at Co-opera-tive teas. She may have liked hobnobbing with Trade Unionists —at intervals—and she certainly set no store by rich food and drink. But amenities, pleasant rooms and efficient service, and, above all, conversation that was brilliant as well as purposeful, was another matter. She would not have been human had she not been pleased to find herself reviving the social successes of her youth while pursuing an object which she felt well worth-while; but only an exceptionally strong and honest mind would have admitted it so frankly.

The Webbs took to "permeation" the more readily because they and Bernard Shaw and a number of other Fabians dis-agreed with Liberals like Lloyd George and with almost all other Socialists on the issue of the South African War, on which they regarded the champions of the Boer Republics as sentimental reactionaries and pointed out (as was of course perfectly correct) that neither Milner's supporters nor Kruger's cared a hoot about the welfare of the great majority of the inhabitants of South Africa—the blacks. They encouraged them to believe that the "Liberal-imperialists" might achieve a re-shuffle of power which would result in a Government whose home policy would run on cautiously Fabian lines. These calculations came to an abrupt end when Campbell-Bannerman won his smashing majority in 1906; the major success of the "permeation" period was the Education Acts of 1902-03, and a minor success Balfour's appointment of Beatrice to the 1905 Poor Law Commission.

The Education Acts were on the face of it a triumph of Fabian policy and method. The original idea, that of transferring primary education from the control of *ad hoc* School Boards to that of the generalised local authorities (strengthened by the

221

inclusion for this purpose of "outside experts") and of solving, or partially solving, the century-old conflict between Church and Chapel by giving, under conditions, support out of the rates to schools run by religious denominations, came from Robert Morant, a Civil Servant; it was recast and written up, in a Tract called *The Educational Muddle and the Way Out,* by Sidney Webb, a Socialist; the Tract was circulated in galley form by a Conservative Minister, Sir John Gorst, to his civil service staff; the resulting Bills were brought in by Balfour, the Conservative Prime Minister; they were passed, and became the basis of the whole present structure of English primary education. But the indignation aroused by them contributed in a small degree to the fall of Balfour's Government and in a large degree to Webb's loss of influence in the London County Council.

Whatever the merits or demerits of the Acts, they serve very well to illustrate certain gaps in the Webbs' political imagination which go far to account for the ill-success of "permeation". Sidney was convinced of the rightness of the policy. Himself an agnostic at the most, he believed, and asserted strongly, that to refuse grant-aid to schools run by religious communities would not merely be unjust but would also mean that the children of such communities would be grievously under-educated. Like Morant, however, he was entirely unaware of the strength of the non-rational nonconformist hatred of Rome and the Anglican Church, derived from a long history of semi-class sectarian warfare, which induced a number of leading Nonconformists to undergo the mild martyrdom of having their goods distrained for refusing to pay the education rate; and he also underrated the disappointment of the enthusiastic members of the London School Board (several of them Fabians) at losing their independence to the L.C.C.

The Webbs discounted, or failed to observe, the emotional strength of the opposition to the Education Bills, as they had previously discounted the emotional strength of the opposition to the South African War. Psychologists may suggest that their own spiritual content with each other had something to do with their failure to appreciate the deeper currents of popular feeling; it is in any event a fact that they were altogether unaware of the growing wave of racialism that was soon to sweep away the Tories in the biggest landslide in British electoral history, and, as a corollary, failed to make connection with the leaders who held the real power in the next decade. They despised Campbell-Bannerman and never got on terms with Lloyd George. The result was that during the exciting years of 1906 to 1910 they were without influence in high politics and to some extent under suspicion as intriguers who had failed; had it not been for the Poor Law Commission that period might have looked very jejune.

THE POOR LAW

"Permeation" of the older political parties together had in fact failed as a policy by the end of 1905. Unless the new Liberal Government could be diverted into Socialism, which in view of its thumping majority and the inclusion in its ranks of politicians like Asquith and Winston Churchill was highly unlikely, the only future for the Socialists lay in the little new Labour Party with its membership of 30, mostly elected by agreement with the Liberals. But in 1906-14 the Labour Party was not Socialist—though it included Socialists—had no defined policy and no individual membership. It did not look at all capable of becoming the government of the country within measurable time, and though the Fabian Society had taken part in its foundation and was officially part of it, the leaders believed it to be of barely marginal usefulness, and some of the rank-and-file, particularly ardent Socialists who joined the Society during the Radical boom, came, under syndicalist influences, to regard it as an actual drag on working-class progress. Sidney, with Shaw, continued to work actively on the Fabian Executive and in producing Tracts, lectures, and propaganda generally, but they took no part in Labour Party politics, and Beatrice's attention was almost entirely occupied by the Poor Law Commission and the national campaign which followed it.

The Royal Commission on the Poor Law, set up by the Balfour Government as almost its dying act, was not the result of any widespread public outcry, but of a general *malaise* and a feeling on all sides that something must be done about the Poor Law. Nominally, the relief of the poor was still conducted according to the Act of 1834—that Act which, rushed through Parliament by a triumphant combination of doctrinaire Utilitarians, Malthusians and enthusiastic bureaucrats, had

223

driven parts of the country nearly to civil war before it could be enforced, and was more bitterly hated by the working classes than any other legislation which remained on the Statute-Book for over a hundred years.

The system had, of course, undergone a good deal of alteration since the days of Brougham and Edwin Chadwick. The original purpose, to make the lot of *anyone* who received *any* relief out of public funds harder and less desirable than that of the worst-paid labourer in employment, and to segregate husbands on relief from their wives, lest they should breed and add to the number of hungry mouths, had been steadily modified, partly because Victorian economic prosperity undermined the theoretical basis for such savagery and partly because growing humanitarianism—combined with such fierce propaganda as Dickens' *Oliver Twist*—made human beings less and less willing to be responsible for it. The system began to leak all through its length. Guardians of the Poor, and their Relieving Officers, refused to tear families apart because the wage-earner had fallen out of work or because illness had eaten up their meagre savings, or to insist that all Personal possessions should be sold or pawned before they would grant any relief, or to make their workhouses correspond as nearly as possible to penal establishments.

This humanising, however much in line with popular feeling, was undoubtedly contrary to the intentions of the original Act, and was, moreover, necessarily a piecemeal effort. If one Board of Guardians strove to discharge its functions in as kindly a manner as might be, and its Relieving Officer to think of himself as a welfare worker rather than a supplementary agent of the police, the next-door Board was pretty sure to have nothing in mind but saving the rates and to employ the nearest possible approach to a Bumble that it could find. There was thus a continuing state of uncertainty—the "shadow of the House"—i.e. the workhouse—darkening the lives of that enormous part of the population which, before the days of social insurance, was always in danger of being suddenly reduced to penury; and the central administrators, the men in charge of the Poor Law at the Local Government Board, also complained that it was impossible for them to carry out their task in any logical mannor if individual Boards of Guardians were sporadically able to alter the conditions of relief and get away with it.

To this general conviction that the system was not working as it ought to work were added three new factors: the revelations of Charles Booth's London enquiry—supplemented by the studies of investigators like Seebohm Rowntree, Lady Bell, and others in the provinces—of the shocking conditions of poverty in which millions of people lived before ever they had recourse to the Poor Law; the big trade fluctuations of 1878 and onwards, which threw out of work many whose characters could not possibly be made to bear the blame for their misfortunes; and the organisation of the unskilled and their uprising on occasions like the London Dock Strike, which induced in the governing class some fear that if no mitigation of living conditions was granted to the rabble they might be led by fiery Socialists and left-wing Trade Unionists to come and take it for themselves. Keir Hardie, "the M.P. for the Unemployed", as he was called, might be howled down by well-fed persons when he rose to protest in the Commons; but cooler heads among the Ministers knew well enough that he would not be howled down outside.

The Government appointed a Royal Commission—a large and representative Commission under the chairmanship of a Tory ex-Cabinet Minister. Nine of its members were poor law administrators; half-a-dozen or so were prominently associated with the Charity Organisation Society, a body of public-spirited persons who endeavoured to regulate indiscriminate and anti-social distribution of alms, and whose tactless zeal often earned them as much hatred as the Poor Law itself. There were four representatives of the Churches, two political economists, a Trade Union official, George Lansbury—and Beatrice Webb.

It is not very certain what the Government intended to be the result of the Commission; possibly they did not know themselves. But certain officials, particularly Mr. James Davy, the head of the Poor Law Division of the Local Government Board, had decided well in advance what the result was to be. They wanted the system tidied up, and they wanted the Commissioners to recommend "reversion to the Principles of 1834 as regards policy, to stem the tide of philanthropic influence that was sweeping away the old embankment of deterrent tests." (Beatrice Webb's *Diaries*). This they were to be gently led to do by evidence carefully arranged and prepared by Davy's own subordinates. Davy, however, in a moment of astonishing

225

incaution, confined his intentions to the one member of the Commission from whom he should have concealed them. "To-day at lunch," wrote Mrs. Webb gleefully, "I put Mr. Lansbury on his guard against this policy."

Her own idea of the Commission was entirely different. She wanted it to call its own evidence, conduct its own investigations, and finally to produce a Report as revolutionary as the Report of 1834, calling for an entirely new treatment of the problem of destitution based on the principle of prevention and the establishment of what the Webbs called The Standard Minimum of Civilised Life. Herein she failed; the majority of her fellow-Commissioners were not prepared either to work as hard as she was, or to undertake stiff fundamental thought about the creation of an entirely new system; even had they been willing it is improbable that they would have come to the same conclusions, not only because Beatrice, as she readily admitted, tended to harry and bully rather than to persuade the slow-moving or hostile minds, but also because what she was suggesting amounted, in fact, to an instalment of Socialism which they were not in the least ready to receive. In fact, during the later years of the commission, she all but abandoned its sittings, devoting herself to making her own enquiries—in which she was helped by an army of secretaries partly paid for by Mrs. Bernard Shaw; and the Report which she got Sidney to write out for her was finally signed only by herself, Lansbury, Chandler the Trade Unionist, and the Rev. Russell Wakefield.

It was a very good thing, both for posterity and for the Webbs' own reputation, that Beatrice stuck so determinedly to her guns and did not soften the outlines of her own scheme so as to secure the adherence of a majority. For there is very little evidence to show that Asquith's Government would have carried out any lesser reform of the Poor Law; even the proposals of the majority were completely shelved. Beatrice's intransigence, however, produced a *Minority Report* which is one of the great State Papers of this century and which, whatever its immediate fate, has been an inspiration and a guide to social workers and social reformers right down to our own day, when the social security, State medical service, and full employment policy for which she then asked are part of the law and practice of the land. It also produced a nation-wide campaign against poverty which, though it failed in its immediate objective, both roused the country and provided political baptism for thousands who subsequently played a part in building up the Socialist movement and the Labour Party. The National Council for the Prevention of Destitution, as the new campaigning organisation was called, reached in a few months a membership of 16,000—more than five times any figure previously achieved by the Fabian Society; it enrolled as speakers and writers distinguished persons from all parties and all walks of life; and the greater part of its day-to-day work, both in London and the provinces was done, unpaid, by hundreds of enthusiastic voluntary workers, many of them very young. Beatrice, presiding over all this activity, writing pamphlets, leaflets and articles for its journal *The Crusade,* organising committees, and taking on lecture tours of considerable strenuousness, enjoyed herself immensely. Up till then, her public life had been lived largely behind the scenes, in private rooms and in discussions with a few; now, at fifty, she suddenly found herself an important figure with a national audience.

She enjoyed herself; but the campaign, as a campaign, was a failure. It could not have been otherwise. For the real purpose of the N.C.P.D., as it developed, was to force upon the capitalist system, by means of a supposedly all-party agitation, the dose of Socialism which Beatrice had failed to induce the Royal Commission to swallow. In a sense, it was to be a noisy "permeation" of the nation by 16,000 persons instead of by a handful of instructed Fabians. But Edwardian England was not at all inclined for a dose of Socialism; it was distressed about starvation and disease, and shocked at the administrative muddles and tyrannies which the Poor Law enquiries had brought to light, but it did not at all accept the view that destitution could not be prevented except by major change. When the Boards of Guardians and the Local Government Board, under stress of the "revelations", made some efforts to put their houses in order, and above all when Lloyd George, realising that something must be done to appease the feeling aroused by the Webbs, went to Germany for inspiration and produced his "ninepence-for-fourpence" contributory insurance scheme, the non-Socialist supporters of the N.C.P.D. sank back with a sigh of relief. Even though the Poor Law was to remain, the destitution due to sickness and (in a few occupations) to sudden storms of unemployment would be at least alleviated—and who, in a competitive world, could ask for more? Why should the Socialists, Webbs and I.L.P. alike, go on grumbling and demanding the *abolition* of the Poor Law and the establishment of a national minimum? Could they not take what they were offered and be reasonably thankful? As Beatrice admitted, "all the steam went out" of her great organisation; the Webbs, never inclined to mourn over lost causes, accepted the event, wound up the N.C.P.D. and *The Crusade,* and, tired with all their efforts, set off on a year's world-tour. Before she left, however, Beatrice had pronounced the final epitaph on their permeative activities. The older parties were hopeless; what was now essential was to form a strong and independent Socialist political party.

FABIAN RESEARCH AND THE LABOUR PARTY

The first movements they made in this direction were unsuccessful. Up to 1914 the infant Labour Party had no Socialist policy —no defined programme at all—and the Webbs barely took account of it; after the 1910 elections, indeed, when the Liberals lost their commanding majority, it was committed to keeping the Asquith Government in office, and many of the most vigorous Trade Unionists, those, for example, who led the great strike wave of 1911-14, openly despised it. The Webbs neither liked nor respected the I.L.P. of Keir Hardie and Ramsay MacDonald, which was much the largest Socialist society; their thought was to build a new Socialist Party out of the Fabian Society and what was left of the N.C.P.D. But they had reckoned without certain factors, of which the most important were the discontent with Parliamentary constitutionalism— shown by such diverse persons as the militant Suffragettes, the Unionists of Ulster, G. K. Chesterton, Hilaire Belloc, and George Lansbury—the slowly rising cost of living, producing "industrial unrest", and the emergence of an anti-collectivist opposition within the Fabian Society itself.

The Fabian Society had shared in the post-1906 Radical revival—a "little boom", as Beatrice rather patronisingly described it in her *Diary*—but the new membership from the first differed considerably from the faithful hardworking hundreds who for nearly two decades had followed the line of *Facts for Socialists* and *Fabian Essays.* It was argumentative, restless, and highly critical of the leaders. H. G. Wells, the Webbs' own recruit, started a vigorous anarchic opposition movement, aimed, insofar as it could be said to be aimed at all, at turning the Fabian Society into a large imposing body with large imposing publications and offices, in which the Samurai of his *Modern Utopia* could be trained; when he indignantly resigned, defeated by Shaw's greatly superior debating powers and Sidney's cruel command of facts, his place was almost immediately filled by one opposition after another, differing in their immediate proposals, but all more or less condemnatory of the leaders. The last of these, the Guild Socialist opposition led by G. D. H. Cole and William Mellor (long afterwards editor of the *Daily Herald*) was the most formidable, both because its protagonists were of very high intellectual quality and of industry as great as that of the pioneer Fabians, and because they had a coherent "functionalist", revolutionary philosophy to oppose to the pure gradualist *Etatisme,* tempered only by some concessions to organised Trade Unionism, to which the Webbs were at that time committed. This opposition, which included a great many of the ex-workers for the N.C.P.D., came on one occasion within one vote of capturing the Fabian Society; it did capture, and staffed with its own supporters, the Fabian Research Department, which—ironically enough—Beatrice had herself created as an organisation in which talented and vigorous young University men might do good work in the collectivist cause, and it certainly was in no mood to be enrolled in a political party controlled and directed by the older Fabians.

The Fabian—later Labour—Research Department had a long and active life, and did a great deal of work, largely in the field of Trade Unionism which had been the Partnership's own first love. And though feelings ran high and harsh words were uttered, the connection was kept up until the L.R.D. came under Communist control; Beatrice, more tolerant on this occasion than Sidney, recognised that these young men, however aggravating, were as enthusiastic and as single-minded as she could have wished, and made real efforts to understand what they were driving at, while they on their part, however much they abused the collectivist pair, never refused either to discuss or honestly to collaborate where they felt collaboration was possible. Nevertheless, during that period, the period of the Webbs' greatest unpopularity, when Wells in *The New Machiavelli* drew his venomous picture of their political factory in their "hard little house", the main contribution they made to the cause they had at heart was neither a political party nor any sort of organisation but the *New Statesman.*

The original idea of the *New Statesman* was in essence "permeatory". The Webbs wanted to create an *independent* journal of opinion which would *independently* lead all intelligent persons to embrace Socialist views; it must therefore not be controlled by any political party or group—even the Fabian Society; and yet it must somehow be assured of sufficient support to get on its feet. The method they devised was (a) to offer reduced annual subscriptions to members of the Fabian Society (which secured for the new journal an initial roll of over 2,000); (b) to promise contributions from the best-known Fabians, including themselves and Shaw; (c) to appoint a young Fabian, Clifford Sharp, as Editor, and to give him practically a free hand for dealing with contributors.

From a prestige point of view the venture was an immediate success, for two main reasons. First, because of the high quality of the individual contributors. Shaw, it is true, found that the paper— and the opinions of the Editor—failed to come up to his standard, and soon ceased to write regularly, though he did give it his famous pamphlet, *Commonsense About the War;* but the names of Sir John Squire, Desmond MacCarthy, S. K. Ratcliffe, Emil Davies, C. W. Saleeby ("Lens"), and Robert Lynd ("Y.Y."), as well as those of the Webbs themselves, and at a later date C. M. Lloyd and G. D. H. Cole, as regular contributors, provided a sufficient guarantee of standard. Secondly, because it was more than a weekly review, but in its famous *Supplements* gave its readers really solid matter to bite on. *Commonsense About the War* was such a Supplement; another was the first study for a League of Nations, produced by Leonard Woolf at the Webbs' instigation; others were weighty research studies on Co-operation, industrial insurance, the professional organisation of teachers, State and municipal enterprise, and so forth—studies longer than Fabian *Tracts,* but not so long as the Webbs' books.

Financially, however, it had to wait for success; to the usual birthpangs was added the difficulty of the 1914 war, breaking out when it was only 18 months old. It was not until long after the war was over that it got itself on to a firm footing, ate up competitor after competitor in the weekly market, and became gradually, as monumental a feature of English life as the London School of Economics, the Webbs watching it grow without interference and with a feeling of friendly pride. Meanwhile, however, world events had made the Webbs, at long last, "clerks to Labour" and had led them to look for their Socialist Party within the Labour Party itself.

Their entry during the war into the counsels of the Labour Party was as nearly accidental as anything can be. No more than the great majority of their countrymen had they foreseen the events of August 1914; they had very little concern with "foreign affairs" as such, though they were mildly interested in Paris municipal government, nationalised enterprises in other countries, and in meeting distinguished foreign Socialists. Their attitude to the issues of war and peace was so little defined that, when war seemed imminent, they were invited to take part both in demonstrating against it and (by the same group a few days later) in a patriotic meeting. They were perfectly prepared, therefore, once war had broken out and its continuance seemed inevitable, to accept it as a fact of nature and try to work within the limits set by war conditions.

This attitude of theirs was, in fact, also the attitude of the bulk of the Labour movement, at least in the beginning. In accordance with anti-war resolutions passed by the Socialist International, the Labour leaders had summoned a great delegate conference, with representatives from the Labour Party, the Socialist Societies, the Trades Union Congress, the General Federation of Trade Unions, the largest individual Trade Unions, the Co-operative movement, and the school-teachers. This was the first really representative gathering of all wings of the working-class; but, by the time it had assembled, war had been declared, Belgium had been invaded, and it was clear that the opportunity for protestations had passed, and that what was now needed was organisation to protect the standards of the workers against wartime encroachments. The Conference, therefore, set up a representative executive called by the clumsy title of War Emergency Workers' National Committee; Arthur

231

Henderson, by then Labour Party Secretary, became its chairman, and Sidney Webb its chief draftsman.

The first and continuing preoccupation of the Committee was to *defend* working-class standards. Few of those who remember only the second world war, in which working-class co-operation was so instantly recognised as essential, and secured by means of price-fixing, rationing, food subsidies and the like without question raised, can really imagine how little of this was suggested in 1914; recruiting meetings and military bands were supposed to be a sufficient inducement to the workers; prices, it was assumed, would rise in a "natural" manner, but any attempt by Labour to cash in on a scarcity situation was unpatriotic, almost treasonable, and should be sternly repressed. So the historian finds the War Workers' Committee initiating campaigns on such subjects as adequate allowances for the dependants of serving soldiers and sailors—including unmarried women and their children; provision of canteens for soldiers and munition workers, and day nurseries for the children; control of rents and of mortgage interest—this, through Webb's ingenuity, being demanded in joint deputation by the workers and the property-owners; fixing of maximum food prices; and the right of the working classes to representation on all official bodies concerned with their problems. At the same time, it was actively supporting, wherever necessary, the struggles of the Trade Unions in the engineering and other industries to prevent the breaking-down of established wage standards by the importation of women at starvation rates.

But as the war went on the Labour movement, and particularly the association of Henderson and Webb, began to reach out to much more positive functions; for this there were two reasons. The first was simply the growth in importance and organisation of the workers, particularly in the war—the membership of the T.U.C. more than doubled between 1913 and 1918. However much their "betters" disliked that fact, they could not ignore it; they might make strikes illegal but they could not jail 200,000 Welsh miners when coal was so urgently needed; they had to bargain and concede, and increasingly to invite the opinion and even the collaboration of Trade Union leaders on new schemes for Government control of industry. This tendency was crystallised in the public mind when Lloyd George invited

Henderson to become a member of his Coalition cabinet; Labour was recognised as a partner, albeit a very junior partner, and one, as later events showed, to be firmly put in its place if it became presumptuous.

Late in the war, however, the second important factor emerged. Particularly after the Russian Revolution, which caused the workers to feel that there was a chance of a people's peace and their rulers to be more determined on a fight to a finish, it began to appear that Labour was developing a definite policy of its own, not merely upon rents, wages, and prices, but upon international and imperial affairs, which was widely at variance with that of the Tory-Liberal Coalition. After Henderson had been virtually frozen out of the War Cabinet because he disagreed with their policy towards Russia, the split became patent, and its first-fruits was the pamphlet *Labour's War Aims* (1917), a statement of policy upon international and colonial affairs, owing much to Leonard Woolf's studies mentioned earlier, which proclaimed to a war-weary world a coherent, intelligible alternative to jungle politics—and laid down a foreign policy faithfully followed by the Labour Party for half a generation, until world unemployment and the Nazis brought the jungle back again.

The eager reception of this pamphlet in many other countries beside Britain encouraged Webb and Henderson and their collaborators to go further and turn the Labour Party into a real Party, a real potential Opposition instead of a pressure group. The result of their efforts, in the last year of the war, was the new constitution of the Labour Party, the comprehensive political programme drafted by Webb under the title of *Labour and the New Social Order,* the departure of Labour, as soon as the war was over, from the Coalition, and its return to Parliament, in the 1918 "coupon" election, as a real Opposition—tiny in numbers but yet larger than Asquith's dissentient Liberals.

The constitution was largely of Webb's drafting, the programme entirely so, as the language shows. The importance of the former was that by creating Divisional Labour Parties, with individual membership, throughout the country, it for the first time enabled persons to join the Labour Party as such, not indirectly through a Trade Union or Socialist Society, and thereby reduced to some extent the dependence of the Party on

233

Q

Trade Union money; the importance of the second needs no stressing. For the first time in its history, the Party had a definite policy—and it was a collectivist-Socialist policy[1]. It was a clear and comprehensive statement—more so than some of those which followed it—and if the electorate, drunk with prospects of hanging the Kaiser and making Germany pay, declined for the moment to accept it, that only indicated the need for more and more intensive Socialist education. And there was Sidney Webb, since 1915 on the Executive Committee of the Labour Party and having come within a few votes of being returned to Parliament for the University of London, ready to embark upon this education—and Beatrice to stand by his side.

COMMITTEES AND BOOKS—SANKEY AND SEAHAM

It should not be thought that the activities of the Webbs, during the war years, were entirely confined to laying the foundations for the new Labour Party. Apart from their (sometimes stormy) collaboration with Guild Socialists in the Labour Research Department, and the writing of books like *How to Pay for the War* (which suggested an extensive programme of socialisation), Sidney, in 1916, was made a member of the enormous After-War Reconstruction Committee, which spawned so many hopeful sub-committees, and in connection with these did a good deal of drafting and writing for the press. Beatrice, after a period of ill-health, served on the Local Government Panel of the same body, to which she reintroduced her eight-year-old proposals for doing away with the Poor Law. "Informed opinion" had moved on since 1909; on this occasion Beatrice effectively carried the other committee members with her to draft the unanimous Maclean Report—which, along with most of the other efforts of the Reconstruction Committee, disappeared in the orgy of "return to normalcy" which followed the war. A similar fate befell her efforts on another official body, the War Cabinet Committee on Women in Industry, set up in 1918 in response to an angry outbreak of propaganda, to report upon whether the Government had or had not observed its pledge that where women were employed on work previously done by men they should be paid

---

[1] "Collectivist" must be emphasised. *Labour and the New Social Order* did little to solve the problem of "workers' control".

at men's rates. The majority of the Committee exonerated the Government; Beatrice, reaching the conclusion that a pledge had been made and been flagrantly broken, wrote a Minority Report in which she went well outside her brief and argued the whole case for equal pay between the sexes. Her report was reissued by the Fabian Society under the title *The Wages of Men and Women—Should They be Equal?* and remains a minor classic, its arguments unrefuted, and its conclusions mostly unapplied, to this day. But in the immediate post-war climate of opinion the work which the two of them did on Government account—including that of Sidney as a member of the Committee on Trusts and Profiteering, which after the end of the war collected so much damning fact about the operations of capitalism *redivivus*—could have very little direct effect. Much more important was Sidney's post-war connection with the Miners' Federation over the Sankey Coal Commission.

It was not only in Russia that the war created revolutionary feeling. Political revolutions happened also in Germany, Austria, Hungary; and among the victorious powers the feeling was only less strong. There were mutinies in the armies in France; the soldiers would not stay enlisted and were expecting a new world for heroes when they came out; in many industrial centres of Britain, particularly Liverpool and the Clyde, there were large and menacing outbreaks; the London police went on strike; the railwaymen demanded nationalisation of the railways and improvement of conditions; and the Miners' Federation, three-quarters of a million strong, asked for wage increases, reduced hours, and the nationalisation of the mines, and threatened a national mining strike if these were not immediately granted.

The overwhelming Parliamentary majority which Lloyd George had secured by rushing an election clearly did not at all reflect the economic mood of the electors; nevertheless, those who had been elected, the "hard-faced men who had done well out of the war", were quite determined to continue to do well and even better out of the peace. Wartime controls, it was certain, would have to yield quickly to the headlong price-and-profits boom which distinguished the next two years; but it looked very much as if industrial strife amounting possibly to civil war and revolution might accompany them.

Lloyd George and his Cabinet played for time; they let the

235

soldiers demobilise themselves anyhow and minimised the resulting confusion by the "cushioning" device of a State allowance, at the unprecedented rate of 29/- per week, to be paid to all workers demobilised from the armed forces or the war industries until they found work; they rushed through an Act to prevent wage reductions and provided subsidies to the local authorities for building houses at whatever prices the building material combines chose to exact; they dealt with individual strikes as best they could. The most formidable threat, however, was that of the Miners' Federation; and this the Government met by setting up a Statutory Commission representative equally of miners and coalowners, with three outside experts appointed by each side, to survey the whole situation. The chairman was the late Lord Sankey, and Bonar Law, speaking as Acting Premier, twice undertook that the Government would carry out the recommendations of the Commission "in the spirit and in the letter."

It is a matter of history how that promise was broken, once the immediate urgency was past and a mining strike no longer a thing to be avoided at all costs; how the majority report recommending nationalisation was discussed for many weary months and finally shelved; and the results of this policy in the General Strike and afterwards. What concerns us here is the part played by Sidney Webb and its results.

The hearings of the Sankey Commission were public, on the crimson benches of the House of Lords; they excited, for a time enormous interest, when distinguished peers who were also royalty-owners were arraigned at the bar to account to society for their incomes; and in Robert Smillie, the Miners' Federation of Great Britain leader, and their three experts, Sir Leo Chiozza Money, R. H. Tawney, and Sidney Webb, the miners had outstanding champions, against whom the representatives of the mineowners could make little headway. Webb was the statistical expert and the best cross-examiner among them; he drove the witnesses remorselessly from point to point; and when all was over the Miners' Federation showed their gratitude first by using their large block vote to return him to the Labour Party Executive at the head of the poll in 1919, and in 1920, after it had become fairly clear that nothing was coming of the Sankey

Report, to ask him to stand for the Parliamentary Division of
Seaham Harbour in Durham.

The request was partly of his own doing. For when, during
the dismal summer of that year, a group of miners' leaders came
to ask what he would advise them to do in face of their industrial failure, he suggested that they should turn to political action
to redress their grievances, that they should send their own men
to Parliament, and men, moreover, to express their views and
drive home their points to a hostile House. Nevertheless, when
they so promptly took him at his word and assured him that the
seat was a safe winner, he found the decision difficult. He was
over 60, not a good age at which to take on a new job, still less
a job so incalculable, so exhausting, and at times so exasperating,
as sitting in Parliament as a member of a small and not very
experienced or gifted Opposition. The days before his marriage,
when an eventual seat in Parliament had seemed a matter of
course, were far behind him; he had built up on different lines a
full and satisfying joint life with Beatrice, which had become
more closely integrated during the past 10 years, after he left
the London County Council and she took to active work in the
Fabian Society and the Labour Party; and the thought of the
hours of physical separation from her which a Parliamentary life
would entail was depressing. Nor could he look to find much
compensation in Parliamentary honours; though an admirable
lecturer, he was no orator (and, in actual fact was not a success
in debate except on subjects like rating which he knew inside
out); and though he might reasonably expect to be a competent
Minister if a Labour Government were ever formed—which in
1920 did not seem likely to happen soon— he had no desire for
office or power, and certainly would become no better known by
it. Parliament, in short, would be no treat to him, and would
leave his wife lonely.

It was thus a real sacrifice of "the good life" that the two of
them were asked to make. How much they hesitated we do not
know; we only know that they came quite firmly to the conclusion that the sacrifice ought to be made, that the interests of the
Labour Party—by then, it will be remembered, accepted by
them as the political party making for Socialism—would be very
ill-served if those who had the ability, could afford the time and
expense, and had won the admiring trust of the industrial

workers, refused, when asked, to serve it in the Parliamentary field. They took the public-spirited course; and it is pleasant to be able to record that the initial stages, at least, turned out much more agreeable than they had anticipated. They found new interests, and in the Durham miners and their wives new friends of the solid working-class "salt-of-the-earth" type whom Beatrice Potter had once known in Lancashire but whom they had scarcely met since *Industrial Democracy* was finished.

For, having taken on the job, they intended to do it thoroughly. They read up the history of mining, Durham mining in particular, till they had it at their fingers' ends; then, before ever they set eyes on the constituency they mapped it out and card-indexed all the organisations—religious, educational, and social—into which they intended to insinuate themselves with lectures on such non-political-sounding subjects as the History of Mining, Social Services, and the like. Many times during the year they took the long journey to Seaham and spent days there lecturing, answering questions, taking classes, or simply having tea with the miners' wives. Beatrice wrote them a weekly News Letter and provided a circulating library of solid literature sent down from London : she called the organisation "the University of Seaham" and often praised the natural good manners and open-minded intelligence of her students there. Sidney, characteristically, produced within a year of his adoption the *Story of the Durham Miners,* to tell his constituents things that they did not know about themselves. After all this intensive activity, it is not surprising that when the election came he was returned with the resounding majority of 11,800 votes, or that Seaham Harbour was his as long as he cared to hold it. If by work in one constituency Socialism could have been built in Britain, the Webbs would have built it.

But, of course, it could not. Apart from the avowed political opponents, who would have to be converted or outvoted, the Labour Party and Labour supporters themselves left a good deal to be desired as instruments of social change. True, the Labour Party was now a real party with a real membership— strengthened on the intellectual side by a number of pacifists, internationalists, and anti-imperialists who had left the Liberal ranks during or after the war; and it was equipped with a vigorous Socialist programme. But it was not so well equipped for carrying it out, either in personnel or in general appeal; a large number of the M.P.s who survived the "coupon" election were pro-war Trade Unionists of no particular skill or brains, their leader being an undistinguished miners' official; they did not really look as though they could be taken seriously in politics.

The Webbs set themselves, patiently and persistently, to remedy this state of things. They urged upon Henderson and other officers reform of the Party organisation so as to make it more efficient, to get more vital research done and more effective propaganda—in view of the slenderness of the Party's purse and the unwillingness of some Trade Union (and other) officials to offer adequate pay or opportunity to brain-workers, this effort made little progress for a good many years. They made it their business to meet and discuss problems and policy with all the leaders who would discuss with them, and not only the leaders, but the rank-and-file M.P.s as well; even when subsequent elections had swollen the numbers of Parliamentary Labour to a comparatively enormous size they still managed to have all the M.P.s in batches to lunch. Beatrice invented a special organisation called the Half-Circle Club, where Labour women, the wives of M.P.s and the wives of Trade Unionists, might meet together for training in social *aplomb;* and the two of them kept a persistent look-out, as they had in Fabian days, for promising young men who might be brought into the movement.

Concurrently, they were writing and publishing a number of books intended to instruct Labour supporters and potential Labour supporters in the past, present, and future of Labour and Socialism. In 1920, they brought out a revised edition of *The History of Trade Unionism*—and distributed it at very cheap rates to branches of Trade Unions, Labour Parties, and adult education classes; in 1921 they produced a big book on *The Consumers' Co-operative Movement.* In 1920, in response to a request from the secretary of the International Socialist Bureau, they wrote their sole blue-print for Utopia, *A Constitution for the Socialist Commonwealth,* and in 1923 they followed this up with a long indignant indictment of existing conditions entitled *The Decay of Capitalist Civilisation,* which drew its examples largely from the information acquired by Sidney during his sessions with the Government Committee on Trusts. In all this activity they were attempting in effect to permeate the Labour movement, actual and potential, with Fabian ideas and Fabian technique, as they had long ago endeavoured to permeate all political parties alike. In his presidential address to the 1923 Party Conference Sidney made it perfectly clear what they hoped to achieve.

He was arguing that the chief fault of the civilisation of his own day was its immorality, its failure to take account of the fact that "morality, like economics, is part of the nature of things", and was saying that any plan for the future of society would fail unless it realised that the free competition postulated by *laissez-faire* Liberals no longer existed, that the "overweening influence" of rich persons in politics and society was a social danger, and that widespread unemployment was not merely socially dangerous but morally intolerable. He proceeded:

> "Let me insist on what our opponents habitually ignore, and indeed, what they seem intellectually incapable of understanding, namely *the inevitable gradualness* of our scheme of change. The very fact that Socialists have both principles and a programme appears to confuse nearly all their critics. If we state our principles we are told, 'That is not practicable'. When we recite our programme the objection is 'That is not Socialism'. But why, because we are idealists, should we be supposed to be idiots? For the Labour Party, it must be plain, Socialism is rooted in political democracy; which necessarily compels us to recognise that every step towards our goal is dependent upon gaining the assent and support of at least a numerical majority of the whole people. Thus, even if we aimed at revolutionizing everything at once, we should necessarily be compelled to make each particular change only at the time, and to the extent, and in the manner in which ten or fifteen million electors, in all sorts of conditions, of all sorts of temperaments, from Land's End to the Orkneys, could be brought to consent to it. How anyone can fear that the British electorate, whatever mistakes it may make or condone, can ever go too fast or too far, is incomprehensible to me. That, indeed, is the supremely valuable safeguard of any effective democracy."

This passage, including the italicised phrase which in after years was so angrily quoted against the Webbs but which, as we have seen was nothing new but inherent in the early Fabian doctrine, expresses with admirable clarity the Webbs' views about the development of democracy and Socialism in Britain up to the time when, influenced partly by the spectacular failure of the second Labour Government and partly by their experiences in the Soviet Union in 1932, they turned over to advocacy of Soviet Communism. This policy was what they were endeavouring to achieve in the Labour Party of the 'twenties; it remains to enquire how far they were successful.

EDUCATING THE LABOUR PARTY

The Webbs could not, of course, have either hoped or wished to have full entire guiding influence on the development of a growing party the bulk of whose strength lay far away from London, in the industrial districts of the north and of South Wales, to hold there the predominance they had held in the London County Council, for example. Apart from the strong influence exercised by the Trade Unions on finance and in counsel, the work of building the Party machine had to be done by hundreds of obscure persons up and down the country with whom they never came in contact. (The Fabian Society, which had been so energetic in the years before the war, after 1918 tended to do its direct political work through membership of local Labour Parties, and though the Webbs remained on its Executive Committee until the 'thirties, there is no evidence that they used it to bring influence upon the Party). Sidney was a member of the Party Executive until he resigned in 1924, and undoubtedly played his part in discussing questions of organisation. but his main contribution lay in persuading the central office to set up a number of Advisory Committees on different aspects of policy— which functioned with varying success according to the extent to which they succeeded in enlisting the services of able people who did not want to be paid. All were hampered by the non-existence of adequate research services.

In the realm of declared policy and programme, the Webbian principles had it almost entirely their own way. Henderson, who became daily a more dominating figure, was in almost complete agreement with them, and *Labour and the New Social Order* remained the Party gospel. Later programmes built upon it—or in some cases watered it down— and emphasised continually "the inevitability of gradualism"; the left-wing opposition, whether of the Guild Socialists and Syndicalists surviving from the war or of the Independent Labour Party clamouring for a more rapid advance, made as little permanent headway as did the new Communist Party attacking from outside. (The Webbs, in the 'twenties, were as anti-Communist and anti-Russian as the most ardent Social-Democrat could have desired). The policy of the Labour Party was firmly established as Fabian.

The newer and more far-reaching suggestions which they made in their own writings, however, received far less acceptance. In the *Constitution for a Socialist Commonwealth* they had proposed, with magnificent disregard for tradition, first, that the House of Commons should be cut into two halves labelled Political Parliament and Social Parliament, and secondly that the local government of Britain should be completely re-designed, that all existing units should be swept away, and their place taken by thousands of new units to be called Wards, which would be arbitrarily grouped, on grounds of convenience, in different ways for the administration of different local services. It must be admitted that both these suggestions disclose an astonishing (in historians) failure to understand or appreciate British tradition and the emotional attachment of the Briton to his Parliament, his city, or even to his parish, and they never had the faintest chance of gaining acceptance; they fired nobody's imagination.

Even their more imaginative appeals, however, fell on pretty stony ground. "Choose equality and flee greed", they called to their fellow-Socialists, echoing Matthew Arnold 40 years before, and they laid tremendous stress on the bad social manners produced by capitalism.

"We do not," they wrote in *The Decay of Capitalist Civilisation*, "think it compatible with the manners of a gentleman to give the governess a cheaper wine than is served to the other persons at table, nor even to put off the servants' hall with cheaper meat. But towards the great unknown mass of our fellow-citizens, *who are really sitting down with us at the world's table*, this principle of good manners is observed only by a tiny minority, even among those who think themselves well-bred."

So far, so good—even if the use of the words "governess" and "servants' hall" did not carry with them a slight *de-haut-en-bas* patronising implication not very pleasing to working-class members of the Labour Party, who did not like to think of them-

selves as part of the servants' hall[1]. But there was also a suggestion—often, no doubt unconscious—that what the Webbs
meant by "good social manners" was a universal living at the
standard of the Webbs, suitably adapted to those of lower
incomes, a ban on extravagance of any kind, and an abolition of
titles, honours, and all the apparatus of snobbery. Beatrice herself certainly felt this very strongly. She had "rational austerity"
in her bones; part, at any rate, of her subsequent falling-in-love
with the Soviet Union was its stern prohibition of unnecessary
luxury to members of the Russian Communist Party. And she
genuinely hated the hierarchical snobbery of London Society;
when, purely for administrative reasons, Sidney agreed to take a
peerage, she firmly refused to make any concessions with regard
to her own name. She was Mrs. Sidney Webb, and Mrs. Sidney
Webb she would remain, however much it upset the heads of the
Colonial Office or the wives of Governor-Generals.

In spite, however, of its past republican principles—now fast
fading as the occupant of the Throne made concessions to
democratic practice which must have made his grandmother
turn in her grave—the inarticulate feeling of the Labour Party
was not with Mrs. Webb. Like a very large number of his fellow-
countrymen, the rank-and-file member had an affection for a
lord—and the party leader, Ramsay MacDonald, shared this to
what later proved an unfortunate extent. Nor did the average
member—still less, of course, those outside the ranks of the party
—feel any strong sympathy with ideas of austere standards of
living imposed as a general social principle and not, as during
wartime, in response to a temporary state of national emergency.

Whatever the cause, Mrs. Webb did have an impression, during the 'twenties, that the Labour Party was failing to give what
she considered an imaginative lead to the country; again and
again in those years visitors to their week-end home at Passfield
Corner, near Liphook (first acquired in 1923) remember her saying—while she was still strongly opposed to the Russian Communist Party and all its works—that if Socialism were to make
real progress and a real appeal to the British people it would

---

[1] Many candidates in election times have discovered the danger
of describing the voter whose support they solicit as "living in
a slum"—even if he does.

somehow have to evolve a dedicated Order, something resembling the Society of Jesus, which should exact a high standard of training, discipline and self-control among its members, and which would furnish, therefore, a leadership of the *élite* to guide the mass of the citizens to a Socialist State. She did not feel that the Labour Party—with whose organisation, it must be remembered, she had not the day-to-day contact which Sidney had—either wanted to be or could be the nucleus of such an Order, and thus, though she remained a perfectly loyal member and M.P.'s wife, she was becoming, if not disillusioned, at least slightly bored, and was developing gradually to the point at which, moved by the Labour collapse of 1931 and the spectacle of Soviet Russia forging ahead, she impatiently told a Fabian audience that "the inevitability of gradualism is dead."

I do not mean to imply that there was any fundamental disagreement within the partnership; there was not. There was only a slight difference of emphasis, increased, possibly, by the fact that as Beatrice grew older she found the physical strain of living in London, with its crowds, its cars, and its noise, increasingly difficult to endure, and tended to retreat more and more often to Passfield Corner, "with no dogs or cocks within hearing", as the advertisement ran, and to stay there in meditation while Sidney went through his political grind. This spelt some loneliness to her, but to the world much advantage, for it was in that retreat that her remarkable and unique autobiography, *My Apprenticeship*, was written.

Of *My Apprenticeship* (1926), the book about which Beatrice was more nervous than she had been about any of her own work since her youthful appearances before the Anti-Sweating Committee—perhaps because in it she had to forego entirely the help from Sidney which had been so readily forthcoming on the public documents which bore her name, and had to stand on her own unaided feet—much could be written if there were space. Here it must suffice to say that as well as being an astonishingly interesting, candid and well-written book, it is much more than a mere autobiography. Its purpose is to tell the story of a fine mind of the late Victorian era searching at once for a profession and a faith to live by; it does this in a series of historical essays into which are woven pieces of vital contemporary description quoted directly from the author's own *Diaries.* It is thus indis-

pensable reading for the student of society; and it may be added
that anyone who wants to get a picture of the character, purpose
and personal idiosyncracies of the Webbs and who finds the
massive style of their long books—for which Sidney must take
the main responsibility—rather hard to get along with, cannot
do better than begin by reading *My Apprenticeship,* followed by
the posthumous *Our Partnership* and the *Diary* volumes and, for
good measure, by *Methods of Social Study* (1932), quoted
above, which was based on a series of broadcast talks given by
her.

MP AND MINISTER

Before *Methods of Social Study* was published Sidney had
become, and had ceased to be, a Cabinet Minister; he had
resigned his Seaham seat (to MacDonald) with the simple words
"It is too much for me, and in two years' time it will be very
much too much for me." They had given up their house in
Grosvenor Road and retired—or so they thought—permanently
to the country; they had completed the last of their great Local
Government volumes, that on the history of the New Poor Law,
had visited the exiled Trotsky on Lake Prinkipo, and thought
very little either of him or of the government which had expelled
him; after the election of 1929 they had reluctantly, at
MacDonald's request, sent Sidney back into harness, as a peer
in charge of the Colonial Office, and seen the ignominious
collapse of the second Labour Government and written its
epitaph. One might well have thought that this second retirement
was final, though, as everyone knows, their last great venture,
and their last great book, was yet to come, and their disappoint-
ments over British politics were to be amply compensated by
what they saw in Soviet Russia.

On Sidney's record as a Cabinet Minister, as on his record in
Parliament, it is not necessary to dwell at any great length. He
was not, at either, an outstanding success, partly, as I have said,
because he was too old when he began, and partly, as it seems
to me in retrospect, because he undertook them not eagerly, but
as a duty he owed to the Labour movement. His enthusiasm was
never deeply engaged, as in the days of the London County
Council and the Technical Education Committee; and one could

detect no trace of regret when his period of service came to an end.

It went without saying, of course, in view of his position in the Party that if and when it was invited to form a Government he would be offered Cabinet rank. When this happened, rather sooner than anyone had expected, he took the Board of Trade, an unspectacular office in which a good deal of his time was occupied in handling tiresome issues left over from the war. As would have been expected, he carried out all his duties with great competence and won the confidence both of his permanent officials and the business executives with whom he had dealings; but the principal event of his tenure of the Board of Trade was the setting-up by him of the Balfour Committee on Trade and Industry which reported so voluminously over a number of years. He played no part in the events which led to the downfall of the first Labour Government, and so deep had he dug himself into the hearts of the voters of Seaham that the ensuing election showed a reduction of less than a thousand in his majority. Returning as an Opposition member, he played a prominent part in the debates on Neville Chamberlain's Local Government Act, the subject of which was of course peculiarly his own; and while fiercely criticising its derating proposals he nevertheless rejoiced that, 20 years after Beatrice's *Minority Report,* the hated Guardians of the Poor, if not the Poor Law itself, were to be abolished.

The Colonial Secretaryship, which he took on in 1929, was a different matter, and far less smooth going than the Board of Trade. It was the Department in which he had himself served as a young civil servant; he knew its ramifications and its problems of old ; he was pleased—and slightly amused—to find himself in charge of such dozens of separate territories, with so many differing forms of government; he liked his staff and got on with them, and he looked forward to being able to do good work in the establishment of greater amenities in the Colonies and the promotion of native welfare. In fact, he did do a good deal, most of a rather unspectacular though useful kind. He started Ceylon on the road to self-government, and saw Iraq made into an independent State; he abolished the system of Mui Tsai (child slave-labour) in Hong Kong, and set on foot enquiries into education, health services, factory acts, juvenile delinquency and

246

a host of other subjects, and the White Paper he wrote on *Native Policy in East Africa* was a good Liberal State Paper —as was shown by the hullabaloo it called forth from white settlers in Kenya and South African leaders who believed that the proper policy towards natives was to keep them well under. But "enlightened" as was his attitude towards Africans in tutelage, he was not really up-to-date in the changes in the outlook of colonial reformers in 40 years, and he quickly gained the reputation of a reactionary among those champions of the Africans who wanted to proceed faster and farther than the white settlers or the Colonial Governors were prepared to go. Webb's lifelong respect for the expert, the man, be he civil servant or bricklayer, who really knew his job, in this situation served him ill; he did not seem to realise, as he would have realised when he was younger, that his official advisers, whether in the Colonial Office or in Kenya or Tanganyika, might be perfectly competent and perfectly wrong.

What overshadowed all his period of office, however, was the problem which has whitened the hairs of many another Colonial Secretary, the problem of Palestine—which one may here add, should never have been put on the shoulders of Colonial Secretaries at all; as a matter of high strategy it was controlled by the Foreign Office and the military authorities. Webb had barely taken office when the troubles between Jew and Arab began, with the riots at the Wailing Wall, and subsequent reports and commissions only made things worse. There is no need to go into details about the propaganda, the wranglings and tergivisations which only foreshadowed the much more tragic happenings that subsequent years had in store; the upshot was that in 1930, after a Cabinet White Paper had aroused a violent Parliamentary storm, the Colonial Secretary was in effect removed from control of the Palestinian question, which was handed over to a committee presided over by the Foreign Secretary.

It was a colossal snub. Anyone else but Webb would have promptly resigned, and some of his friends regretted that he did not do so, but he acquiesced in his own supersession. One of the reasons was undoubtedly his own genuine personal humility; he would always have strongly disliked taking overt action on a question of personal prestige. Another, however, was that when it came to the point he did not really greatly care; he was not on the side of either Jew or Arab and was inclined to think, if not to say, "a plague on both of your houses", and would not have regarded a difference of opinion over Palestine as a reason for resignation, for breaking up the Labour team. I am inclined to think, also, that by that date—the winter of 1930, when the bankruptcy of Labour policy with regard to increasing unemployment was already painfully apparent—that he was already coming nearer to Beatrice's state of doubt and disillusionment with the Labour Party, and beginning to share her increasing interests in Russia. But this is conjecture.

Whatever the truth, his confidence in MacDonald, never very great, was by no means increased by that statesman's treatment of him; and he—and Beatrice—received with hardly a tremor of surprise the events of the following summer, when MacDonald, having presented his Cabinet with a programme of cuts in the pay of Government servants and the unemployed which they refused to accept, tendered their and his own resignation, and reappeared next day as head of a Government composed almost entirely of their enemies; one would almost have imagined that they had expected nothing else. They were rather astonished by the thumping majority secured by MacDonald in the election, therein, as more than once before, completely misjudging popular emotional reactions; but they were not much moved. Their faces were set eastwards.

THE SOVIET UNION

For a good many years the Webbs had nothing good to say of the Soviet State. When the Bolsheviks first took command they regarded them as a new and unpleasing variety of anarchists or syndicalists such as had made up the various oppositions within the pre-war Fabian Society; and so long as they were trying to make the Labour Party into a workable instrument of Socialism they had no use for anyone who called its leaders "social traitors." Neither the enlightened labour laws, the social reforms set on foot, the sex equality of the new Russia, nor the panegyrics of visitors like George Lansbury, moved them at all; they thought it all merely revolutionary romanticism. Even the start, in 1928, of the first Five-Year Plan, which might have been expected to excite their interest, did not do so : they were not looking in that direction.

But in the middle of 1930, when Sidney was in the Cabinet and Beatrice alone at Passfield Corner, she began to read books about the Soviet Union, and what she read gradually excited her more and more. Could it be that there, in the most backward part of Europe, was developing a really Socialist society, a society based on production for use and not for profit, a society where the people collectively owned the means of production and their exploitation was collectively planned, a society which had abolished unemployment and was putting into effect, as fast as conditions allowed, a programme of social services which might have been taken straight from Fabian Tracts, a society which fostered, and encouraged Trade Unions, Co-operative Societies, and municipal enterprise, a society which denied supernatural religion and replaced its values by a Religion of Scientific Humanism, a society, finally, which was effectively run by a trained and dedicated Order—the Communist Party? Could such things be? The Russian Ambassador said they were, and produced consular reports; foreign observers of trained intelligence said they were; soon the Webbs' old friend Bernard Shaw, went on a trip to Russia and came back bubbling with excitement. The western countries, in the icy grip of unemployment, falling production, and reaction—almost of Fascism— seemed to prove clearly the utter bankruptcy and hopelessness of the capitalist world. They would go to Russia themselves and see whether there was really a Socialist sun rising in the East.

In May, 1932 they landed in Leningrad—two people well over 70 years old—and were received with almost regal honours, as befitted the authors whose *History of Trade Unionism* Lenin had translated in jail. In August they returned—after Beatrice had fallen ill and tested the Soviet health services from the consumer angle—and set to work on their *Soviet Communism,* the most enormous political guide-book in history; and it is no exaggeration to say that, from the moment they set foot on Russian soil, the rest of the political world, even including Nazi Germany, for them had thenceforward only a comparatively shadowy existence.

For those of us who have lived on after their death, and have watched the changes which Fascism and world-war have worked upon the Soviet political system which they hailed so joyfully, it is easy enough to feel superior and to smile a rueful pitying smile

249

R

at the aged Webbs falling so passionately in love (as they always readily admitted) with the institutions of the country which has altered so much from what they thought they found. But it is important not to be too wise after the event. Russia was in 1932, and for many years afterwards remained, literally the hope of the world for the working classes—witness the leap-up in British war production which took place after June 22nd, 1941, when Hitler made the Russian workers into allies of the British; it is at least worth noting that in *Soviet Communism,* the most uncritical of all their books, the Webbs came nearer to the heart of the ordinary worker than in all their major works and their political efforts put together; it is of some significance that a taxi-driver who took them, long afterwards, to a dinner at the Soviet Embassy kept them waiting while he expressed his admiration of that book.

The book itself, moreover, was not as uncritical as some who have not taken the pains to read it through have imagined. Granted that in the Soviet Union the Webbs thought they had found something very like the perfect Fabian State, and so advertised it, they did not swallow the whole apparatus : they observed and permitted themselves publicly to criticise aspects of the regime which they thought bad—the occasional outbursts of chauvinism against the west, for example, the enforcement of Marxist orthodoxy, the hostile policy of the Comintern to the outside world, and the repressive remains of the Tsarist police state. Where they went wrong, and many with them, was in taking at face value the time-honoured Marxist assertions that these inevitable concomitants of a proletarian revolution achieved by violence would in a comparatively brief while "wither away" and disappear. As Beatrice told an interviewer[1] :

---

[1] "Even in our casual contact with members of the Communist Party, the repression of free thought and free expression, in all that concerns the structure of human society, was obvious; it was in fact openly defended as a necessary 'war measure' to ensure national unity in the presence of a powerful enemy at home and abroad. More sensational, but I think, *more likely to disappear,* is the occasional physical terrorism, the trapdoor of disappearance of unwanted personalities; the ostracism and persecution of innocent but inconvenient workers."

They did not disappear, the power of the State has not "withered away", in Moscow or anywhere else. But that was in the future.

As the above extract, which is only one of several which might have been selected, shows quite clearly, the Webbs did not travel through the Soviet Union in blinkers. As honoured guests, they were naturally shown the best the country had to display; but its failures were not concealed from them, and they did their best to keep their eyes open, though on a matter of agriculture, which in 1932 was paying very heavily for the first ill-considered experiments in collectivisation, they were no experts and did not see what was happening. The most that can be alleged against them is, having all their lives—however little they realised it— cared more for equality and efficiency than for personal freedom, they took much too lightly the threat of the Communist system to the human liberties of individuals. Here again, though, they erred in very good company—in 1932.

The criticisms they originally made, however, were considerably less emphasised as the years went on. The first edition of *Soviet Communism* bore the sub-title *A new Civilisation?* : it is significant that in subsequent editions the query disappeared and polemical prefaces were added defending the Soviet Union root-and-branch. This is not really surprising, for the march of events was steadily hardening capitalist and liberal opposition. The great Russian treason trials began the year after the book was published; then came the long drawn-out failure of east and west to come together over foreign policy, culminating in the Soviet-German Pact, Russian neutrality in the war and the attack on Finland. Throughout the period, the Webbs held stoutly to their faith—Sidney rather more stoutly than Beatrice, who was obviously perturbed both by the circumstances of the trials and by the Russian language of friendship to Hitler. But she never seriously wavered, and she never allowed any misgivings she may have had to find public utterance. The more the outside world vilified Soviet Russia, the more stoutly she defended it, so that visitors to Passfield during the late 'thirties were sometimes inclined to feel that they had been fed entirely on information about things Russian. But it is certain that she

[1] *Clarion.* October 8, 1932.

was as relieved at heart as the bulk of the British working class when Russia became an ally; and she lived long enough to learn of the triumphant defence of Stalingrad.

CONCLUSION

The rest is epilogue—a happy, tranquil, interested old age at Passfield Corner, cared for by faithful Scottish maidservants. Beatrice's last public position was that of President of the revived Fabian Society, which she held from 1939 until 1941, when the blitz finally made visits to London an impossibility; she did not think, of course, that it was the dedicated Socialist Society of her dreams, but she regarded it as the most hopeful political venture in the Britain of '39. "Long live the Fabian Society," she wrote in her last presidential message, and she continued to take interest in it and its doings until her death. Sidney, after a serious illness in 1938, retired completely from public life.

This did not mean, however, that they took no further interest in politics and society; far otherwise. Apart from the absorbing delights of Soviet Communism, they read and discussed incessantly, wrote articles and reviews, and took holidays at home and abroad (trying air travel in 1937, to their great pleasure!). Beatrice had broadcast with some success, and more than one University saluted her with honorary degrees. Later, as their physical energies waned, they tended more and more to remain at Passfield Corner and to be visited by streams of persons, small and great, who were either bidden to talk and to be questioned or came to pay their homage—on one occasion over a 100 of the descendants of Beatrice's sisters attended a tea-party on her lawn. The most vivid memory, indeed, which most of the present generation have of the Webbs is of week-end visits to Passfield Corner, of Beatrice's tall figure welcoming them at the open door, of walks over the rough grass and heather of the common-land, of long regulated sessions of talk in the lounge, Sidney reclining with his feet up, and Beatrice on a low stool, with skirt drawn up and hands stretched out to the fire, discoursing about "holism", Toynbee's philosophy of history, "modern" novels, and what not, canvassing the merits of present and prospective leaders of Labour, or simply gossiping, in her amusingly acid manner, about Asquith and Haldane and other figures of her prime.

Beatrice died in the spring of 1943 after a very short illness; Sidney in the autumn of 1947. After her death the Order of Merit was conferred on him in explicit recognition of the work of the Partnership; in December 1947 the ashes of both were laid in Westminister Abbey.

There is no space, even if it were not something of an impertinence, to evaluate here the work of the Partnership. A few things however, must be said. The greatest concrete contribution of the Webbs to British political life is to be found in research and in the building of institutions. As research workers they were original, purposeful, and magnificently thorough; they had a remarkable sense of what, from the social angle, needed to be undertaken; they blazed many trails, and were untiring in the pursuit of facts and extremely scrupulous in both verifying and giving their references. Not everyone, naturally, would agree with all their conclusions, but there is not the faintest likelihood that the work they did upon local government and Trade Unions, to take only two examples, will ever be upset.

The same is the case with institutions; as *founders* they were almost uniquely successful. They knew exactly how to do it; they knew how to make plans, how to obtain initial support, and—by careful and thoughtful study—how to enlist others, from the millionaire to the small Trade Union branch, and how to keep them interested. They were experts in all organisational devices, and never too proud to learn from others. Moreover, they possessed two very valuable qualities not always found in brilliant organisers; they could recognise a failure and cut their losses, and, in the much more frequent case of a success, they knew when to sit back and let it alone. They never fussed over their spiritual children or attempted to keep them in tutelage; and the London system of higher education, the London School of Economics, the *New Statesman,* and the Fabian Society stand as monuments to their foresight and self-restraint.

In the realm of politics direct they were less successful, mainly because of a certain failure to understand and appreciate the irrational emotions of men—not merely of men in the mass, but of individual men whom they hoped to influence. Most of their general political agitations, whether "permeation" or nationwide campaign, failed in the short run, and the Utopia they wrote struck a spark in nobody's heart; when the purposes of their agitation were eventually achieved, it was through other agencies than theirs. It was this lack of emotional understanding, this blind spot in their remarkable mental equipment, which caused them to be taken by surprise by outbursts of popular feeling, over the South African War, for example, or in 1931. It also accounted, in part, for the bitterness shown by a few who disagreed with them and who cried out, with obvious sincerity, that the Webbs were not democratic at all, but illiberal old bureaucrats without a spark of humanity; it may, as I have suggested, have played a part in their uncritical advocacy of Soviet Communism.

But if that is admitted, it must also be admitted that to accuse them of lacking common human kindliness is stark nonsense. Not merely did they devote their lives to disinterested service for the public good, and swallow—and forgive!—attacks and insults, even from their fellow-workers, which lesser spirits would have furiously resented; they were also, personally among the kindest people in the world. They cast off no friends, nor spared themselves trouble to help them in difficulty; they were endlessly interested in younger workers in the same field, and often regarded them with real affection that looked for no return. Furthermore, they never displayed either arrogance or any conviction that they had said the last word, even upon the subjects they had made peculiarly their own, or that the truth would die with them; even in their 'eighties they never posed as Great Persons who ought not to be contradicted—and of how many Great Persons in our history could this have been said?

They combined personal modesty of this kind with a deep conviction that on the whole they were right. This conviction, by and large, has been supported by events. On particular issues, no doubt, they made mistakes, like other human beings. But— and this is the final word—on general principles and the future of the modern world, the shape they gave to political thought, the demand for Socialist planning and organisation, for an essential minimum of civilised existence, for standards of measurement and publicity in human affairs, for tolerance, accuracy, and devotion among servants of the community, has never been seriously called in question; and among architects of British society in the mid-twentieth century two of the names which most unmistakeably stand out are those of Beatrice and Sidney Webb.

BIBLIOGRAPHIES

THOMAS PAINE. Moncure Conway edited a complete collection of Paine's works in 1894-96, *The Writings of Thomas Paine* (4 Vols.). A more recent collection is that of Philip S. Foner (New York, 1945, 2 Vols.). *The Rights of Man* is available in Penguin Books, 1969. All the important works are included in Howard Fast (ed.), *Selected Works of Tom Paine* (1945) and in Sidney Hook (ed.), *The Essential Thomas Paine* (1969).

There are numerous lives of Paine. Most of the early works are unreliable with the exception of Moncure D. Conway, *The Life of Thomas Paine* (1892). Of the more recent works, the best are: M. A. Best, *Thomas Paine, Prophet and Martyr of Democracy* (1927); W. E. Woodward, *Tom Paine, America's Godfather* (1946); A. O. Aldridge, *Man of Reason, the Life of Thomas Paine* (1960), is based on original research in England, France and the United States. Howard Fast's novel *Citizen Tom Paine* (1949) is also of interest.

For background, the most useful books are P. A. Brown, *The French Revolution in English History* (1918); H. N. Brailsford, *Shelley, Godwin and their Circle* (1913).

FRANCIS PLACE. Graham Wallas, *The Life of Francis Place* (1898, revised 1918) remains the only full life of Place. Before this book appeared, Place was almost entirely unknown. Recently, Place's manuscript *Autobiography* (ed. Thale, 1972) has been published.

The British Museum has several hundred volumes of material collected by Francis Place. This includes newspaper cuttings, pamphlets, letters, etc. dealing with the movement to reform parliament, with the working-class movement, etc., as well as manuscript material of unfinished works by Place. Some of this has now been published, notably Francis Place, *London Radicalism 1830-1843—A Selection of Papers* (1970). Place's one major work *Illustrations and Proofs of the Principle of Population* (1822), was re-published in 1930 with an introduction by Norman E. Himes. This work, which was one of the earliest books to advocate birth-control, was reprinted in 1967.

ROBERT OWEN. The literature both by and about Robert Owen is enormous and no attempt can be made here to give a full bibliography. Attention is however drawn to three existing bibliographies and to the most important of recent books, most of which are still available. The National Library of Wales, *Bibliography of Robert Owen the Socialist 1771-1858* (2nd Edn. 1925) contains an excellent list of Owen's own writings. Appendices E and F to G. D. H. Cole's *The Life of Robert Owen* (1930, 3rd Edn. 1965) are an adequate guide to material published before 1930. The bibliography contained in J. F. C. Harrison's *Robert Owen and the Owenites in Britain and America* (1969) includes numerous works not mentioned in either of the above.

A good selection of Owen's most important works can be found in *A New View of Society* (edited by G. D. H. Cole) in the Everyman Library. There is also a Penguin selection *A New View of Society & Report to the County of Lanark* (ed. V. A. C. Gattell, 1970).

For the life of Robert Owen, the first source is *Life of Robert Owen by Himself* (reprinted by Charles Knight, 1971 with a remarkable introduction by John Butt which attempts to "strip the man of legends"). Frank Podmore's *Robert Owen* (1906) is a very detailed and accurate account. Margaret Cole's *Robert Owen of New Lanark* (1953) takes account of new material which has come to light since G. D. H. Cole's *The Life of Robert Owen* (1930) was first written. The autobiography of Robert Dale Owen, *Threading my Way* (1874, reprinted 1967) is also of great interest, as are *Robert Owen on Education* (ed. Silver, 1969) and John Butt (ed.) *Robert Owen: Prince of Cotton Spinners* (1970), a number of essays based on recent research.

WILLIAM LOVETT. The main source for the life of Lovett is his autobiography *Life and Struggles of William Lovett* (1876). This was reprinted in 1920 with an excellent preface by R. H. Tawney. Unaccountably, an edition published in 1967 omitted three chapters from the original.

In 1840, Lovett in collaboration with John Collins wrote *Chartism, a New Organisation of the People*. A number of pamphlets by Lovett, bound in one volume, formerly the author's property, can be found in the British Museum (8138a55).

For the Chartist background see Mark Hovell, *The Chartist Movement* (revised 1925); R. C. Gammage, *History of the Chartist Movement 1837-1854* (1894, reprinted 1969); Julius West, *History of the Chartist Movement* (1920).

JAMES KEIR HARDIE. The standard life of Keir Hardie is *J. Keir Hardie: A Biography* (1925) by William Stewart. For his early years see also *From Pit to Parliament: The story of the early life of James Keir Hardie* (1923) by David Lowe. A good short life is *Keir Hardie* (1935) by Hamilton Fyfe. More recent biographies have added little that is new. Fred Reid's *Keir Hardie's Conversion to Socialism* is an important essay to be found in *Essays in Labour History 1886-1923* (edited by Asa Briggs and John Saville, 1971). For comment on *Keir Hardie's Biographers,* see F. Reid in the *Bulletin of the Society for the study of Labour History,* No. 16 (1968) p. 30 ff. Fred Reid's doctoral thesis, *The Early Life and Political Development of James Keir Hardie, 1856-92,* (Oxford, 1969) covers new ground.

There has been no recent collection of Hardie's own writings, the most important of which are: *Keir Hardie's Speeches and Writings 1888-1915* (3rd Edn. 1925); *From Serfdom to Socialism* (1907)—a brief exposition of Hardie's socialism; *India* (1909)—an account of British rule in India based on impressions formed during his visit there; and numerous pamphlets especially: *Can a Man be a Christian on a Pound a Week?* (1901); *My Confession of Faith in the Labour Alliance* (1909); *The I.L.P.—All about it* (1909); *Socialism* (1907); and *Killing no Murder: The Government and the Railway Strike* (1911). For a history of the I.L.P. in its early days see Henry Pelling, *Origins of the Labour Party* (2nd Edn. 1965).

JOHN BURNS. The most detailed account of the life of John Burns is William Kent, *John Burns: Labour's Lost Leader* (1950). Earlier lives like A. P. Grubb, *From Candle Factory to British Cabinet* (1908) are unreliable and incomplete. J. Burgess, *The Rise and Progress of a Right Honourable* (1911) is a sustained attack from the Labour side.

Other material for the life of Burns can be found in Tom

Mann, *Memoirs* (1932, reprinted 1967); H. Llewellyn Smith and V. Nash, *The Story of the Dockers Strike, 1889* (1889, reprinted 1971); H. H. Champion, *The Great Dock Strike* (1890); Ben Tillett, *History of the Dockers' Union* (1910) and *Memories and Reflections* (1931); Beatrice Webb's *Our Partnership* (1948) also contains shrewd comments on Burns, as do other books by the Webbs.

Burns wrote no books but he wrote numerous articles and made many speeches, some of which have been reprinted. Most famous is his speech for the defence in the 1886 sedition trial *The Man with the Red Flag* (1886). Burns own account of the great dock strike has been printed in Frow and Katanka, *Strikes —A Documentary History* (1971). In 1893 the Fabian Society published Burns' pamphlet *The Unemployed* (Fabian Tract No. 47). The files of *South-Western Star,* Battersea's oldest local newspaper, are a useful source for Burns' speeches and activities.

BEATRICE AND SIDNEY WEBB. For the life of the Webbs see Beatrice Webb, *My Apprenticeship* (1926); *Our Partnership* (edited by B. Drake and M. I. Cole, 1948); M. I. Cole (ed.) *Beatrice Webb's Diaries 1912-1924* (1952) and *Diaries 1924-1932* (1956). Other biographical material is contained in M. A. Hamilton, *Sidney and Beatrice Webb* (1933); Margaret Cole, *Beatrice Webb* (1945); and M. I. Cole (ed.), *The Webbs and their Work* (1949). On Beatrice Webb, see also Muggeridge and Adam, *Beatrice Webb—A Life 1858-1943* (1967).

Sidney Webb joined the Fabian Society in 1885, he contributed to *Fabian Essays* (1889) and wrote numerous *Fabian Tracts* throughout the series. Beatrice Webb's first book was B. Potter, *The Co-operative Movement in Great Britain* (1891). After their marriage in 1892 their major works were written jointly. They include : *The History of Trade Unionism* (1894, revised 1920); *Industrial Democracy* (1897), new Edn. (1920); *English Local Government* (8 Vols. 1906-1929) includes *English Poor Law History* (3 Vols.); *The Break Up of the Poor Law* (1909); *English Poor Law Policy* (1910); *The Prevention of Destitution* (1911); *A Constitution for the Socialist Commonwealth of Great Britain* (1920); *The Consumers' Co-operative Movement* (1921); *The Decay of Capitalist Civilisation* (1923);

Methods of Social Study (1932); *Soviet Communism: A New Civilisation* (1935, 3rd Edn. 1945).

A considerable collection of the Webbs' papers, letters and writings can be found at the British Library of Political and Economic Science (L.S.E.), London W.C.2.

NOTES ON CONTRIBUTORS

COLE, GEORGE DOUGLAS HOWARD, author of the Fabian Biographical Tract on *J. Keir Hardie* (first published January 1941) and *John Burns* (first published June 1943) was the outstanding socialist writer and thinker of his day. Throughout his life he combined important academic work with the propagation of advanced political and social views in numerous books, pamphlets, articles and speeches. At the same time he took an active part in trade union and political organisations and adult education.

G. D. H. Cole was born in Cambridge in 1889, was educated at St. Paul's School, Hammersmith and Balliol College, Oxford. In 1912 he obtained a prize fellowship at Magdalen College. In 1913 he published his first political work *The World of Labour*. During World War I he became research officer of the Amalgamated Society of Engineers and Honorary secretary of the Fabian Research Department and helped to prepare the Labour case in a number of industrial disputes. After the war Cole returned to teaching and writing as his main occupations. After a period in adult education he returned to Oxford in 1925 as a fellow and tutor of University College and as university Reader in Economics. In October 1944 he was made Chichele Professor of Social and Economic Theory and Fellow of All Souls. In 1957, on retirement from the Chichele Chair, he was made Honorary Fellow of Balliol and Research Fellow of Nuffield College, Oxford.

He married Margaret Postgate in 1918 and in the same year began his regular association with the *New Statesman* which was to last until his death. In 1931 he founded the New Fabian Research Bureau, which, in 1939, amalgamated with the Fabian Society, of which Cole was Chairman (1939-46) and (1948-50). From 1952 he was its President. In the period after 1931 his most important contribution to politics was the lead he gave in research towards framing new and coherent policies for the Labour Party after the 1931 *débâcle*. G. D. H. Cole died in 1959.

Of the hundreds of books and pamphlets by G. D. H. Cole,

261

many of them written in collaboration with Margaret Cole, the most important are : *Self-Government in Industry* (1917); *The Payment of Wages* (1918); *Workshop Organisation* (1923, reprinted 1972); *Life of William Cobbett* (1924, new Edn. 1947); *Life of Robert Owen* (1925, new Edn. 1965); *Short History of the British Working-Class Movement* (1925-7, new Edn. 1948); *Intelligent Man's Guide through World Chaos* (1932); *What Marx Really Meant* (1934, revised 1948 as *The Meaning of Marxism*); *The Condition of Britain* (1937); *Persons and Periods* (1938); *The Common People*—with Raymond Postgate (1938, revised 1946); *British Working Class Politics* (1941); *Chartist Portraits* (1941); *Opinions of William Cobbett*—ed. with Margaret Cole (1944); *A Century of Co-operation* (1944); *History of the Labour Party from 1914* (1948); *History of Socialist Thought* (5 Vols., 1953–1960); *Attempts at General Union* (1953); *Case for Industrial Partnership* (1957).

The biography by Dame Margaret Cole, *The Life of G. D. H. Cole* (1971), gives details of many other publications, including the titles of over 20 detective novels. Cole's substantial collection of material on the history of the labour movement is now in the Library of Nuffield College, Oxford.

COLE, MARGARET ISABEL, author of the Fabian Tract on *Beatrice and Sidney Webb* (first published September 1955), was born in Cambridge in 1893. She was educated at Roedean School, Brighton, and Girton College, Cambridge. She married G. H. D. Cole in 1918. After teaching Classics for two years during the First World War, she became assistant secretary of the Labour Research Department from 1916–1925. From 1925 to 1949, Mrs. Cole was a lecturer for university tutorial classes in London and Cambridge, while writing numerous books and pamphlets and contributing to newspapers and journals. She has held many posts in the Fabian Society, was Hon. Secretary of the New Fabian Research Bureau 1935–1939 and of the Fabian Society 1939–1953. She became its Chairman in 1955 and was appointed President in 1963. She has been a member of the London County Council, an Alderman (1952) and Chairman of its Further Education Committee.

Among her many books are *Women of Today* (1937); *Marriage—Past and Present* (1938); *Beatrice Webb—A Memoir*

(1945); *Makers of the Labour Movement* (1948); *Growing up into Revolution* (1949), an autobiography; *Robert Owen of New Lanark* (1953); *Servant of the County* (1956); *The Story of Fabian Socialism* (1961) and *The Life of G. H. D. Cole* (1971). She has edited *The Webbs and their Work* (1949); *The Diaries of Beatrice Webb* (2 Vols., 1952–1956). In addition she has written jointly with G. D. H. Cole, around 40 detective novels and a number of works on politics.

ERVINE, ST. JOHN GREER, author of the Fabian Tract on *Francis Place* (first published October, 1912) was a playwright, novelist, biographer, journalist and dramatic critic. Born in Belfast in 1883, he fought and was wounded in the First World War, managed the Abbey Theatre, Dublin, for a brief period, was one of the earliest members of the Irish Academy and was appointed Professor of Dramatic Literature by the Royal Society of Literature.

His early plays, produced before 1914 were socially realistic dramas. The first, *Mixed Marriage* (1911), dealt with Catholic-Protestant relations in Ulster. Ervine's later plays were mainly conventional domestic comedies. In 1947 he wrote a play against nationalisation, *Private Enterprise*.

He was dramatic critic of *The Observer* for many years, wrote several novels and contributed widely to newspapers and journals. His non-fiction includes several books on the theatre; a long adulatory biography of his fellow-Fabian *Bernard Shaw: His Life, Work and Friends* (1956, re-issued 1972), a sketch of *Parnell* (1925); a political biography *Sir Edward Carson and the Ulster Movement* (1915); a biography of General Booth *God's Soldier* (1934) and a hostile study of *Oscar Wilde: a present-time appraisal* (1951). Ervine died in 1972.

HAMMOND, L. BARBARA, author of the Fabian Tract on *William Lovett* (first published May, 1922), was the wife and collaborator of J. L. Hammond, the historian and journalist. They were married in 1901. Barbara Hammond, born 1873, was the daughter of a Headmaster of Haileybury College and won first-class honours in Classics at Lady Margaret Hall, Oxford.

J. L. and Barbara Hammond collaborated in writing a

number of historical works, the most important of which were the great trilogy *The Village Labourer* (1911), *The Town Labourer* (1917) and *The Skilled Labourer* (1919) covering the period of the industrial revolution from 1760 to 1832. These books were distinguished for their research and literary sensitivity and profoundly affected the interpretation of this important period. Both authors were awarded the Honorary Doctorate of Literature on the same day by the University of Oxford (1933).

Other works written by the Hammonds were *Lord Shaftesbury* (1923); *The Rise of Modern Industry* (1925); *The Age of the Chartists: a Study of Discontent* (1930)—sections of this book were published as *The Bleak Age* in 1934 and again, further enlarged as a Penguin in 1947; *James Stansfield* (1932).

HUTCHINS, Beatrice L., author of the Fabian Tract on *Robert Owen, Social Reformer* (first published November, 1912), was a historian of the factory system and a prominent member of the Fabian Women's Group for whom she wrote pamphlets and gave lectures on various aspects of women in industry. In 1903 she published, under the aegis of the London School of Economics, *A History of Factory Legislation*—together with A. Harrison (1903, 2nd Edn. revised 1911). Among her other writings is *Home-work and Sweating: The Causes and the Remedies* (1907, Fabian Tract No. 130); *What a Health Committee Can Do* (1910, Fabian Tract No. 148); *The Working Life of Women* (1911, Fabian Tract No. 157). She contributed to several joint Fabian publications notably *Socialism and the National Minimum* (1909), *Women in Modern Industry* (1915), and edited *Women's Industrial News*.

MARTIN, Kingsley, author of the Fabian Tract on *Thomas Paine* (first published July, 1925), was born in 1897 the son of a Unitarian minister. He was educated at Mill Hill School and Magdalene College, Cambridge. After several years as a lecturer at the London School of Economics, he joined the editorial staff of the *Manchester Guardian*. In 1931, he was appointed Editor of the *New Statesman and Nation,* a post he held until 1960. He remained Editorial Director until his retirement in 1962.

Among the books written by Kingsley Martin were : *The Triumph of Palmerston* (1924, new Edn. 1963); *The British*

Public and the General Strike (1927); *French Liberal Thought in the 18th Century* (1929, reprinted 1955); *Low's Russian Sketch-book* (in collaboration with David Low) 1932; *The Magic of Monarchy* (1937); *Propaganda's Harvest* (1942); *The Press the Public Wants* (1947); *Harold Laski, A Memoir* (1953); *Critic's London Diary* (1960); *The Crown and the Establishment* (1962).

Kingsley Martin wrote two volumes of his autobiography, *Father Figues* (1966) and *Editor* (1968) but died in 1969 before completing the third. *Kingsley Martin—Portrait and Self-Portrait* (ed. Mervyn Jones, 1969) is a collective tribute to his memory. A book by C. H. Rolph, *Kingsley—The life, letters and diaries of Kingsley Martin* is announced for 1973.

BIBLIOGRAPHICAL DETAILS OF THE FIRST PUBLICATION OF THE TRACTS INCLUDED IN THIS VOLUME

1. THOMAS PAINE (1737–1809) by Kingsley Martin (Fabian Tract No. 217, Fabian Biographical Series No. 10). First published July, 1925, pp. 24.
2. FRANCIS PLACE THE TAILOR OF CHARING CROSS (1771–1854) by St. John G. Ervine (Fabian Tract No. 165, Fabian Biographical Series No. 1). First published October, 1912, pp. 28.
3. ROBERT OWEN SOCIAL REFORMER (1771–1858) by B. L. Hutchins (Fabian Tract No. 166, Fabian Biographical Series No. 2). First published November, 1912, pp. 24.
4. WILLIAM LOVETT (1800–1877) by Mrs. L. Barbara Hammond (Fabian Tract No. 199, Fabian Biographical Series No. 8). First published May, 1922, pp. 24.
5. JAMES KEIR HARDIE (1856–1915) by G. D. H. Cole (Fabian Biographical Series No. 12, not included in Tract series). First published January, 1941, pp. 36.
6. JOHN BURNS (1858–1943) by G. D. H. Cole (Fabian Biographical Series No. 14, not included in Tract series). First published June, 1943, pp. 36.
7. BEATRICE AND SIDNEY WEBB (1859–1947, 1858–1943) by Margaret Cole (Fabian Tract No. 297, Fabian Biographical Series No. 15). First published September, 1955, pp. 47.

CHECK-LIST OF FABIAN BIOGRAPHICAL SERIES

INDEX